I0099652

RECONSTRUCTING JAPAN'S SECURITY POLICY

*This book is dedicated to my wife, Parveen, and
my daughter, Kohana.*

RECONSTRUCTING JAPAN'S SECURITY POLICY

The Role of Military Crises

Bhubhindar Singh

EDINBURGH
University Press

Edinburgh University Press is one of the leading university presses in the UK. We publish academic books and journals in our selected subject areas across the humanities and social sciences, combining cutting-edge scholarship with high editorial and production values to produce academic works of lasting importance. For more information visit our website: edinburghuniversitypress.com

© Bhubhindar Singh, 2020, 2022

Edinburgh University Press Ltd
The Tun – Holyrood Road, 12(2f) Jackson's Entry, Edinburgh EH8 8PJ

First published in hardback by Edinburgh University Press 2020

Typeset in 10/12.5 Adobe Sabon by
IDSUK (DataConnection) Ltd

A CIP record for this book is available from the British Library

ISBN 978 1 4744 4622 8 (hardback)
ISBN 978 1 4744 4623 5 (paperback)
ISBN 978 1 4744 4624 2 (webready PDF)
ISBN 978 1 4744 4625 9 (epub)

The right of Bhubhindar Singh to be identified as the author of this work has been asserted in accordance with the Copyright, Designs and Patents Act 1988, and the Copyright and Related Rights Regulations 2003 (SI No. 2498).

CONTENTS

ACKNOWLEDGEMENTS

This book is a culmination of my interest in explaining change in Japanese security policy between the Cold War and post-Cold War period. This interest started when I was pursuing my doctoral studies at the University of Sheffield. In my first book, entitled *Japan's Security Identity: From a Peace State to an International State*, I examined the role of identity as a cause of change in Japanese security policy between the two periods. In this book, I examine the external military crises factor as a policy window and attempt to argue that this external factor was critical in explaining the significant security policy initiatives that have made Japan an engaged security actor in post-Cold War strategic affairs.

I would like to take this opportunity to thank many important people who were instrumental in the completion of this book. I would like to thank the senior leadership at the S. Rajaratnam School of International Studies (RSIS), Nanyang Technological University (NTU), which includes Ambassador Ong Keng Yong, Executive Deputy Chairman; Ralf Emmers, Dean; and Joseph Liow, former Dean, for their constant support during the entire research and writing process. Also from RSIS and NTU, I would like to thank Pascal Vennesson, Anit Mukherjee and Kei Koga for reading through selected chapters and sharing very insightful comments that improved the manuscript. I would like to thank Ang Cheng Guan for his constant support since I was a junior researcher, and never failing to ask for updates on this book.

I would like to thank Katahara Eiichi for his support for my Visiting Fellowship at the National Institute of Defense Studies (NIDS), Tokyo, Japan, in 2012, and Deepa Ollapally for hosting me at the Elliott School of International Affairs, George Washington University, under the Fulbright Award in 2015. Both research fellowships were instrumental in allowing me to concentrate on my writing and gathering the important information I required for the book.

I am deeply thankful to Sumit Ganguly, Ian Clark and Linus Hagström for reading various versions of the book proposal and offering valuable insights that strengthened the argument of the book. I would like to thank all the interviewees in Japan and the United States for taking time off their busy schedules to answer my numerous questions. Their responses have been a very important resource for me to unpack and understand the complexities in Japanese security policy practice.

I would like to thank Sarah Teo for her assistance in compiling the references and bibliography, and Sarah Corradini for her research assistance, especially for Chapter 6. At the Edinburgh University Press, I would like to thank Jenny Daly, Sarah Foyle, Bekah Dey, Joannah Duncan and Camilla Rockwood for their patience and professionalism.

Last but not least, I would like to thank Parveen, my wife, who painstakingly edited all the chapters, and Kohana, my daughter, for being such a joy. Both are pillars in my life and their love, support and encouragement were absolutely critical in the completion of the project. This book is dedicated to them.

LIST OF ABBREVIATIONS

ACSA	Acquisition Cross Service Agreement
ADIZ	Air Defense Identification Zone
APEC	Asia-Pacific Economic Cooperation
ARF	ASEAN Regional Forum
ASDF	Air Self-Defense Force
ASEAN	Association of Southeast Asian Nations
ATSML	Anti-Terrorism Special Measures Law
BMD	Ballistic Missile Defense
CDPJ	Constitutional Democratic Party of Japan
CLB	Cabinet Legislation Bureau
CPTPP	Comprehensive and Progressive Agreement for the Trans-Pacific Partnership
CRIO	Cabinet Research and Information Office
CSIS	Center for Strategic and International Studies
DDF	Dynamic Defense Force
DP	Democratic Party
DPJ	Democratic Party of Japan
DPRI	Defense Policy Review Initiative
DPRK	Democratic People's Republic of Korea
DSP	Democratic Socialist Party
EASR	East Asian Strategic Review
EPA	Economic Partnership Agreement
FOIP	Free and Open Indo-Pacific
GOJ	Government of Japan
GSDF	Ground Self-Defense Force
HADR	Humanitarian and Disaster Relief
IAEA	International Atomic Energy Agency
ICB	International Crisis Behaviour
IPCL	International Peace Cooperation Law
ISR	Intelligence, Surveillance and Reconnaissance
JCG	Japan Coast Guard
JCP	Japanese Communist Party
JDA	Japan Defense Agency

JIP	Japan Innovation Party
JSP	Japan Socialist Party
KEDO	Korean Peninsula Energy Development Organization
LDP	Liberal Democratic Party
MITI	Ministry of International Trade and Industry
MLIT	Ministry of Land, Infrastructure, Transport and Tourism
MOD	Ministry of Defense
MOF	Ministry of Finance
MOFA	Ministry of Foreign Affairs
MSA	Maritime Safety Agency
MSDF	Maritime Self-Defense Force
MTDP	Mid-Term Defense Program
NDPG	National Defense Program Guidelines
NDPO	National Defense Program Outline
NGO	Non-Governmental Organisation
NPA	National Police Agency
NPT	Treaty on the Non-Proliferation of Nuclear Weapons
NSS	National Security Strategy
ODA	Overseas Development Assistance
OEF	Operation Enduring Freedom
OIF	Operation Iraqi Freedom
PLA	People's Liberation Army
PMO	Prime Minister's Office
PSI	Proliferation Security Initiative
RCEP	Regional Comprehensive Economic Partnership
SCC	Security Consultative Committee
SDF	Self-Defense Force
SDP	Social Democratic Party
SDPJ	Social Democratic Party of Japan
SEALD	Student Emergency Action for Liberal Democracy
TMD	Theater Missile Defense
TPP	Trans-Pacific Partnership
UNAVEM II	UN Angola Verification Mission II
UNCLOS	UN Convention on the Law of the Sea
UNHCR	UN High Commission for Refugees
UNPCC	UN Peace Cooperation Corps
UNPKO	UN Peacekeeping Operations
UNSC	UN Security Council
UNTAC	UN Transitional Authority in Cambodia
USFJ	United States Forces, Japan
WMD	Weapons of Mass Destruction
WTC	World Trade Center

I

A CASE FOR CRISIS IN JAPANESE SECURITY POLICYMAKING

In a speech delivered at the Center for Strategic and International Studies (CSIS) in Washington, DC in February 2013, Japanese Prime Minister Abe Shinzo confidently declared: 'Japan is back' (Abe 2013). One of the main goals of this statement was to reinforce Japan's place as a responsible contributor to regional and international security affairs. Since returning as Japan's prime minister in December 2012, Abe and his government have taken bold steps to achieve this objective.

In December 2013, the Abe government, for the first time, published a National Security Strategy (NSS) document outlining Japan's basic national security policy (Prime Minister of Japan and His Cabinet 2013a). This was introduced together with an updated set of National Defense Program Guidelines (NDPG) outlining five- and ten-year targets for Japan's defence policy (Prime Minister of Japan and His Cabinet 2013b). These documents called for the strengthening of Japan's naval, air force, patrol and surveillance capabilities, as well as acquiring new capabilities such as the amphibious island defence force. In order to support these measures, the Abe government reversed an eleven-year declining trend by increasing Japan's defence budget. To complement the internal force modernisation efforts, the Abe government also updated its alliance with the United States (US) through a revision of the Guidelines for Japan–US Defense Cooperation in April 2015. This not only widened the areas of defence cooperation but also, for the first time, authorised the Self-Defense Force (SDF) to use force to defend the US and other friendly countries even when Japan was not attacked – referred to as collective self-defence missions (Ministry of Defense of Japan [MOD Japan] 2015a).

Though Abe's return to power in 2012 hastened Japan's security policy expansion, the initiatives discussed above are best understood as part of an ongoing incremental transformation of Japan's security policy since the onset of the post-Cold War period. After the demise of the Soviet Union the Japanese leadership became cognisant that its minimalist security policy, formed during the Cold War, was inappropriate for the post-Cold War strategic environment. The minimalist version entailed a dominant reliance on economics as a tool of security policy, as well as to achieve its security interests. This resulted in Japan's limited involvement in external security affairs and reliance on its alliance partner, the US, to fulfil its international responsibilities to ensure peace and stability. Since the onset of the post-Cold War period, the Japanese security policymaking elite has taken significant steps to transform Japan's security policy away from its minimalist version. The outcome has been Japan's security policy expansion, which entailed a wider use of the military to achieve its security policy goals, as well as a more active participation in external security affairs through a range of measures that can be divided into those implemented outside of the US–Japan alliance and those implemented within the alliance framework.

Outside of the US–Japan alliance, an early measure was the incorporation of humanitarian and disaster relief (HADR) duties, including peace-keeping, into the SDF's mandate in the early 1990s. The foundation was laid by the passage of the 'Law Concerning Cooperation for United Nations Peacekeeping Operations and Other Operations' (also known as the International Peace Cooperation Law or IPCL) in 1992, which for the first time authorised the SDF's deployment to UN-mandated peacekeeping operations (UNPKOs). After a successful experience in Cambodia in 1992–3, the SDF was deployed in various peacekeeping operations and humanitarian missions in Mozambique, Rwanda, the Golan Heights, East Timor, Nepal, Sudan/South Sudan and Haiti. These missions subsequently increased in frequency, becoming more complex in terms of duties and spanning a wider geographic area. Another milestone was Japan's participation in international anti-piracy efforts in the Gulf of Aden from 2009. In coordination with other states, Maritime SDF (MSDF) destroyers were deployed off the coast of Somalia to escort commercial vessels from Japan and other countries, and P-3C planes conducted patrols over the affected area to support the destroyers. In support of the MSDF's long-term commitment to this mission, Japan set up its first full-scale overseas military base in Djibouti in 2011. This base became the operational centre not only for anti-piracy activities but for all SDF's activities in Africa and the Middle East, such as rescuing Japanese citizens during contingencies in the Middle East, collecting terrorism-related information, conducting surveillance during emergencies and serving as a base for SDF's disaster relief and UN peacekeeping activities in the region (Fukui and Miwa 2015). Japan's security policy expansion has also entailed the diversification of its strategic partnerships beyond the US. It developed military cooperation with countries in the south of its immediate region, namely with Australia, Indonesia, India, Vietnam, the Philippines, Malaysia and several other states (Wallace 2013).

Within the US–Japan alliance, the SDF's mandate expanded from solely focusing on national defence to accepting a greater burden-sharing role in the maintenance of regional and international peace. This was the outcome of several key developments from the mid-1990s. The first was the signing of the 1996 Japan–US Joint Declaration on Security between President Bill Clinton and Prime Minister Hashimoto Ryutaro in April 1996 and the subsequent revision of the 1978 Guidelines for US–Japan Defense Cooperation, which led to the SDF's authorisation to provide active logistical support to US forces not only during a direct attack on Japan, but also during contingencies in the Asia-Pacific region that would have an important impact on Japan's peace and security. The SDF's responsibilities within the alliance broadened even further in the context of the US-led war on terrorism. The SDF was deployed to the Indian Ocean to offer non-combat support to the US and other militaries involved in the Afghanistan campaign, and to Iraq to provide non-combat logistical and reconstruction support. Following these missions, the commitment to augment the capability of the bilateral relationship to address diverse global security challenges expanded. Both Japan and the US pushed for greater integration between their militaries in a range of areas including interoperability of the two militaries, policy and operational coordination during periods of both peace and crisis, and information sharing (see Ministry of Foreign Affairs of Japan [MOFA Japan] 2005, 2010, 2011). These efforts laid the foundation for the decision to upgrade the bilateral defence guidelines in 2015 to include collective self-defence missions for the first time, following Cabinet approval of the reinterpretation of Article 9 on 1 July 2014.

This book examines the means through which Japan's security policymaking elite achieved security policy expansion over the post-Cold War period. This is of interest because this expansion occurred despite the existence of domestic and regional constraints that have consistently precluded the legitimate use of the SDF as a tool of security policy and an expansion of Japan's military role in external strategic affairs. The domestic constraints refer to the anti-militaristic social and legal constraints that emerged during the postwar period. Although these constraints have gradually eased, social and legal limits remain resilient in shaping the Japanese security policymaking process in the post-Cold War period (Oros 2008, 2017; Singh 2013). The regional constraints refer to the problem of the 'burden of history', where Japan's neighbours – notably China,

South Korea and some Southeast Asian countries – have consistently opposed Japan's security policy expansion. Their experience of Japanese atrocities during World War Two, along with their dissatisfaction with Tokyo's failure to express remorse for its wrongdoings, continue to be a source of suspicion against Japanese security policy expansion. Of these two types of constraints, the domestic constraints have been the more influential in shaping Japanese security policy debates, and this continues to be the case. Although regional constraints remain a consideration for the Japanese government, their impact has weakened as a result of the increasing uncertainty in the strategic environment around Japan.

The research question this book aims to address is: how did Japan's security policymaking elite negotiate these stringent domestic constraints and somewhat less influential regional constraints to expand Japan's security policy practice in the post-Cold War period? The answer lies in the external military crises factor. In order to understand the deep and significant changes in Japan's security policy, it is essential to examine why and how the Japanese security policymaking elite successfully used a number of external military crises in the post-Cold War period as policy windows to push for security policy expansion. This was arguably the main policy instrument that helped the security policymaking elite overcome the multiple overlapping constraints that made it so challenging to expand Japan's security policy.

THE DEBATE

Japan's shift away from its minimalist post-Cold War security policy has not gone unnoticed in the extant literature. A large body of theoretical and policy literature, namely from the realism and social constructivism theoretical persuasions, has attempted to explain its security policy expansion. The following discussion elaborates these arguments by identifying the main factors that have driven Japan's security policy expansion in the post-Cold War period.

Realism

Realism-based arguments have mostly been critical of Japan's minimalist security policy during the Cold War period. For them, it was 'unnatural' for Japan to rely on this policy during the post-Cold War period. Neorealist scholars argued that Japan would transform its vast economic power into military power owing to the worsening structural pressures of the post-Cold War period compared to the Cold War period (Layne 1993; Waltz 1993, 2000).[1] There were two main reasons for this. The first source of increasing structural pressure was the uneven distribution of power characterised by US unipolarity. The unipolar order was understood as causing intensified competition between states, as states would challenge the unipolar power (see Waltz 2000). The second source was the uncertainty of the post-Cold War East Asian security environment caused by escalating tensions on the Korean Peninsula, China's strategic rise, and the instability resulting from Japan's territorial disputes with China (Senkaku/Diaoyu Islands), South Korea (Takeshima/Tokdo Islands) and Russia (Kurile Islands/Northern Territories). Faced with these structural pressures, neorealism contended that Japan would strengthen the full spectrum of its capabilities, pursue 'strategic autonomy' from the US and even develop nuclear weapons (Layne 1993: 37; Waltz 1993: 66–7, 2000: 34). Since 2010, this logic of analysing Japan has gained further ground. In response to the shifting distribution of military and economic power in China's favour, along with Chinese aggressive behaviour (particularly in the maritime domain), Japan is argued to have adopted a 'hard hedge' approach in its security policy (Grønning 2014; Hornung 2014; Hughes 2016).

A second set of realism-based arguments is influenced by the assumptions of neoclassical realism. These arguments accept the importance of the structural pressures or international structure alone, but also underscore the importance of domestic factors to explain changed security policy behaviour (see G. Rose 1998). For scholars of neoclassical realism, a new national purpose emerged in Japan during the post-Cold War period. This resulted in Japan showing willingness to play a more active strategic role in external affairs both within and outside the alliance (Drifte 1996; Green 2000, 2001; Green and Self 1996; Midford 2000, 2002; Pyle 1992; Saltzman 2015). This group of scholars has seen an increase in publication since 2004, as Tokyo has implemented bold security policies in response to the US-led war on terror, involving the SDF in the Operation Enduring Freedom (OEF) and Operation Iraqi Freedom (OIF) campaigns, and the US–Japan alliance has subsequently been bolstered (see Hughes 2004, 2009; Hughes and Krauss 2007; Pyle 2007; Samuels 2007). Unlike the neorealists, those subscribing to this view do not argue for Japan's acquiring greater strategic autonomy or security independence from the US. Instead, these publications argue for the continued strengthening of the US–Japan security relationship in the post-Cold War period with Japan widening its duties alongside the US, as the Japanese security policymaking elite recognises the strategic importance of the US–Japan alliance for Japan's national defence and security policy expansion.

Apart from the uncertainties of the regional security environment outlined by the neorealist scholars above, the neoclassical realism-based arguments rely on a range of domestic factors to explain Japan's security policy expansion. Probably the most important ones are those related to the changing Japanese domestic political environment, which became more conducive to an expanded security policy in the post-Cold War period. The post-Cold War environment saw the demise of the Japan Socialist Party (JSP) – the main opposition party during the Cold War period – as a political force, after it reversed its long-standing opposition to the existence of a US–Japan alliance and the constitutionality of the SDF in the mid-1990s. Although this shift was necessary for the JSP to join the ruling coalition with the Liberal Democratic Party (LDP), it led to its long-term supporters abandoning the party. This resulted in security policy debates becoming dominated by the conservative LDP, who largely supported an expanded security policy for Japan. Moreover, the JSP's place as the main opposition party to the LDP was taken over by the Democratic Party of Japan (DPJ) or Democratic Party (DP), which supported a security policy posture that was more similar to the LDP than the JSP (and later renamed the Social Democratic Party of Japan (SDPJ)), especially in terms of the expanded use of the SDF to achieve foreign and security policy goals (Pekkanen and Krauss 2005: 437).[2] This critical change removed the strong 'psychological and political obstacles' within the National Diet that had precluded the introduction of an expanded security policy during the Cold War (Kohno 2007: 40).

Within the conservative LDP, defenders of Japan's minimalist security policy shaped by economics, known as the mainstream conservatives, saw their dominance over the security policymaking process significantly reduced.[3] These individuals included prominent LDP politicians such as Miyazawa Kiichi, Gotoda Masaharu, Kaifu Toshiki, Kato Koichi, Kono Yohei, Koga Makoto and Nonaka Hiromu. Their position was taken over by more conservative LDP politicians, known as the 'normal nationalists', who supported an expanded security role for Japan.[4] The rise of the normal nationalist politicians, as reflected by the accession to power of prime ministers Hashimoto Ryutaro, Mori Yoshiro, Koizumi Junichiro, Abe Shinzo and Aso Taro, demonstrated a strong political will to expand Japan's security policy beyond the minimalist version of the Cold War. Their position was strengthened by the implementation of institutional and administrative reforms carried out during the period 1996–2001. These reforms strengthened the central authority of the Japanese government (namely the prime minister and his cabinet) over the policymaking process – a shift that has been referred to as the presidentialisation of the office of the Japanese prime minister (Boyd and Samuels 2005: 36–8; Krauss and Nyblade 2005; Shinoda 2007).[5] The confluence of the rise of the normal nationalist prime ministers within the security policymaking elite and the centralisation of the policymaking process were critical to explain Japan's security policy expansion in the post-Cold War period.

Social Constructivism

Earlier seminal publications that adopted a social constructivist approach, such as those by Peter Katzenstein, Thomas Berger and Glenn Hook, argued for the continued practice of a minimalist security policy for Japan in the post-Cold War period. This was due to the enduring presence and constraining effect of social and legal norms and the culture of antimilitarism on Japanese security policy (Berger 1998; Hook 1996; Katzenstein 1996). As the security policy expansion became more visible in the 2000s, more observers began relying on ideational factors – namely identity, norms and risk – to explain either the overall expansion in Japan's post-Cold War security policy, or specific policies that supported security policy expansion.

In terms of identity, Japan's security policy expansion has been explained by a transformation of its security identity from 'peace state' to 'international state'. Japan's security policymaking elite recognised that its Cold War approach to security policy, influenced by the peace-state security identity that had supported its minimalist security policy, was inappropriate in the post-Cold War period. Being a member of the international community, Japan carved out a responsible role in regional and international security affairs with an expanded military role in its post-Cold War security policy that was shaped by the inter-national-state security identity. This shift in identity was illustrated in three main areas that defined and shaped its security policy: Japan's definition of national security; Japan's contribution, in military terms, to regional and inter-national security affairs; and the composition of the Japanese security policy-making regime (Singh 2013). Authors have also utilised the identity concept through a relational identity approach, referring to how 'Japan is constructed vis-à-vis particular "Others"' to explain the change in Japanese security policy practice (Hagström and Gustafsson 2015). This approach has been used to explain Japan's stronger approach to North Korea (see Hagström and Hanssen 2015), Japan's foreign policy approach to South Korea in the context of the Takeshima/Tokdo territorial dispute (see Bukh 2015) and Japan's security pol-icy expansion through the decline of pacifism within Japanese state and society (see Gustafsson et al. 2018).

Scholars have used international norms and conventions to explain Japan's security policy expansion in the post-Cold War period, especially in reference to specific security policy initiatives. David Leheny has argued that Japan adopted international norms to address local security concerns. More specifi-cally, he explained that the Japanese government used the counter-terrorism policies implemented following the September 11th attacks not only to dis-play unity with the US but also to address threats faced by Japan, namely from North Korean spies and foreign criminals. The counter-terrorism policies became accepted internationally and hence offered legitimacy to the Japanese leadership's intention to strengthen its security posture to address its own primary national security threats – in this case, to address the threat posed by North Korea (Leheny 2006). Others have argued that international norms were responsible for Japan's implementation of the peacekeeping policy – a milestone in the Japanese security policy expansion of the early 1990s. Dobson (2003) and Kurashina (2005) illustrate how the normative structure of the post-Cold War period defined by the norms of collective security (which entailed a military intervention by international society in civil conflicts to preserve human rights and global peace) convinced Japan's security policymaking elite to become amenable to the deployment of its military for UNPKOs.

The risk factor was also used to explain Japan's move away from its minimalist security policy in the post-Cold War period. The argument was that Japan's security policy expansion is explained by a shift in how risks from the challenges Japan is facing in the regional security environment were perceived and recalibrated by the Japanese state, market and society. The risk narrative – derived from both external and domestic challenges including North Korea's missile and nuclear programmes, the unresolved state of Japanese abductees by North Korea, China's strategic rise, the relocation of US bases in Okinawa, Japan's territorial disputes with Russia, South Korea and China, the terror attacks of 11th September 2001, transnational environment issues and natural disasters – has resulted in the broadening of Japanese security policy options (Maslow et al. 2015; Mason 2014).

Problematising the Literature

The realist and social constructivist factors discussed above have successfully explained specific aspects of the story of Japanese security policy expansion in the post-Cold War period. At the international level, the material and normative shifts of the post-Cold War context have directly affected Japan's behaviour. Although regional uncertainties in the security environment are not a post-Cold War phenomenon, the intensity of security challenges stemming from North Korea's adamant pursuit of ballistic missiles and nuclear capabilities coupled by its unpredictable behaviour, China's strategic rise and Japan's territorial disputes has markedly worsened for Japan. These concerns, along with fears of a reduction of US military presence in Japan and East Asia (especially during the early 1990s, but a persistent feature of Japanese security policy debates), led Japan's security policymaking elite to perceive the post-Cold War environment as more complicated than the Cold War (Izawa, personal communication, 19 September 2012). Together with the emergence of collective security norms, both material and normative factors at the international level have motivated Japan to implement an expanded security policy that was more suitable to the conditions of the post-Cold War period.

At the same time, material and normative shifts at the domestic level were important for the weakening of the entrenched minimalist version of Japanese Cold War security policy. The shift in the balance of power in the Japanese political system in favour of the normal nationalist conservatives resulted in the increased importance of security issues on the national agenda and the implementation of security policy expansion through a renegotiating of constraining social and legal norms. Such an environment not only expanded the Japanese MOD's influence over the security policymaking process, but all ministries within the government became involved in the discussions involving security issues – a clear sign of the higher status of security issues on the national agenda (Shimada, personal communication, 21 November 2012). Moreover, Japanese society has become more amenable to an expanded security policy, made visible in its increasing support of the SDF's deployment for humanitarian and disaster relief and peacekeeping duties, and increased acceptance of the SDF as a critical institution of the Japanese government.

Though the authors above have rightly captured the trajectory of Japanese post-Cold War security policy, these analyses have fallen short in explicating change in Japanese post-Cold War security policy. Both the material and normative factors at international and domestic levels discussed above are at best 'background variables' (Ollapally and Mochizuki 2011: 198) or 'underlying causes' (Lebow 1981) that reveal the context within which Japan expanded its security policy practice through the incorporation of a greater military dimension. In these explanations, there is often a gap between the proposed causes and the actual process that leads to Japanese security policy expansion. They do not specify the policy mechanisms through which the factors discussed above end up transforming security policies. For example, the structural pressures that cause an unfavourable shift in the balance of power for Japan are not a sufficient cause for change to Japanese security policy, as not every perceived threatening act by China or North Korea triggers a change in Japanese security policy in the post-Cold War period. Many incidents take place in the East Asian security environment that threaten the status quo and Japan's security – some important, others not. Only certain incidents or acts that are viewed as threatening offer Japan an opportunity or policy window to expand its security role in external security affairs. In the same way, the emergence of normal nationalist politicians and charismatic prime ministers in the Japanese political system and government, along with the administrative and institutional reforms that served to confer greater power to these individuals in the security policymaking process, do not result in the expansion of Japanese security policy through the incorporation of the military dimension in Japanese security policy practice.

This is important because any explanation of change in Japanese security policy must illustrate the means through which the proposed factors circumvented or negotiated the domestic (social and legal constraints defined by antimilitarism) and regional (problem of the 'burden of history') constraints. The existing analyses, especially those located in the realist tradition, fail to identify the political processes/mechanisms that occur within the changed context of the post-Cold War period to examine how the Japanese security policymaking elite was able to pursue security policy expansion despite the existence of constraints.[6] These analyses do not demonstrate how exactly, through the uses of which policy tools and the calculation of what specific timing, these leaders actually enact their objectives. This is a crucial missing piece, because the trajectory and development of Japanese security policy have been shaped by the presence of these very constraints.

Social constructivists who have emphasised the role of international norms and risk are somewhat exceptions to this criticism. Leheny's work relied on the higher legitimacy levels from international norms and escalated levels of danger/fear during crisis periods to demonstrate how social and legal norms were circumvented to recast Japanese security policy. Those utilising risk also underscore the importance of circumventing social and legal constraints to justify an expanded security policy. However, the argument I present here differs from Leheny's, as discussed in detail below. In contrast to the risk-based arguments, my project differs in two important ways. First, rather than 'risk', I underscore the importance of external military crises as providing a policy window for change. Risk is an effect, and it cannot be treated as a stand-alone causal factor. What this means is that publications that utilise risk have failed to account for where the risk comes from. Second, instead of risk, I use the notion of 'threat' arising from serious military crises.

In short, policy and scholarly debate on change in Japanese post-Cold War security policy has introduced a range of international and domestic as well as material and ideational dynamics. They identify a number of necessary conditions for the expansion of Japan's security policy over the years, but as such these conditions are not sufficient to account for change. To put it differently, a number of background factors have operated as permissive causes of Japan's security policy expansion but they are not sufficient to explain how the security policy changes came about, despite the existence of social and legal constraints at domestic and regional levels. To explain the expansion of Japan's security policy requires us to examine the specific circumstances of security policymaking, notably the policy tools that the security policymaking elite put to the task to overcome the serious obstacles they faced, and the timing.

A Case for External Military Crises

I argue that the Japanese security policymaking elite, comprising politicians, bureaucrats and others who support an activist security policy, relied on *external military crises* to achieve the desired objective of expanding Japanese security policy.[7] With the background factors explained above being the permissive conditions, external military crises offer productive conditions for change in Japan.[8] Following Soifer's argument that both types of conditions must be present for change in a state's policy, an explanation that combines the effects of background factors and external military crises is required to understand the shift in Japan's security policy. On the one hand, the background factors explain why external military crises occur; more importantly, they set the stage for Japan's security policy expansion due to the changes of conditions at the international and domestic levels for Japan. The external military crises, on the other hand, are not just, in the words of Robert Sutter, a 'reinforcing mechanism' (Sutter, personal communication, 16 April 2015), but reveal the negative impact of the background factors and serve as conduit, justification and opportunity for a policy shift within Japan's security policy. This argument takes advantage of the duality of the crisis feature, where it has a disruptive effect as well as provides an opportunity for change.

External military crises refer to specific military incidents that disrupt the peace and stability of the regional and international security environment. These crises can be global (for example, the 1991 Persian Gulf War or the September 11th attacks that triggered the US-led global war against terrorism), where the impact is felt by the international community, or regional (for example, the 1996 Taiwan Strait Crisis and the 1998 Taepodong Crisis), where the negative impact is isolated to the region. This book adopts two definitions of crisis: a crisis defined by a single identifiable incident, and a crisis defined by a series of incidents that occur in quick succession over a period of time triggered by the same larger issue. The single-incident-based military crises studied here are the 1991 Persian Gulf War, the 1994 North Korean Nuclear Crisis, the 1996 Taiwan Strait Crisis, the 1998 Taepodong Crisis and the September 11th terrorist attacks on the US. The 'series of incidents' crisis definition is applied to the way Japanese security policymakers have internalised the threat posed by China in official debates following China's increasingly assertive maritime behaviour and the militarisation of the Senkaku/Diaoyu Islands territorial disputes. The height of Japan's concerns took place during the 2010–13 period and were caused by the September 2010 fishing trawler incident – in which a Chinese fishing vessel deliberately rammed into two Japanese Coast Guard (JCG) ships near the disputed Senkaku/Diaoyu Islands – and the September 2012 nationalisation of those same islands, which resulted in Chinese maritime and military vessels making frequent incursions into Japanese sea and air spaces. The maritime incidents were followed by the locking of fire-control radar on Japanese military vessels by the Chinese military, and China's announcement of the Air Defense Identification Zone (ADIZ) in November 2013. All of these incidents not only raised bilateral tensions, but also collectively influenced Japan's security policy expansion during the 2010–15 period.

To answer the 'how' question, the argument focuses on the notion of 'threat' as perceived or constructed by the Japanese security policymaking elite from the external military crises. Those responsible for security policymaking highlight the threat element(s) of a crisis to create a context that supports the strengthening of Japanese security policy. This narrative is underscored by elements of threat inflation, when the stated level of threat from a particular crisis is higher in intensity than the alternative threat narratives expressed by other relevant domestic or external actors; and less frequently, threat deflation, when the stated level of threat is lower than the other competing narratives expressed by other domestic and external actors and even by the security policymaking elite related to the same military crises. In this way, the Japanese security policymaking elite has been able to circumvent domestic and regional constraints in order to achieve its security policy objectives.

In essence, two mutually reinforcing processes form the explanatory mechanism that shows the interaction between external military crisis and Japan's security policy expansion. The first is the military crisis–threat construction, which refers to how the Japanese security policymaking elite constructs threat elements from an external military crisis as directly affecting both national and international security – referred to here as the two levels of the threat construction process. The national level connects the threat elements from the crises to Japan's national security, and the international level connects the threat elements to regional and international security. The combined effect of highlighting threats at the national and international levels underscores the 'danger' from the crisis to Japan, the weaknesses in Japan's security posture towards addressing the stated threats from the crisis, and a justification for Japan to pursue a stronger security posture against the 'danger' to Japan. Moreover, the international level has an added importance, especially as a source of legitimacy for the security policymaking elite to justify Japan's expanded security role. The second process is the threat construction–security policy development, which refers to how military crises facilitate the development of security policy initiatives that strengthen both Japan's national security and its contribution to the external security environment in military terms. The argument is represented graphically as follows:

EXTERNAL MILITARY CRISES	THREAT CONSTRUCTION	JAPANESE SECURITY POLICY EXPANSION
→	→ →	
(STRUCTURAL DETERMINANT)	(PROCESS & MECHANISM)	(DIRECTION/ OUTCOME)

Source: Adapted from Haferkamp and Smelser (1992: 2)

The notion of crisis as an impetus for change in Japanese security and foreign policy study is not new. An early work was Kent Calder's 1988 *Crisis and Compensation*, which focused on change in Japanese public policy, namely in non-industrial areas such as agriculture, small business, welfare, land use and regional policy. His focus on crisis had a domestic element, especially regarding the stability of the ruling conservative LDP. In order to prevent a 'crisis', which is referred to as a threat to LDP's pre-eminence in the Japanese political system, the LDP offered a routinised pattern of compensation to its opponents in the form of income, entitlements and subsidies (Calder 1988a). For David Leheny, international crises were critical in implementing an expanded security policy for Japan to address proximate threats to its national security. By raising fears within Japanese society in relation to international crises, the government gained support for the application of international norms to address threats more relevant to Japan's national security. An example provided by Leheny is Japan's utilisation of the internationally accepted counter-terrorism policies that followed the September 11th attacks to address the threat by North Korea (Leheny 2006). Richard Samuels has studied the impact of the triple disasters of 11 March 2011 on Japanese politics and public (Samuels 2013). Not only did this crisis start a debate on the future of Japan, it was a tool used by Japanese elites from ideologically variant political camps to shape national interests and direct future Japan towards their preferred paths. Samuels focused on the impact of the crisis in three areas: national security, energy and local governance. Finally, Yong Wook Lee also utilised crisis, specifically the Asian Financial Crisis, to explain a shift in Japan's policy in relation to East Asian financial regionalism (Y. W. Lee 2012).

This book agrees with the importance of crisis in understanding change in Japan as outlined above. Underscoring the importance of crisis in Japan, Clyde Prestowitz, a seasoned analyst of Japan, has said: 'Without a crisis, Japan may not be able to change' (Takahara 2015). However, this book differs from the above-mentioned authors in several ways. Unlike Calder, Samuels and Lee, I focus on external crises that are military in nature, and I analyse their impact exclusively on the security policy of Japan over the post-Cold War period. This focus on the post-Cold War period is deliberate, although the same argument could also be applied to Japanese security policy during the Cold War (Auslin, personal communication, 5 May 2015; Przystup, personal communication, 16 June 2015). This is because a clear shift in Japanese security policy from a minimalist to an activist security policy practice is visible in the post-Cold War period, especially in terms of the widening use of the SDF as a legitimate tool in Japanese security policy. While Leheny focuses on the events following the September 11th attacks (namely, targeting North Korea as part of the larger global war on terror), I cover a wider spectrum of crises and policies over the post-Cold War period, resulting in a more systematic account of how external military crises are critical aspects of change in Japanese security policy – a missing element in the Japanese security policy literature. Unlike Calder and Samuels, the argument here focuses on how external military crises are used to bring about significant change to Japanese security policy in the post-Cold War period, both outside and within the alliance.

To illustrate the critical role of external military crises in causing change in Japanese security policy, four key developments in Japanese security policy are selected as case studies.

The first is Japan's incorporation of an international security role within security policy practice in the form of peacekeeping missions. For this development, the 1990–1 Persian Gulf Crisis provided the impetus or policy window. Japan's experience in the Persian Gulf Crisis underscored the need for Japan to contribute to the formation of the new world order as challenged by the Gulf Crisis through the notion of international contribution. Since the military remained an important factor in shaping international relations, Japan had to expand its contribution not only in the economic area but also in military affairs. The Persian Gulf Crisis was a critical event which the security policymaking elite relied on to achieve the objective of expanding Japan's role internationally by widening the SDF's mandate. The foundation for an international contribution was laid with the 1992 passage of the IPCL, authorising for the first time the deployment of the SDF to UNPKOs. Following a successful experience in Cambodia, the SDF was deployed in various UNPKOs and humanitarian missions to perform an array of complex duties. Peacekeeping has become not only a permanent but a primary mission of the SDF, alongside territorial defence.

The second area is the incorporation of regional defence for the SDF within the US–Japan security alliance in the mid-to-late 1990s. The 1994 North Korean Nuclear Crisis, the 1996 Taiwan Strait Crisis and the 1998 Taepodong Crisis were critical determinants for this development. The 1994 North Korean Nuclear Crisis and the 1996 Taiwan Strait Crisis stressed to Japan that the mission of the SDF would no longer be to defend Japan alone, but also to address regional security challenges of the post-Cold War period through the alliance. Though this was first outlined in the 1995 National Defense Program Outline (*New Taiko*), this role became the centrepiece of the update of the US–Japan alliance following the signing of the 'Japan–US Joint Declaration on Security – Alliance for the 21st Century' by US President Bill Clinton and Prime Minister Hashimoto Ryutaro in April 1996 (MOFA Japan 1996a). This further led to a decision by both the American and Japanese governments to revise the 1978 Guidelines for US–Japan Defense Cooperation. However, it was the 1998 Taepodong Crisis that pushed the Lower and Upper Houses in Japan to pass bills in 1999 that legally authorised the SDF to provide active rear-area support to US forces not only during a direct attack on Japan (as stipulated by the 1978 US–Japan Defense Cooperation Guidelines and Article 5 of the US–Japan Security Treaty) but also during contingencies in the Asia-Pacific region that have an important influence on Japan's peace and security. Another important consequence of the Taepodong Crisis related to regional defence was Japan's decision to join the US-led Ballistic Missile Defense (BMD) project. The deployment of the BMD would protect not only Japan but also the East Asian security environment from the threat of ballistic missiles – strengthening Japan's contribution to regional defence duties.

The third area is the further expansion of Japanese responsibilities within US–Japan defence cooperation to include global missions during the first decade of the 2000s. The impetus for this was the 2001 September 11th attacks and the subsequent global war on terrorism involving the OEF and OIF missions. Not only did Japan show undivided support for US objectives and operations in both OEF and OIF, it also contributed prominently to the US-led war on terrorism, with the deployment of the SDF to the Indian Ocean to offer non-combat support to the US and other militaries following the passage of the Anti-Terrorism Special Measures Law (ATSML) by the National Diet in 2001. Japan was again deployed to Iraq to provide non-combat logistical and reconstruction support following the passage of the Iraqi Reconstruction Law in 2003. Following these missions, the commitment to address diverse global security challenges was augmented. Both Japan and the US have since pushed for greater integration between their militaries in a range of areas that include policy and operational coordination during periods of peace and crisis, information sharing and intelligence cooperation, and ballistic missile defence cooperation (MOFA Japan 2005).

The fourth area is the incorporation of collective self-defence missions into the SDF's mandate in 2014–15 – a historic event that has been compared to Prime Minister Yoshida Shigeru's conclusion of the Japan–US Security Treaty in 1951 and Prime Minister Kishi Nobusuke's revision of the security pact in 1960 (Kuromi 2015). The formal incorporation started with the Cabinet's approval of the reinterpretation of Article 9 to authorise the SDF to perform collective self-defence missions in July 2014. Collective self-defence missions were incorporated into the 2015 bilateral defence guidelines, and were later formalised with the passage of security bills by the Lower and Upper Houses in 2015. This development created a legal framework authorising the use of force by the SDF to assist any friendly country, namely its ally, the US, engaged in regional contingencies through limited measures. For this development, the impetus or policy window was provided by a series of military incidents involving China in the maritime domain during the 2010–13 period. These included the September 2010 fishing trawler incident; the September 2012 nationalisation of islands, leading to frequent incursions of Chinese maritime and military vessels into Japanese waters and airspace; the fire-control radar locking incident; and China's announcement of the ADIZ. Even though the reality of China destabilising the region emerged in the mid-1990s, these incidents led to an understanding that the China threat was directed at Japan, and China's actions were perceived as militarising the East China Sea territorial dispute. This in turn led to a radical shift in Japanese security policy, including the authorisation of collective self-defence missions for the SDF.

CONTRIBUTION

The contribution of this research lies in three main areas. The first relates to the critical role of Japan in the strategic context of the post-Cold War period relative to the Cold War period. During the Cold War, Japan's importance lay mainly in its position as the largest economy in Asia (and second largest in the world) and its close security relationship with the US. Japan's rapid economic ascendancy from the 1960s onwards contributed to the development of other Asian economies through its high levels of investments, trade and aid. Moreover, Japan's security relationship with the US, which involved Japan hosting the largest US troop deployment in Asia, was described as the cornerstone of peace and stability in East Asia. Nevertheless, other than hosting the US military, Japan's strategic contribution to regional and international affairs was limited and mainly concentrated in the area of economics.

However, this has changed in the post-Cold War period, as Japan's strategic importance has grown significantly. Its prolonged economic stagnation, and the increased instability of the East Asian security environment – notably China's rise and North Korea's belligerent behaviour – forced Japan to debate possible ways that it might contribute to regional and international security affairs. The outcome has been a gradual expansion of Japan's contribution in the area of security affairs. The military-strategic dimension has assumed a permanent place in Japanese security discourse. This initially occurred under the banner of 'international contribution', as the Japanese government had successfully expanded the use of the SDF to contribute to the maintenance of peace and stability in regional and international security affairs, both in the contexts of the US–Japan security relationship and UNPKOs and subsequently also in the form of affecting the balance of power in the region. This has materialised through force modernisation to strengthen Japan's military; strengthening of the US–Japan alliance; diversification of its security partnerships beyond the US; and the provision of material equipment to states such as the Philippines and Vietnam to ensure they are able to defend themselves against China. As Japan becomes a more engaged security actor in the regional security environment it is important to study Japanese security policy, as its evolution will be crucial in determining the peace and stability of the East Asian strategic environment in light of the intensifying US–China strategic struggle.

The second important aspect of this research is manifest in terms of the introduction of external military crises as an important determinant of Japanese security policy practice. As outlined above, a large body of work has been produced to explain the causes of change in Japanese post-Cold War security policy practice through various factors, such as international structure, domestic politics, security identity and norms. These have undoubtedly enriched the study of Japanese security policy. This research attempts to incorporate the external military crisis factor to this list. For Japan, this factor has a more decisive impact due to the constraining domestic and regional constraints that have precluded any expansion of Japanese security policy since the postwar period. It is important that we understand how external military crises are utilised by the Japanese security policymaking elite to justify and formulate a security policy that can address the challenges of the post-Cold War period through both empirical and theoretical perspectives.

The third important aspect of this research is a challenge to the dominance of realism since the 2000s in explaining Japanese security policy practice. Japan's enhanced role in regional and international security affairs has facilitated the rising dominance of the realist approach to capturing contemporary changes in Japanese security policy. While realist analyses relying on international and domestic material factors have correctly captured the trajectory, they do not extend their investigations deep enough to capture the complex processes that negotiate the domestic and regional constraints to bring about change in Japanese post-Cold War security policy. This research attempts to offer a nuanced analysis that not only accepts the positive contribution of realism but also incorporates a social constructivist perspective as a means of capturing the significant changes taking place in Japanese security policy practice, through analysing the interaction between Japanese security policy changes and external military crises. The main point to emerge from the use of this factor is that crises are indeed social constructions based on a state leadership's perceptions and intentions; and the Japanese security policymaking elite has relied on external military crises to pursue security policy expansion in the post-Cold War period.

STRUCTURE

To illustrate the argument, the book is organised in the following manner. Chapter 2 analyses the role of crisis in explaining security policy change through several steps. First, I explain how crisis is understood in international relations, including the definition and key features of military crises. Second, I introduce the analytical framework that connects military crises to Japanese security policy expansion, known as the threat construction process. This section outlines the key actors involved in the threat construction process, the key crises that are studied here, the type of threat elements utilised by the security policymaking elite, and the process adopted by the security policymaking elite to use military crises to bring about security policy expansion. Third, I identify cases that show the effects of various crises on Japanese post-Cold War security policy. Finally, I conclude with a brief discussion of the sources and method used in the analysis.

Chapters 3 to 6 are the case study chapters. Chapter 3 focuses on Japan's incorporation of international contribution through peacekeeping missions into its security policy practice; Chapter 4 focuses on the adoption of the regional defence role by the SDF within the US–Japan security alliance; Chapter 5 focuses on the adoption of global missions by the SDF within the US–Japan security alliance; and Chapter 6 discusses how the collective self-defence role was incorporated into Japanese security policy practice. The concluding chapter summarises the research findings, discusses the implications of the argument and makes sense of Japan's role in the intensifying competition or rivalry between the US and China.

NOTES

1. For neorealism's theoretical assumptions, see Waltz (1979).
2. The DPJ/DP lost its position as Japan's main opposition party to the Constitutional Democratic Party of Japan (CDPJ) following the Lower House election in October 2017. As the CDPJ is a more left-leaning political party compared to the DP/DPJ's amalgam of conservatives, liberals, and former socialists, it supports a less activist security policy for Japan.
3. For a detailed explanation of the mainstream conservatives, see Chapter 2, fn. 8.
4. For a detailed discussion of normal nationalists, see Chapter 2, pp. 24–5.
5. Relatedly, electoral reform of the early 1990s was another factor to explain the widened focus on national security issues by conservative politicians (see Catalinac 2016).
6. One exception in offering a determinate analysis was Midford (2002), who argued that balance of power considerations are relevant but insufficient as Japan's enhanced security role raises negative reactions from its Asian neighbours based on historically rooted fears. Hence, Japanese decision-makers face the difficult task of balancing the perception of threat from its neighbours with the need for Japan to fulfil that role. This is achieved by the Japanese government through the adoption of reassurance strategies to dissuade the Asian neighbours from balancing against it.
7. Many interviewees agreed with the importance of crisis in shaping Japanese security policy. These included present and previous government officials (Asari, personal communication, 25 September 2012; Kano, personal communication, 29 November 2012; Kimura, personal communication, 29 November 2012; Kokubun, personal communication, 30 October 2012; Serizawa, personal communication, 29 November 2012; Takahashi, personal communication, 2 October 2012; Takamizawa, personal communication, 28 September 2012) and leading analysts of Japanese security policy (Akutsu, personal communication, 14 November 2012; Funabashi, personal communication, 24 September 2012; Michishita, personal communication, 21 September 2015; Szechenyi, personal communication, 18 June 2015).
8. For permissive and productive conditions, see Soifer (2012).

2

'CRISIS IS WHAT A STATE MAKES OF IT'

The notion of crisis has been analysed in multiple fields, such as disaster relief, sociology, public administration and political science, among many others (Dayton 2004). For the international relations discipline, crises are an inherent part of the international state system that is mainly, but not exclusively, made up of sovereign states (Snyder and Diesing 1977: 3–4). As this system is governed by the condition of anarchy (where there is no higher authority above the states), states are engaged in constant competition.[1] To mitigate the negative effects of anarchy, states devise rules, structures and processes to peacefully manage the negative consequences of the competitive element of the international system. Nevertheless, states are always concerned about any challenge to the stability of the strategic environment or, in the words of Snyder and Diesing, 'the shadow of war' (Snyder and Diesing 1977: 4). There is always a possibility that the strategic system will be upset by events, such as crises, or by a potential war/conflict. Since one of the main goals of states is to maintain independence (national survival), they remain sensitive to military crises and adopt measures to strengthen their preparedness towards their negative effects.

International relations and strategic studies scholars have noted the utility of the crisis factor in unpacking the complexity of state behaviour. First, the behaviour of states becomes clearer during crises periods as opposed to peace times. The reason for this is that power configurations, national interests, perceptions and alignments become 'more sharply clarified' during crisis periods compared to any other situations, including peace times

(Gourevitch 1986: 9; Snyder and Diesing 1977: 4–5). Second, the crisis factor is important to understand change in a state's foreign and security policy (Gustavsson 1999; Hermann 1990). Samuels noted that a crisis situation triggers a battle of ideas within a state on how it should respond or which path it should take. He wrote:

> Crises provide the stage on which groups battle to define the situation and so to control it. In this competition for control of how the crisis is to be understood, populations can be made anxious or they can be calmed. In either state, they can be led in new directions. (Samuels 2013: 26)

Third, not just to explain change, Gustavsson noted that the crisis factor resolves the difficulty in explaining the timing of foreign and security policy change (Gustavsson 1999: 85). Fourth, in studying the causes of war, Ned Lebow notes the importance of crises as an immediate or proximate cause of war. He argues that occurrences of war are not determined by underlying or long-term factors alone. Instead, immediate or proximate factors, such as crises, can influence and change the course of a state's foreign and security policy (Lebow 1981: 1–3). The study of the Cuban Missile Crisis recognises this position. While long-term factors related to structural competition repeatedly resulted in a negative reading of the bilateral competition between the US and the Soviet Union during the Cold War, the experience of the Cuban Missile Crisis mitigated their aggressive strategies towards each other and resulted in an unexpected détente between the two competitive powers (Lebow 1981: 4).

There are many definitions of crisis.[2] Hay defines crisis as a 'moment of decisive intervention' and 'process of transformation' (Hay 1996: 254–5). Walby defines crisis as 'an event that has the potential to cause a large detrimental change to the social system and in which there is lack of proportionality between cause and consequence' (Walby 2015: 14). There is a well-established literature on external military crises that has attempted to devise a more specific definition that could differentiate a military crisis situation from a non-crisis situation or a 'situational change' (see Brecher 1977: Brecher and Harvey 1998; Parker 1977; Snyder and Diesing 1977; Tanter 1978). Michael Brecher and his colleagues at the International Crisis Behaviour (ICB) Project, which was established in 1975 at McGill University, offer the most developed theory of international crisis behaviour as well as a definition of international crisis.[3]

At the ICB Project, the concept of a crisis is approached in a bifurcated way: at the macro level (international/system) and the micro level (state/actor) (James 2004: 357–8). An *international* crisis is defined as having the following two necessary and sufficient conditions:

(a) a change in type and/or an increase in intensity of *disruptive*, that is, hostile verbal or physical, *interactions* between two or more states, with a heightened probability of *military hostilities*; that, in turn,

(b) destabilises their relationship and *challenges* the *structure* of an international system. (Brecher and Wilkenfeld 2000: 4–5, emphasis from original)

At the state/actor level, a crisis, essentially a foreign policy crisis, is a situation with three necessary and sufficient conditions deriving from a change in the state's external or internal environment. It becomes a foreign policy crisis when the highest-level decision-makers of the actor concerned perceive the following three conditions:

(a) a *threat to one or more basic values*;

(b) an awareness of *finite time for response* to the value threat; and

(c) a *heightened probability of involvement in military hostilities*. (Brecher and Wilkenfeld 2000: 4–5, emphasis from original; also see Brecher 1977: 43–4; Dowty 1984: 1–2)[4]

International and foreign policy crises are closely connected. Each international crisis begins with and is made up of one or more foreign policy crises. Both levels, systemic and actor, have a complementary role in the crisis definition for the ICB Project. While the international level concentrates on actions and events *per se*, the actor level focuses on how leaders as participants perceive the state's involvement (see Brecher and Harvey 1 998: 8; James 2004: 358).

Using the ICB Project's definition of international and foreign policy crises as a foundation, the way military crises are understood in this book requires the addition of two more features. First, to add to the ICB Project's focus on a singular event as crisis, it is important to recognise that a crisis can also comprise a series of incidents around a similar issue over a period. Murray Edelman wrote that '[m]ore often than not a crisis is an episode in a long sequence of similar problems' (Edelman 1988: 31). Colin Hay concurred when he wrote: '[t]he discursive construction of crisis can thus be seen as a process involving the mapping together of a great variety of disparate events unified through the identification of some *common essence* – the over-extension of the state, etc.' (Hay 1996: 266, italics added). It is important to note that such an understanding of crisis does not weaken the definition of a crisis but strengthens it. While the core features of crisis discussed above remain relevant, the broadening of this definition reflects the nature of crises today that could be defined by a series of incidents or episodes over a specific period. This understanding of crises has been applied to financial crises, as noted by both Calder and Ye and Walby, but should also be extended to military crises (Calder and Ye 2010: 46; Walby 2015).

Second, my understanding of crisis underscores the subjective notion of a crisis (Hart 1993; Hay 1996). This work aligns with Hart's power-critical approach, which recognises the importance of not only the functionalist (for example, policies implemented in response to crises), but also social constructivist elements (for example, the crisis managers' various constructions of reality in relation to the crises) in studying the impact of crisis on state behaviour (Hart 1993: 37). The crisis managers' interpretation is a key element in understanding the interaction between external military crises and changes to a state's security policy (Weldes 1996: 278–9). This point is about the security policymaking elite having the ability to attach crisis-like features, in appropriate conditions, to non-crisis events, and non-crisis features to crisis events. The way this occurs is dependent on the security environment and the objectives of the security policymaking elite. Arjen Boin refers to this approach as the 'political-symbolic' perspective of crisis research, namely 'how crisis managers and the rest of us make sense of the crisis' (Boin 2004: 167). The subjective element is important because, as Boin noted, 'we can only speak of a crisis if the actors in question perceive the situation as such' (Boin 2004: 167). At the same time, as Murray Edelman noted, the creation of a crisis is a 'political act' that allows any incident to be elevated to a crisis causing instability (Edelman 1988: 31). Therefore not all states react to crises in a similar way, and a state can react to a certain crisis in a more exaggerated way than other crises that could potentially be more threatening to its national security. This impact of the crisis is expressed through narrative and discourse (Hay 1996: 255).

The subjective aspect of crisis leads us to the opportunistic notion of crisis. Crisis offers a 'policy window' (see Keeler 1993) when the security policymaking elite can inflate the seriousness of issues in a way that would not have been possible during non-crisis periods. The aim is to convince others internally (within the state and society, especially those who oppose a new policy or path proposed by the security policymaking elite) and externally (states/institutions that are suspicious of the intentions/behaviour of the new policy or proposed path) of the constructed reality that requires action as suggested by the security policymaking elite, sometimes even circumventing democratic processes.[5] Paul 't Hart refers to crisis periods as 'opportunity spaces' for the security policymaking elite to take charge of shaping the strategic debates that justify policies which challenge the existing principles that shape the state's security policy (Hart 1993: 36). Moreover, crises are times when not only is consensus fractured, as argued by Walby, but also the security policymaking elite can fracture the consensus so as to achieve the desired vision of those in power who do not agree with the existing vision or principles of a state's security policy (Walby 2015: 16).

THREAT CONSTRUCTION PROCESS

The subjective and opportunity aspects of crisis are important to my argument, which explicates *how* external crises played an integral role in the reorientation of Japanese security policy in the post-Cold War period. To ask the 'how' question, as Jeffrey Checkel argued, is to think about mechanisms that form the possible relationship between cause and effect (Checkel 2005: 805). For our purposes here, the proposed cause is external military crises and the observed effect is Japanese security policy expansion, entailing a widened use of its military as a tool of security policy. The explanatory mechanism to show the relationship between the cause and effect is the threat construction process surrounding military crises. In elucidating the process of threat construction, this section addresses: the actors involved in the threat construction process; the military crises studied here; the type of threat elements the security policymaking elite used in the process; and how the threat construction process takes place.

The Actors

The lead actor in the threat construction process is the Japanese security policymaking elite. This group is responsible for identifying what it sees as the 'appropriate' course of a state's security policy, and undertaking efforts related to the conceptualisation, formulation, implementation and operationalisation of Japan's security policy. The security policymaking elite is also responsible for identifying moments when a new course should be charted for Japan in response to the changes in the external strategic environment. In introducing change, the security policymaking elite utilises various tools to legitimise the proposed change in security policy. I show that this group has the power to respond, identify, define and give meaning to a crisis (Hay 1996: 255).

In general, the Japanese security policymaking elite in the post-Cold War period includes the Prime Minister, officials of the Prime Minister's Office, the Cabinet Secretariat, the Chief and Deputy Chief Cabinet Secretaries, the Minister for Foreign Affairs, the Director-General of the Japan Defense Agency or Minister of Defense, the National Security Advisor, and officials from the Ministry of Foreign Affairs (MOFA), Japan Defense Agency (JDA) or Ministry of Defense (MOD), National Security Council, and the Cabinet Legislation Bureau (CLB). Outside of the bureaucracy, the security policymaking elite group also includes members of the political parties. The main party has been the conservative LDP that has ruled Japan for most of its postwar history, except in 1993–4 (for ten months) and 2009–12 (see Krauss and Pekkanen 2011). The other important political parties that have also contributed to debates on security policy expansion are the DPJ or Democratic Party (formed in March

2016 with the merger of the Democratic Party of Japan and Japan Innovation Party), the New Komeito or Komeito, Japanese Socialist Party (JSP), Kino no To (Hope), Assembly to Energize Japan, the New Renaissance Party, and the Party for Future Generations, among several others. The participation of opposition parties in the security policy expansion process has occurred in various forms, such as by taking over the reins of the government whether independently or through a coalition, especially in the case of the JSP and DPJ; through being part of the ruling coalition with the LDP and finally, through sharing the LDP's objectives relating to security policy expansion. Other key actors of the security policymaking elite are members of academia who have contributed to national security debates through various means, such as serving in the bureaucracy, as advisors to the prime ministers and other leaders in the government, and on committees to review Japan's security policy.

Compared to the Cold War period, the security policymaking elite has become more diverse in the post-Cold War period.[6] First, security policymaking is no longer the domain of the MOFA and the economics-focused ministries (Ministry of Finance and Ministry of International Trade and Industry (MITI)) alone, as it was in the Cold War period. Other ministries, such as the MOD and Ministry of Land, Infrastructure, Transport and Tourism, have become prominent in the security policymaking process in the post-Cold War period. Second, politicians have expanded their control over the security policymaking process in the post-Cold War period, resulting in the weakening of the bureaucracy's traditional dominance since the onset of the Cold War. This came about following the implementation of institutional and administrative reforms in the mid-1990s by politicians. The outcome was the centralisation of power within the Kantei (Prime Minister's Office), which allowed the politicians to assume a larger coordinating role over security policy matters (see Shinoda 2007; Singh 2016).

Third, there is a change in the type of politicians dominating key positions within the security policymaking elite.[7] Mainstream conservatives, who were supportive of a minimalist security policy that was defined by economic interests and a low profile for Japan in military-strategic affairs, lost their dominance in the post-Cold War period.[8] Their place was taken over by politicians who preferred security policy expansion with a wider use of the SDF as a security policy tool. Samuels refers to this group as the 'normal nationalists'. For the normal nationalist conservatives, Japan's minimalist security policy was incongruent to the post-Cold War security environment. They aimed to transform the assumptions that determine Japan's role in external security affairs and introduce what they saw as the 'appropriate' course for Japan's security policy in the post-Cold War period. They initiated debate and introduced an alternative formulation of Japan's security policy that favoured Japanese security policy expansion with a wider use of the SDF as a tool of security policy.

Undoubtedly, there are competing views within the normal nationalists on what would be the best course for Japan. Samuels divided the normal nationalists into three groups: the globalists, the realists and the revisionists. The globalists supported the expansion of the SDF's role in global security affairs commensurate with its economic wealth. They called for the SDF's deployment only under the aegis of the UNPKOs, a move that does not require a revision to Article 9. The realists argued that Japan should expand its security role in global affairs through a strengthened military, UN-centric diplomacy and US–Japan security relationship. Japan should assume responsibility for its action in World War Two and avoid any provocation of its neighbours through its actions, such as the textbook reforms and prime ministers' visits to the Yasukuni Shrine (Samuels 2007: 124–5). The revisionists shared the same premise as the realists in terms of strengthening Japan's security policy through military terms, but believed that Japan had to move beyond the postwar regime. Japan had apologised sufficiently for its past misdeeds and controversies related to the history issue, such as the textbook issue and Yasukuni Shrine. Moreover, these issues were viewed as internal matters that should not concern China and the Koreas (Samuels 2007: 125–6). Samuels' division of the normal nationalists term into the three groups is useful in highlighting the transfer of power from the globalists to the realists and subsequently to the revisionists over the course of the post-Cold War period. This is directly related to the gradual strengthening of Japan's security posture through the implementation of incrementally bolder policy initiatives in the post-Cold War period, as discussed in the case studies.

Military Crises

My analysis focuses on external military crises. These include both singular crisis events, and crises that are defined by a series of events surrounding a particular strategic concern. The singular events studied are the 1991 Persian Gulf War, the 1994 North Korean Nuclear Crisis, the 1996 Taiwan Strait Crisis, the 1998 Taepodong Crisis, and the September 11th attacks. The series definition of crisis is applied to the China-related maritime incidents in the East China Sea. The incidents include the September 2010 fishing trawler incident, the September 2012 nationalisation of islands, Chinese maritime and military vessels' repeated entry into Japanese sea and air spaces following the 2010 and 2012 incidents, the radar locking incident, and China's announcement of the controversial ADIZ in November 2013. All these situations created security crises for Japan, as well as serving as policy windows for Japanese security policy expansion in the post-Cold War period.

In this analysis, only military crises that affected Japan are selected. There were other international military crises, such as in Rwanda and Darfur, that took place in the post-Cold War period. However, these did not affect

Japanese security policy debates in the manner that the regional and global crises introduced above did. This is for two reasons. First, these crises did not occur in Japan's immediate environment. This is an important point, as Yuki Tatsumi from the Stimson Centre argued: that the trigger for change in Japan is always not far from Japan's shores, asserting the point that regional dynamics have traditionally been the main cause of change in Japanese security policy (Tatsumi, personal communication, 27 April 2015). Second, these crises did not affect Japan's national security or question Japan's role within the US–Japan security alliance. These two conditions are important for Japan's participation in crises beyond the region. The inclusion of crises beyond the region, such as the 1990–1 Persian Gulf War and the 2001 September 11th attacks, is based on the critical impact these events had on debates at home relating to Japan's role as a reliable ally of the US and a responsible actor in regional and international affairs.

Not all military incidents that could be construed as crisis by others, such as the 1995 Chinese nuclear tests and the 1999 North Korean ship intrusions into Japanese waters, are included in this analysis. The 1995 Chinese nuclear tests did not amount to an international crisis, nor did the Japanese leadership frame them as a security policy crisis. The nuclear tests were a reassertion of China's status as a nuclear power and did not trigger significant developments in Japan's security policy. The March 1999 North Korean ship intrusions were a significant military incident that led to Japanese destroyers firing, for the first time since 1954, on North Korea spy boats disguised as fishing vessels. While this incident is not treated as a separate crisis here, its effects are incorporated into the threat narrative surrounding the 1998 Taepodong Crisis. These ship intrusions occurred while the Japanese state and society were still recovering from the 'shock' of the Taepodong Crisis and debating the revision of the bilateral defence guidelines to authorise the SDF to adopt a regional defence role within the US–Japan alliance. The incident intensified the security policymaking elite's threat construction processes related to the Taepodong Crisis.[9] The 2006, 2009, 2013, 2016 (twice) and 2017 nuclear tests by North Korea are also not discussed separately. These events do not constitute military crises and the outcome of the tests reinforced existing threat perceptions within Japanese security policymaking elite of the North Korean threat. The impact of the Great East Japan Earthquake on 3 March 2011 is also excluded. This tragedy, like the 1995 Great Hanshin Earthquake, changed Japanese society's perceptions of the SDF due to their relief efforts. However, these are not domestic crises and fall outside the scope of this book, which is on external military crises.

Threat Elements

According to Maoz, a threat 'reflects an anticipation of loss to some currently possessed values or assets as a result of some observed environmental cue'. The magnitude of threat perception is dependent on the 'magnitude of anticipated losses' and 'the probability of loss to those values' (Maoz 1990: 62).[10] Unlike realism's understanding of threat being determined by power politics and exogenously given factors (Walt 1987), the understanding here is that threat is socially constructed based on historical, political, cultural and economic contexts. Its meaning(s) is/are constitutive of social structures formed when states attach meaning(s) through practices that create and instantiate one structure of identities and interests over another (Wendt 1992: 395). States are constantly engaged in threat construction processes, as they discern the outlook of the external strategic space and discuss means to address the challenges that could harm their national security as well as destabilise the external strategic environment. The main difference between everyday threat construction processes and those associated with crises is the intensity of the threats perceived. The threat perceived or constructed from a crisis has a higher level of danger/fear and urgency. This is when the security policymaking elite realises that a 'decisive intervention', in the words of Colin Hay, has to be made for change to take place (Hay 1996: 254–5).

What types of threats are constructed in the threat construction processes related to the military crises? Japan is a constitutive member of the regional and international security environment. It engages with other states and non-state actors to collectively construct the strategic environment. Such construction identifies the different actors in the international strategic environment, including identifying Japan's friends and enemies (Weldes 1999: 231). These constructions of the representations of the international strategic environment are based on the interests and values Japan supports. The Japanese government chooses the appropriate representations for its security policy because it not only represents the interests pursued by state officials but these representations are also a source of legitimacy for public support of the security policymaking elite's desired security policy (Weldes 1999: 257, fn. 19).

Broadly speaking, Japan (like other states) has dual representations of the security environment – positive and negative representations.[11] They are dual because one cannot exist without the other. Japan's preferred vision of the security environment is based on the 'other' (the undesired vision). The positive view of the international order for Japan would be defined by a US-led global security order, where there is peace and stability of the international strategic environment, determined by peaceful states and Japan's security partners; and states' adherence to international law and norms that are supported by Japan and its security partners (see Abe 2014).[12] The negative image would be determined by acts that destabilise the peace and stability of the US-led global security order by hostile states that contravene accepted international laws and norms. The Japanese government, like all other like-minded governments, is constantly working towards creating a security environment that conforms to the positive representation. This entails constant vigilance for signs that might steer the security environment towards the negative representation. This is because an unstable security environment threatens Japan's objectives and national survival.

One such sign is the occurrence of military crises. The occurrence of crises informs the Japanese government that there is instability in the regional and international strategic environment that threatens its national security. The security policymaking elite engages in a threat construction process related to a crisis that entails representations of reduced security for themselves and others (Weldes 1999: 233). The notion of threat construction through crises, like all social facts, is a social construction and without the threat-based interpretation, a crisis would not be a crisis. Threats do not exist in a vacuum. They are constructed from events, speeches, history, the behaviour of others, and many other sources. Threats do not just appear, but political actors portray them in such negative terms to convince the audience (Stone 1989).

When referring to the phrase 'threat construction', this does not mean that the threats faced by Japan are artificial or not real (Walby 2015: 14). Crises are 'real', as Japan does face existential threats to its national security in the region and beyond, such as from the ballistic missile and nuclear programmes of North Korea and the repeated intrusions of Chinese maritime and military vessels into Japanese territorial sea and airspace. However, crises are also socially constructed, as they are open to various interpretations. This refers to how the Japanese security policymaking elite understands and expresses its threat perceptions during external military crises. Subotić noted that crises are events that allow for selective narrative activation to bring about change through introducing a narrative that would 'make policy change comprehensible and acceptable' (Subotić 2015: 616). The threat narrative was an important process undertaken by the security policymaking elite targeted at the domestic and external audiences to overcome the domestic and regional constraints against Japanese security policy expansion.

As Yong Wook Lee noted, not all crises result in policy change. Only those crisis-defining ideas that are related to threat perceptions result in security policy change (Y. W. Lee 2012: 794–5). Lee writes: 'By constructing a crisis or policy failure in a certain way, crisis-defining ideas enable/constrain actors in a position of institutional authority to engage in defining, diagnosing, and explaining the crisis as an event that calls for a particular course of action' (Y. W. Lee 2012: 793). The objective here is to explicate the process through which the security policymaking elite frames specific events (crises) through language to achieve their desired ends (Hart 1993: 37–41). To achieve this, the threat construction process is defined by threat inflation – where the stated level of threat from a particular crisis is higher than the accepted level of threat perceived by either domestic or external actors – or threat deflation, where the stated level of threat voiced by the Japanese security policymaking elite is lower than the accepted level of threat perceived by others, or even expressed by the security policymaking elite in other contexts (Walby 2015: 14).[13]

The framing of the crisis through the use of language in a particular incident allows one to recognise an incident as a crisis (Edelman 1988: 31). The framing is through a threat-based discourse that occurs at two levels: national (threats are constructed around the subject Japan) and international (threats from the crisis are connected to the regional and international security environment). The justification for the national level in the threat construction process is obvious, as the connection of the threat to the subject's national security suggests a necessary response from the Japanese security policymaking elite to enhance the state's security. The international level in the threat construction process is important for Japan as it recognises itself as a constitutive member of the regional and international security environment, where Japan's national security is connected to the larger external strategic environment. To safeguard its national security and be a responsible member, Japan has to participate in the collective protection of the peace and stability of the regional and international security environment. The international dimension of the threat construction process also reduces the suspicion and fears of Japan's neighbours in relation to its intentions and legitimises Japan's security policy expansion.

At the national level, the threat construction process involves three kinds of threat elements, as discussed in the case study chapters. The first kind of threat construction involves the direct impact of military crises on Japan's national security. These include tying Japan's national security to a particular military crisis; highlighting the threat to Japan's national security based on its close geographic proximity to the crisis; and exposing the vulnerability of the Japanese territorial state and society to the threats exposed by the crisis, such as international terrorism, North Korea's advanced nuclear weapons and ballistic missile programmes, Japan's dependence on Middle East oil, China's maritime assertiveness, and Japan's inability to address negative effects of the crises due to its unprepared security posture (such as in gray zone situations that have not been provided for in the US–Japan security debates). The second kind of threat construction focuses directly on the behaviour of the crisis initiator. Examples include China's use of force and coercive actions; China's missile inventory; China's uncertain intentions; China's attempts to change the status quo; and North Korea's belligerent behaviour, which was described as 'insincere' or 'irresponsible'. The final kind of threat construction relates to issues that were indirectly implicated by the crises but have a direct impact on Japan's national security. These include the uncertainty in the US–Japan security relationship as well as the uncertainty related to the sustainability of the US military presence in East Asia, and the issue of Japan being internationally isolated due to its passive response to crises; the danger of weapons of mass destruction (WMD) falling into the hands of international terrorists if the international community, including Japan, did not intervene in Iraq militarily; and the drawing of linkages of nuclear weapons proliferation between Iraq and North Korea – the latter being more dangerous to Japan's national security.

The security policymaking elite's threat constructions at the international level have assumed several features. Some were general in nature, such as the crises causing uncertainty in the post-Cold War security environment, and even challenging the extant status quo. The threat construction process at the international level also focused on specific actors, usually when there was an international consensus that these actors were deemed as 'dangerous' to the international community, namely North Korea and Iraq. Since 2012, the Japanese security policymaking elite has repeatedly declared China's assertive behaviour in the maritime domain as a serious concern to the regional and international community. It has argued that Chinese actions infringed the international legal order and were a risk to the global commons. The threat construction process also specifically identified issues that challenged regional and international peace and stability, such as North Korea's nuclear weapons and ballistic missile programmes, Chinese maritime assertiveness, international terrorism and the proliferation of missiles and nuclear weapons.

The Process

The intervening mechanism that outlines the flow from external military crises to Japan's security expansion is the threat construction process. The threat construction process is made up of two sub-processes – the *military crisis-threat construction* and the *threat construction-security policy development*. This process illustrates the key stages involved in the way states use crises, as identified by Paul 't Hart: (1) individuals/groups become aware of changes to their environment ('perceptual' stage); (2) the extant situation is questioned, anxiety is raised and vulnerability is escalated ('affective' stage); (3) particular established principles within the state and society are questioned ('de-legitimation' stage); and finally (4) new paths are opened ('opportunity' stage) (Hart 1993: 39–40). Although the two sub-processes will be discussed independently below, it is important to note that they are both constitutive of each other – one cannot exist without the other.

Military Crisis-Threat Construction: There must be a relationship between the military crises and the threat construction processes. When a crisis occurs, the security policymaking elite made of the normal nationalist politicians recognise the importance of either showing active participation in the resolution of the crisis or taking active measures to address the negative effects of the crises on Japan's national interests. This could be due to several factors, such as pressure from the international community to respond appropriately to the resolution of the crisis; the recognition that Japan should respond responsibly along with other states to contribute to the peace and stability of the extant

US-led international/regional order; and the realisation that Japan requires a stronger security policy that is prepared to address the negative effects from the military crises. However, Japan's response is usually restricted by institutional and societal anti-militaristic structures and norms. This results in the security policymaking elite forming a relationship between the occurrences of a crisis and Japan's national security. At the same time, the security policymaking elite also recognises the opportunity or policy window the crisis presents for implementing a policy initiative that would lead to an expanded security policy.

The relationship between the military crises and the threat construction process is obviously negative, as the focus is on threat. The negative relationship is represented at two levels: the national level (how the crisis exposes a threat towards Japan's national security and, in turn, how Japan's security policy, based on its previous minimalist security policy, is ill-equipped to deter that threat) and the international level (how the crisis destabilises the peace and stability of the international/regional security environment). Though the threat elements associated with the military crises studied here show diversity at both the national and international levels, two main points are common to all threat construction processes: first, the threat construction process at the national level exposes Japan's vulnerability in relation to the threat posed by the military crises; and second, the threat construction process at the international level reveals the uncertainty of the strategic environment, which in turn exacerbates Japan's vulnerability.

In analysing Japanese security policy, the threat construction process is mostly inflationary, as in the security policymaking elite's threat representations are more alarming than those of the other internal groups who oppose a proactive security policy, along with other countries involved in the crises. This is because the security policymaking elite's objectives are to highlight the 'danger' from external military events and how Japan's extant security policy is insufficient to address these challenges. Inflated threat representations are used to circumvent the normative constraints as well as the domestic and regional opposition towards an expanded security policy. This was the case for all four case studies.

However, the threat construction process could also be deflationary. In this book, the deflationary effect is explained through the security policymaking elite's downplaying of the negative effects of the policy initiatives that support security policy expansion. This was visible in two cases – Japan's participation in the OIF, and the passage of the collective self-defence security bills. Both cases incorporated the inflationary and deflationary types of threat construction elements. The common feature of these two cases was that both were controversial decisions made by the security policymaking elite that faced strong, vehement opposition. The OIF was opposed by most states at the international level, and Prime Minister Koizumi's decision to support the

US received widespread criticism from various segments of Japanese state and society. To overcome opposition towards SDF's deployment to Iraq, he played up the humanitarian aspect of this deployment to underplay the dangers that the SDF could face in its Iraq mission. The security bills passed in September 2015 were controversial due to the lifting of the long-time ban on collective self-defence missions for the SDF. As discussed in Chapter 6, this move by the Abe government faced strong opposition from various segments of Japanese society. Even though these bills were arguably in response to China's increased assertiveness in the maritime domain, the security policymaking elite worked hard to detach the bills from Japan's concerns related to China during the debates in the National Diet and underplayed the risks from the SDF's engagement in collective self-defence missions. Instead, the Japanese security policymaking elite emphasised how the ability to engage in collective self-defence made Japan safer and reinforced Japan's identity of being a responsible actor in global affairs.

Threat-Policy Development: There must be a relationship between the threat elements of the threat construction processes and the implementation of security policy initiatives that support Japan's security policy expansion in the post-Cold War period. In this phase, the external crisis creates a crisis at the domestic level. The domestic political environment becomes a 'marketplace of ideas' (Kaufmann 2004) where there is intensive debate between the security policymaking elite's representations of the crisis and those of the opposition groups; hence, showing the interactive relationship between the external and domestic levels.

Based on the entrenched social and legal norms defined by antimilitarism, the opposition parties (namely the JSP, the Japanese Communist Party (JCP) and elements within the DPJ/DP), nongovernmental organisations, civil society groups and segments of Japanese society usually oppose the security policymaking elite's intent to implement policies that challenge the minimalist version of security policy and result in greater risk for the SDF and Japan's national security. In addition, the security policymaking elite could also face stiff opposition from within the LDP, such as during the debate leading to the passage of the IPCL in 1992. Apart from the Japanese public, the security policymaking elite's threat construction processes accompanying military crises are also targeted at Japan's Asian neighbours, who are traditionally suspicious about an expanded security role for Japan.

The threat construction processes from the military crises empower the security policymaking elite to steer the negotiation process in favour of Japanese security policy expansion. To circumvent the opposing view, the government makes a successful case for the threat posed by the crisis to Japan's national security. Despite the opposition, the government manages to use threat-based representation to implement and legitimise policy initiatives that support security policy expansion by circumventing the social and legal constraints on Japanese security policy. The more the security policymaking elite aims to win over the support of those in the opposing camp, the higher the threat level (or the anticipated loss of values or assets) constructed.[14] The threat elements introduced by the security policymaking elite underscore the 'danger' Japan is in and are frequently inflated compared to the visions offered by opposition groups. Samuels wrote: 'It is not surprising . . . that the rhetoric of crisis is so often an exercise in excess, prone to over-vilification and over-glorification' (Samuels 2013: 28). As mentioned above, the security policymaking elite could also deflate the threat when it would like to push a specific policy. To win over the support of the opposition group, the security policymaking elite underplays the threat environment and possibility of the Japanese military being involved in a potential conflict, underscoring the international dimension of the security policy expansion.

It is important to note that the security policymaking elite is not always successful in achieving its objectives, nor is the process always as straightforward as described above. Those who favour the expansion of Japanese security policy must always negotiate the social and legal constraints supported by opposing groups by devising strategies to address challenges in the strategic environment. Hence the security policymaking elite's proposed policy changes are usually not as ambitious as hoped by the Japanese security policymaking elite, the US and other states that support an expanded security policy for Japan. In fact, any new security policy expansion always comes with limits in relation to what the SDF is authorised to do independently or alongside the US.

The proposed security policy initiatives of the security policymaking elite are usually implemented during the crisis or during a post-crisis phase. For example, the Anti-Terrorism Bill was implemented while the crisis in Afghanistan was ongoing, and the bills authorising a regional defence role followed the 1994 North Korean Nuclear Crisis and the 1996 Taiwan Strait Crisis, and were passed after the 1998 Taepodong Missile Crisis by the National Diet. Due to the political difficulties stemming from the social and legal constraints, along with the 'political immobilism' feature associated with the Japanese security policymaking process (see Calder 1988b; Grimes 2003; Hellman 1977), the debate between the security policymaking elite and the opposition has frequently extended into the post-crisis stage. As a result, Japan has frequently been accused by the US and other concerned states of failing to contribute to international efforts to resolve crises. The 1991 Persian Gulf Crisis and the 1994 North Korean Crisis are good examples. However, the post-crisis phase served as an important stage for the security policymaking elite to discuss ways that Japan could have reacted to a preceding crisis and ways to make Japan more secure from threats posed by future crises. This usually results in a debate that is defined by the threat construction process and leads to the successful implementation of active measures to support Japanese security policy expansion.

At this point, it is important to note that the intensity of the debate at this stage has fluctuated over the course of the post-Cold War period. On the one hand, the opposition that adhere to the minimalist security policy within the security policymaking process has lost power. This especially coincided with the gradual decline of the JSP (which constantly challenged the LDP's attempts to expand Japan's security policy since the early postwar period) as the main opposition political party within Japan's political environment since 1996. The DPJ/DP, which subsequently became the main opposition party, supported an expanded security policy that was similar to the LDP, but in limited terms. Moreover, the opposition within the LDP has weakened over the course of the post-Cold War period. This is due to the increasing dominance of the revisionist normal nationalist politicians within the LDP, as well as increasing support within the LDP for a stronger security posture to address the escalating uncertainty in the strategic environment facing Japan. With these changes, the security policymaking elite has been able to enact policy initiatives to support security policy expansion in a shorter span of time – a point that will be made evident in the comparison of Japan's responses to the 1991 Persian Gulf War and the OEF/OIF. On the other hand, in response to the revisionists' increasingly bold initiatives to expand Japan's security policy, the opposition has also become fiercer in some ways over the course of the post-Cold War period. For example, the decision to reinterpret the collective self-defence triggered the largest demonstrations from Japanese society since the protests in 1960 against the revision of the Treaty of Mutual Cooperation and Security between the United States and Japan pushed by revisionist Prime Minister Kishi Nobusuke.

CASES

To show the impact of crises, four key developments of Japanese security policy expansion are selected: the incorporation of international peacekeeping into the SDF's mandate following the passage of the IPCL in 1992; the incorporation of the regional defence role for the SDF within the US–Japan security alliance following the revision of the Guidelines of Japan–US Defense Cooperation in 1997; the incorporation of global missions into the US–Japan security relationship in the mid-2000s; and finally, the incorporation of collective self-defence missions into the SDF's mandate in 2014–15. These policy initiatives, as argued here, are the most important developments in expanding the use of the SDF as a tool of security policy through expanded roles, capabilities and missions both individually and within the US–Japan alliance in the post-Cold War period.

International Peacekeeping

The first major policy for Japan's post-Cold War security policy was the incorporation of peacekeeping into the SDF's mandate. To be sure, the idea of Japan pursuing a peacekeeping policy is not a post-Cold War phenomenon. It was debated by Japanese officials and politicians as early as the late 1950s and has remained on the national security agenda ever since (see Heinrich et al. 1999; Pan 2005). For the conservative politicians and bureaucrats in Japan, peace-keeping was regarded as the most appropriate and least controversial means through which Japan could widen its contribution to the international secu-rity environment. Despite the frequent proposals from the LDP and MOFA (see Pan 2005), the SDF's participation in UNPKOs was never authorised dur-ing the Cold War due to its controversial status within the Japanese political system, even though progress was made at the tail end of the Cold War period through only civilian participation.

A major shift came in the post-Cold War period, when the SDF was authorised to perform peacekeeping duties. This policy came through the passage of the IPCL in 1992, which authorised the deployment of the SDF to UN-mandated HADR and peacekeeping missions overseas. This development was a curtain-raiser for Japan's increasing involvement in contributing to the regional and international security environment. Following its successful first deployment to Cambodia in 1992, the SDF was deployed in various UNPKOs and humanitarian missions, such as in Mozambique, Rwanda, the Golan Heights, East Timor, Nepal, Sudan/South Sudan and Haiti. These missions have increased in frequency, becoming more complex in terms of duties and spanning a wider geographical area. The deployment of Japanese troops is no longer restricted to regions where the con-flict had ceased, as stated in the IPCL, but has widened to where the conflict is ongoing, such as the SDF's deployment to Iraq. In fact, HADR and peacekeeping duties have become one of the core mandates of the SDF.

The impetus of this policy was the 1990–1 Persian Gulf Crisis – the first international crisis of the post-Cold War period. The unique feature of the Gulf Crisis was the collective manner in which the international community reacted to Iraq's forceful takeover of Kuwait. From the outset of the crisis, the interna-tional community voiced universal condemnation of Iraq's belligerent behav-iour as expressed in the various resolutions issued by the UN Security Council (UNSC). The breach of the international norm of sovereignty made it possible for the US to rapidly assemble a multinational military force of twenty-eight states under the auspices of the UN to liberate Kuwait. With the participation of other militaries, it was clear that other nations were willing to join the US to put their soldiers in harm's way to evict Iraqi forces from Kuwait (Mazarr et al. 1993: 3). With the participation and support of the international community (US, Soviet Union, most of the Arab countries, the Europe Commission, and Asian countries) the collective security mechanism worked extremely well to quell the first military crisis of the post-Cold War period.

However, this did not apply to Japan. While Japan did not behave as if the Persian Gulf Crisis was a military crisis, the events on the Gulf certainly caused a 'foreign policy crisis' within Japan. In spite of the geographical distance, the

Persian Gulf Crisis was important in influencing internal debates on not only the kind of role that Japan/the SDF could assume in the multinational effort to free Kuwait from Iraqi control, but also a broader debate on the kind of security role Japan could and should play in post-Cold War security affairs. A leading diplomat, Yanai Shunji, said that the Persian Gulf Crisis was the most important event to cause a shift in Japanese post-Cold War security policy (Yanai, personal communication, 24 May 2006). Funabashi Yoichi stated that the Persian Gulf Crisis discredited Japan's one-country pacifism (Funabashi, personal communication, 24 September 2012) and according to James Przystup, it forced Japan's reconsideration of its role in regional and international security affairs (Przystup, personal communication, 16 June 2015). Jim Schoff from the Carnegie Endowment for International Peace mentioned that the Persian Gulf Crisis changed the mindset of the Japanese by forcing them to think about practical ways that Japan could contribute to regional and international affairs (Schoff, personal communication, 20 May 2015). A defence ministry official summed it up aptly, describing the Persian Gulf Crisis as a 'wake-up' call for Japan (Kimura, personal communication, 29 November 2012). Since the military remained an important factor in the resolution of the Iraqi crisis, Japan became aware that it had to contribute to global security affairs not only through economic means but also through military means (Green 1998: 13).

Regional Defence

Despite the serious questions surrounding the utility of the US–Japan security alliance following the end of the Cold War, both the US and Japan worked tirelessly to update the alliance to make it more relevant to the challenges of the post-Cold War period. The first update began in the mid-1990s in the face of the North Korean nuclear and ballistic missile programmes and China's incipient rise challenges. This led the Japanese security policymaking elite to conclude that the SDF's passive role in the alliance was insufficient for the post-Cold War period. The outcome was the SDF's adoption of a regional defence role to strengthen US–Japan defence cooperation. According to Michishita Narushige, a leading security policy expert, the SDF had already adopted such roles during the Cold War, namely in the form of contributing to the US maritime strategy through providing sea-lane defence to identify the choke points for the Soviet Union's submarines. Rather than defining these roles as contributing to the US regional defence strategy, the security policymaking elite used the national defence logic to authorise these roles during the Cold War (Michishita, personal communication, 21 September 2015). However, it was only during the post-Cold War period that the security policymaking elite was able to institutionalise the regional defence role for the SDF within the alliance.

Though first outlined in the 1995 National Defense Program Outline (*New Taiko*), this role became the centrepiece of the update of the US–Japan alliance following the signing of the joint declaration between US President Clinton and Prime Minister Hashimoto in April 1996 (MOFA Japan 1996a). This was followed by the decision of both states to revise the defence guidelines – for the first time since 1978 – to authorise the SDF to provide active rear-area support to the US military not only during a direct attack on Japan, but also during contingencies in the Asia-Pacific region that have an important influence on Japan's peace and security.

To achieve this outcome, the Japanese security policymaking elite relied on the 1994 North Korean Nuclear Crisis, the 1996 Taiwan Strait Crisis and the 1998 Taepodong Crisis. The North Korean Nuclear Crisis was an international crisis. Although this crisis had regional and international implications, especially related to the issue of a nuclearised Korean Peninsula as well as the threat of nuclear proliferation, Japan did not adopt crisis-like behaviour during the North Korean Nuclear Crisis initially. However, this changed subsequently, especially during discussions on how Japan could contribute more effectively to the US–Japan alliance. Tanaka Hitoshi, a former top diplomat, has said that this crisis led Japan to start formulating plans for a regional contingency which did not exist before (H. Tanaka, personal communication, 8 September 2012). This crisis subsequently became important for Japan during its negotiations related to the reaffirmation of the US–Japan security relationship and the revision of the US–Japan defence guidelines.

The Taiwan Strait Crisis was another international crisis. This crisis showcased the kind of threat China could pose to Japan and regional security (Kokubun, personal communication, 30 October 2012). Like the North Korean Nuclear Crisis, the Taiwan Strait Crisis was important for Japan during the negotiations related to the recalibration of the US–Japan security relationship in the post-Cold War period, especially for expanding the SDF's support role of the US military during regional contingencies. In fact, according to Takamizawa Nobushige, a high-ranking defence ministry official, the Taiwan Strait Crisis was more important in understanding the kind of role the US would adopt in a regional contingency (Takamizawa, personal communication, 28 September 2012). The urgency of this crisis was also appreciated by the Hashimoto government (1996–8), which adopted crisis-like behaviour during the Taiwan Strait Crisis.

The Taepodong Crisis was not an international crisis but a foreign policy crisis for Japan. It accentuated Japan's vulnerability of being geographically close to North Korea. The Japanese leadership framed the incident as a crisis and subsequently behaved like it was a security crisis, even though analysts argued that the 1993 medium-range (Rodong-1) missile tests were more threatening to Japan's security than the suspected Taepodong launch (Akutsu, personal communication, 14 November 2012; Michishita, personal communication, 21 September 2015). This crisis came at an opportune time, when the security policymaking elite was hoping to overcome the impasse in the debate to pass the bills authorising the SDF's expanded regional defence role within the alliance in the National Diet.

Global Missions

The broadening of the US–Japan defence cooperation from a regional to a global focus occurred in the 2000s, especially in the first decade of the 2000s. Both Japan and the US pushed for greater integration between their militaries for global missions to address diverse global security challenges. This came in a range of areas that included policy and operational coordination during both peace and crisis periods, information sharing and intelligence cooperation, and BMD cooperation. A clear outcome of this shift resulted in the security policy-making elite's authorisation of SDF deployments to US-led coalition missions, such as in Iraq, and not just to UN-led ones.

The impetus for this broadening of the US–Japan alliance was the attacks of September 11th, 2001. The September 11th attacks were arguably the most significant and all-encompassing event to have occurred in the industrialised world during the twenty-first century, and they created an international crisis. The events not only renewed the severity of the threat posed by international terrorism but also had an profound impact in economic, political, cultural, psychological and military terms, both for the US and the entire international community. September 11th changed the nature of conflict, reshaped diplomatic relations, raised the levels of insecurity, led to the curtailment of civil liberties, tightened security within states, and led to a recognition and appreciation that the threat posed by international terrorism could only be countered through international cooperation and coordination (Hoge and Rose 2001: xi–xiii). These attacks launched a global war on terror beginning with the OEF, which was meant to dismantle the Taliban regime, and followed by, more controversially, the OIF, which was designed to overthrow Saddam Hussein's regime based on the suspected connection between international terrorism and his regime's quest for WMD.

For the September 11th attacks, Japan adopted a crisis-like position. The attacks changed Japan's perceptions of the world and the way it defined its global role in strategic affairs (Funabashi, personal communication, 24 September 2012). Not only was the crisis responsible for the incorporation of global missions in the US–Japan alliance, it also led to the emergence of a debate on a permanent law of troop deployment overseas (Schoff, personal communication, 20 May 2015). The urgency in Japan's response was manifested in the quick passage of the Anti-Terrorism Special Measures Law by the Diet authorising the dispatch of the SDF to the Indian Ocean to support the US and other militaries. A similar response, but more controversial, was adopted to show support and participate in the OIF at the request of the US. This led to the deployment of the SDF to conduct reconstruction duties in Iraq.

Collective Self-Defence

The fourth policy selected is the lifting of the collective self-defence ban for the SDF – a milestone in the postwar history of Japanese security policy. Sase Masamori, professor emeritus at the National Defense Academy, described this as an 'epochal event' (Kuromi 2015). Though permitted by Article 51 of the United Nations Charter, Japan had interpreted Article 9 in such a way as to ban any engagement in collective self-defence missions, as this went beyond self-defence and the minimum necessary level of force that Japan was able to maintain. When Abe came to power in 2012, he was keen to lift this ban as part of his own mission to implement political reforms and strengthen the US–Japan alliance. In this context, the lifting of the ban on collective self-defence missions became a central issue for Abe.

To achieve this goal, Abe and his government utilised the series of China-related incidents in the maritime domain that collectively signalled an increased militarisation of the East China Sea by China. These incidents were the September 2010 fishing trawler incident; the September 2012 nationalisation of islands; Chinese maritime and military vessels' repeated entry into Japanese waters and airspace, which included serious encounters; the locking of fire-control radar on Japanese military vessels by the Chinese military; and China's announcement of the ADIZ in November 2013. The 'common essence' in this series of incidents was the negative impact of the rise of China's assertive behaviour, and each of these incidents was a 'symptom' of the larger development surrounding China's behaviour.

It is argued here that China's assertive behaviour was a more important consideration for the Abe government than the threat posed by North Korea's nuclear and ballistic missile threat. As discussed in Chapter 6, China's actions revealed its intention to change the status quo of the East Asian security order, which was detrimental to Japan's security interests. Hence, Chinese actions in the maritime domain described above significantly impacted Japan's defence strategy and the way it responded to instability in the maritime domain (Asari, personal communication, 25 September 2012). Not only was the coast guard used more frequently, but the incidents saw a greater involvement of the Japanese navy and air force in defending Japan's sovereignty against the incursions of Chinese maritime vessels and military. The Japanese government strengthened the defence of the south-western region of Japan, introduced a new defence strategy known as the 'Dynamic Defense Force', acquired amphibious capability for island defence, and incorporated 'gray zone' missions or disputes into the SDF's mandate. The security policymaking elite raised the defence cooperation within the US–Japan alliance through seeking US support for Japan's territorial claims and pushed for the first revision of the bilateral defence guidelines after eighteen years. The outcome was a strengthened US commitment towards the defence of the Senkaku/Diaoyu islands as well as a revision of the US–Japan defence guidelines in April 2015, which provided for SDF's engagement in collective self-defence missions and the incorporation of the defence of gray zone situations into the guidelines. Abe and his government achieved a milestone when the security bills authorising the SDF's adoption of a collective self-defence role were passed by the Lower and Upper Houses in September 2015.

Sources

The relationship between external military crises and Japanese security policy expansion in the case study chapters is elaborated through the process-tracing research method (Collier 2011; George and Bennett 2005; Mahoney 2010). The appropriateness of this method lies in its effort to achieve careful descriptive and causal inference through identifying a sequence of events within a particular case study. Additionally, the appropriateness is explained by the method's ability to detect critical mechanisms at work that under certain conditions connect the proposed cause and the observed outcome (George and Bennett 2005: 3–36). As noted by George and Bennett: 'The process-tracing method attempts to identify the intervening causal process – the causal chain and causal mechanism – between an independent variable (or variables) and the outcome of the dependent variable' (George and Bennett 2005: 206).

To support the process-tracing approach to illustrate the government, I rely heavily on empirical data and analyses to achieve in-depth knowledge for all the cases. More specifically, empirical data from the following four areas was collected and analysed for all the case studies. First, data was collected that represented Japanese security policy expansion in the post-Cold War period, compared to the Cold War version. This data focused on policies and initiatives that support Japan's security policy expansion, especially in relation to the four key security policy developments selected as case studies. Second, data was collected on the military crises under study. These focused on what happened during the crises and how Japan responded. Third, empirical data on how the security policymaking elite attached (or not) 'threat' meanings to the military crises were collected. At the same time, data was also collected on how other actors who were involved in the crises perceived the crises. Fourth, empirical data was collected on how the security policymaking elite was able to transform and later strengthen Japanese security policy as a result of the threat construction process related to the military crises. Here, the empirical data relating to the debate between the security policymaking elite and the opponents of the security policy expansion was the main focus. Fifth, data was also collected on the implementation process of the security policies identified as case studies.

To illuminate the security policymaking elite's representations of the security environment, as well as Japan's vulnerability and Japan's threat perceptions, the research relies on Japan's official statements. It involves compiling and analysing policy statements of the Japanese government before, during and after the crises. Other than government sources, and secondary sources such as Japanese newspapers (from various political ideological sides), policy reports and scholarly analyses have also been important sources for empirical data. Information was also gathered from more than fifty interviews conducted in Japan and the US during the 2005–18 period. These interviews were with present and former officials as well as academics based in universities and government-linked think-tanks.

To illustrate the effect of the military crises on Japanese security expansion, the case study chapters are each organised into five sections. Each chapter begins with a brief introduction to the crisis, namely a discussion on what happened during the crisis and Japan's response to the crisis. The second section focuses on how a particular crisis was perceived as a crisis by the Japanese security policymaking elite, and an introduction on the debate between the security policymaking elite and those with competing views. The section illustrates how the security policymaking elite had a relatively higher sense of concern towards the crises vis-à-vis internal groups, as well as countries that are involved in the particular crisis. The third section is a discussion of the threat construction process carried out by the security policymaking elite in relation to the crisis under study. This section highlights the inflated threat elements at both the national and international levels, as well as the means by which the security policymaking elite deflated the risks surrounding controversial policy initiatives and missions. The final section is a detailed discussion of the way the security policy development was implemented.

NOTES

1. There is general consensus amongst the main theoretical schools of international relations on the impact and influence of anarchy on a state's behaviour. For neorealism's interpretation, see Waltz (1979); for neoliberalism's interpretation, see Keohane (1984); and for social constructivism's interpretation, see Wendt (1992, 1999).
2. Other than 'crisis', two other terms have been used to describe critical events that change the course of policy – 'critical juncture' and 'punctuated equilibrium'. Critical juncture is widely used in the historical institutionalism literature to reflect a redirection of a path-dependent institutional stability caused by a brief phase of 'institutional flux' (Capoccia and Kellemen 2007: 341). This brief period of institutional flux makes greater options available to the actors whose decisions have a greater impact on the state's policy (Capoccia and Kellemen 2007: 343). 'Punctuated equilibrium' refers to a 'short burst of rapid institutional change followed by long period of stasis' – an understanding of change that challenges the continuous and incremental understanding of institutional change (Krasner 1984: 242). Whichever term is used, the main point here is that events are critical to understanding change. Events offer leaders opportunities to implement new policies and take the country

on a different path not possible before. For excellent theoretical discussions on crisis, see Calder and Ye (2010: 38–42); Samuels (2013: 24–30).

3. The International Crisis Behaviour (ICB) Project and database is hosted by Duke University and the University of Southern California. For a comprehensive collection of data on inter-state crises, see ICB Project (n.d.).

4. One of the earliest definitions was by Charles Hermann, when he described a 'crisis' as possessing the following three elements: (1) threatens high-priority goals of the decision-making rule unit; (2) restricts the amount of time available for response before the decision is transformed; and (3) surprises the members of the decision-making unit by its occurrence (Hermann 1969: 414). While the notions of *threat* and *time* have been accepted as important components of a 'crisis', the notion of *surprise* is contested. As Michael Brecher noted, most studies saw *threat* and *time* as greater determinants of crisis behaviour than *surprise*. For Brecher, the *surprise* element is subsumed in the time pressure and probability of war features (Brecher 1977: 54; also see fn. 7 for a detail critique of the element of *surprise*).

5. On the circumventing democratic processes, see Agamben (2005).

6. For Japan's Cold War security and foreign policymaking structure, see Baerwald (1977); J. C. Campbell (1989); H. Fukui (1977); Rix (1988).

7. For detailed discussions on various camps in Japanese security policy debate, see Boyd and Samuels (2005: 27–41); Deming (2004: 5–6); Mochizuki (1983/4); Samuels (2007: 18–36); Togo (2010).

8. The mainstream conservatives' (or pragmatists') position was based on Yoshida's vision of Japan as a merchant nation. It envisaged Japan directing all efforts towards achieving the main goal of economic development and technological autonomy, while keeping a low profile in military-strategic affairs (Berger 1996: 336–7). This group supported the retention of Article 9 of the Peace Constitution and used it to deflect US pressure on Japan to acquire military capabilities that went beyond Japan's defensive needs. The mainstream conservatives also resisted US pressures for any participation in international military missions. They were committed to the strengthening of the US–Japan security relationship, as developing an autonomous defence capability was understood as an economically and politically costly option (Berger 1998: 104; Boyd and Samuels 2005: 26; Samuels 2007: 32–3).

9. When Takahashi Sugio, a Deputy Director, MOD, was asked about the 1999 North Korean nuclear spy ships, he said this incident could not be analysed individually. For North Korea, the analysis would have to assess the collective impact of the series of events that define the North Korean threat for Japan (Takahashi, personal communication, 2 October 2012). When MOFA Deputy Press Secretary Okada Masaki was asked if Japan's resolute response to the intrusion of the two unidentified ships was related to the debate in the Diet to revise the defence guidelines that was being carried out when the intrusion occurred in March 1999, he responded by saying 'You might still clearly remember the launch of missiles from North Korea,' suggesting that Japan had become 'more sensitive to the security issues in recent years' after the Taepodong Crisis (MOFA Japan 1999a).

10. Instead of the term 'threat', other terms such as 'insecurities' and 'risk' and phrases such as 'representations of danger' have been used in the extant literature. For

'insecurities', see Weldes et al. (1999); for 'risk', see Maslow et al. (2015); and for 'representations of danger', see D. Campbell (1998). The use of the term 'threat' is privileged, as it is a study of Japan's security policy expansion through using military crises as policy windows. The security policymaking elite usually represents the 'danger' from military crises as 'threats' to both the national and regional and international security.

11. Obviously a state can have more than two representations of the security environment. However, two are stressed here for comparison purposes.

12. The importance of the US in Japan's positive representation of the security environment was widely noted during the interviews and in Japanese official documents. In fact, a high-ranking official from Japan's MOD added that it is important to keep the US entrenched and welcome in the region. It is important that the US maintains close policy coordination with countries in the region, including Japan. He added that without the US's entrenched presence, it would be difficult for Japan to win support from the Japanese public for the expansion of its security policy (Tokuchi, personal communication, 14 September 2005).

13. For a rigorous definition of 'threat inflation', see Kaufmann (2004: 8–9).

14. Theoretically speaking, studies on democratic politics show that leaders in a democracy are often able to lead public opinion to the desired outcome (see Page and Shapiro 1992; Zaller 1992). The public acquire information and form opinions from the information offered by leaders. This gives the elite space to influence public opinion in a democratic regime by persuading members of the policy elite and key actors that form the elite, such as the executive branch, experts from the media, academia and research foundations and interest groups (Takeuchi 2014: 10). This is even more the case in the area of foreign policy where the information available to the public is more limited (Takeuchi 2014: 10–11).

3

INTERNATIONAL PEACEKEEPING

The first key security policy development in Japan's post-Cold War security policy was the passage of the IPCL in 1992, authorising the SDF to participate in international peacekeeping. This chapter shows the importance of the 1990–1 Persian Gulf Crisis to this development, and how the security policymaking elite utilised this crisis as a policy window to achieve their objective of expanding the SDF's mandate to include international peacekeeping missions.

The Crisis

On 2 August 1990, Iraqi tanks invaded Kuwait and occupied all its territory within hours.[1] With the use of the UN, the international community, led by the US (along with support from the Soviet Union), took swift action to condemn Iraq's aggression. An emergency meeting at the UNSC was called on the same day as the invasion and it issued Resolution 660. This resolution condemned Iraq's behaviour and called for Iraq's immediate and unconditional withdrawal. On 6 August 1990, the UNSC issued Resolution 661, which imposed a trade and financial embargo against Iraq. Another resolution, Resolution 662, was passed on 9 August, which declared Iraq's attempted annexation of Kuwait null and void. This was followed by a massive gathering of military personnel and equipment in Saudi Arabia by the US and other allied states under the operation name Desert Shield. This military presence served to enforce economic sanctions and the embargo against Iraq, as well as to prepare for a potential offensive operation to liberate Kuwait.

As the potential for a negotiated settlement between Iraq and the US dimmed, the UN adopted Resolution 678 on 29 November 1990, authorising the use of force against Iraq if it failed to withdraw by 15 January 1991. As Iraq failed to comply with the UN resolution, the US-led multinational force launched Operation Desert Storm on 17 January 1991 with an air campaign to destroy Iraq's air defences and command and control structures. After gaining air superiority and inflicting a massive amount of damage on Iraq's military personnel and installations, the multinational force launched a ground offensive in Kuwait on 24 February 1991. The war ended on 28 February 1991, when the coalition forces banished the Iraqi forces and assumed control of Kuwait.

Japan's initial response to Iraq's invasion of Kuwait was quick and decisive. It wasted no time in joining the international community to condemn Iraq's act of aggression. Not only did the Japanese government support the series of UN resolutions, it also froze Iraqi and Kuwaiti assets in Japan on 3 August 1990 and announced a four-point package of economic sanctions against Iraq (an oil-import embargo, an export embargo, a suspension of economic aid and a freeze on investment and loans) two days later (Purrington and A. K. 1991: 308). These sanctions were independently imposed by Japan two days before the UNSC sanctions were passed. Japan's early action led the US and the rest of the international community to form positive impressions about Japan's proactive response to the crisis (Armacost 1996: 99).

However, these positive impressions turned negative as the Japanese government failed to provide support beyond efforts that came to be known as 'chequebook diplomacy'. After facing intense pressure from the US government, as well as Japanese government officials and high-ranking LDP members hoping for Japan to contribute proactively to the resolution of the crisis, the Japanese government led by Prime Minister Kaifu Toshiki announced a comprehensive package on 29 August 1990. This package announced that Japan would: (1) loan planes and ships for transporting food and medical supplies to the multinational forces; (2) send a fact-finding medical team to the region and subsequently dispatch a 100-member team composed of private sector personnel; and (3) extend emergency financial assistance to Jordan, Egypt and Turkey, including US$10 million for refugees in Jordan. Despite these efforts, the Kaifu government relied on financial means to support the US-led Gulf effort. The reason was that it faced severe obstacles in authorising a military deployment to the Gulf. By the middle of September 1990, the total value of aid provided by Japan to allied forces, frontline states, and refugees reached US$4 billion.

During the September–November 1990 period, the Japanese government attempted to authorise a 'human contribution' to the US-led multinational effort. It proposed the United Nations Peace Cooperation Corps (UNPCC) bill, which was designed to make a non-military contribution to the multilateral forces in the Persian Gulf. However, this draft bill was revised to incorporate the SDF deployment provision due to immense pressure from government officials and high-ranking LDP members who supported the SDF deployment to the Gulf. Following intense debate, the Japanese government announced in October 1990 that the SDF would serve in the Peace Corps to provide logistical support to multinational forces and be allowed to carry small firearms to defend themselves. However, the bill failed to gain passage in the National Diet.

The failure of the UNPCC Bill coincided with the US increasing its military presence in the Gulf as the deadline for Iraq's withdrawal drew closer. As Japan could not make a human contribution, the Kaifu government pledged another US$9 billion on 24 January 1991 as additional aid to the US-led multinational effort. On 6 March 1991, the Diet passed the supplemental budget, making Japan the largest financial contributor to the war effort apart from Saudi Arabia and Kuwait. Despite immense opposition at home, Japan did eventually make a military contribution to the Persian Gulf Crisis after the conflict had ceased. On April 1991, the government authorised the dispatch of minesweepers to the Gulf to aid in the clearing of Iraqi mines from strategic waterways. It sent four minesweepers, a flagship, and two supply ships, which arrived at the Gulf on 3 June 1991 – making this Japan's first overseas military mission since the Korean War (see Ushiba 1992).

The 'Crisis' in the Crisis

Iraq's invasion of Kuwait caused a foreign policy crisis within Japan. Japan's response to the Persian Gulf Crisis was far from structured and planned. Instead, it was 'lost', as described by a high-ranking official from Japan's MOD (Takamizawa, personal communication, 28 September 2012), and it was not prepared for what was expected in terms of crisis resolution efforts (H. Tanaka, personal communication, 8 September 2012). From the outset of the crisis, the US had made it clear that it expected not only political and financial support, but also a 'physical presence' (understood as military presence) from Japan (Niksch and Sutter 1991: 5). Despite being aware of the constraints the Japanese leadership faced, the US (and other states) expected Japan to move away from its economics-based security policy and expand its political/security role in the post-Cold War period commensurate with its status as the second largest economy in the world. Moreover, the US and members of the coalition force thought that it was 'natural' for Japan to want to play an active military role in the resolution of the Persian Gulf Crisis, as any instability in the Middle East would disrupt the oil supply that is critical for Japan's economic development.

However, Japan did not fulfil these expectations (see Ozawa 1994: 37–9). The first post-Cold War Japanese government led by Kaifu avoided addressing the possibility of Japan's military participation in security affairs, and believed that Japan's security role expansion would come in economic and technological areas. This was in response to the mood of optimism ushered in by the end of the Cold War, which pointed to the military becoming a less important determining factor in international relations. This perspective was reflected in Kaifu's vision for post-Cold War Japan published in *Foreign Policy* in 1990, when he wrote that 'dialogue and cooperation [are] now replacing missile and tanks as the tools for achieving order' and that 'the role of military might in the balance of power is diminishing and the importance of dialogue and cooperation is growing'. As a result, he believed that Japan would use its 'economic and technological strength, along with its store of experience and its conceptual ability' in facing the challenges of the post-Cold War order (cited in Blaker 1993: 17). Such a vision clearly meant the continuation of the Cold War-based minimalist security policy for Japan in the post-Cold War period.

Hence, when Iraq invaded Kuwait, the Japanese government did not perceive it as a crisis at first (Bono, personal communication, 26 August 2005). Just like the Cold War, the Japanese government analysed the Gulf Crisis strictly in economic terms. This was evident from Japan's responses, especially in three aspects. First, Japan played down the impact of the Gulf Crisis on its national security as a result of its decreased dependence on Middle East oil for its energy needs as compared to the past (Blaker 1993: 18). One day after Iraq's invasion of Kuwait, Kaifu told reporters that the Gulf Crisis 'would not have much effect' on Japan, as the decision to diversify Japan's oil supply after the 1973 oil crisis had left Japan in a stronger position (Bennett et al. 1994: 62; Inoguchi 1993: 98–9; *FBIS Daily Report* as cited in Niksch and Sutter 1991: 6). Moreover, the Japanese government and the business community were generally calm about the effects of Iraq's invasion on the world's oil market. They argued that Iraq would have to eventually sell the oil, and the Japanese economy was strong enough to withstand higher oil prices caused by Iraq's control over Kuwait's oil (Niksch and Sutter 1991: 18). The Japanese Consul-General in New York, Hanabusa Masamichi, articulated this attitude when he said, 'experience tells us that whoever controls oil will be disposed to sell it. We are prepared to pay' (Blustein 1991). Business leaders, including the *Keidanren* (Japan Business Federation), argued that Japan should take an independent path from the US and avoid war at all costs, as Japan's economic interests would be threatened by a war and it would 'alienate Arabs from the industrial nations for many years to come' (Brown 1991: 6).

Second, Prime Minister Kaifu, following strong resistance from the MOFA, cancelled a diplomatic trip to Egypt, Jordan, Oman, Saudi Arabia and Turkey which was scheduled to commence on 15 August 1990. This cancellation deprived Japan of the opportunity to play a leading diplomatic role by using its influence within the West and the Arab world to mediate the conflict and demonstrate Japan's potential to fulfil the 'global partnership' it had forged with the US in 1990.[2] Apart from the fear of endangering the hundreds of Japanese trapped in Iraq and Kuwait,[3] Prime Minister Kaifu postponed the trip citing that his visit 'could offend Iraq' and damage Japan's economic interests with Iraq (Bennett et al. 1994: 62; Unger 1997: 139).

Third, Japan expressed hesitation in imposing economic sanctions against Iraq when Kaifu met with his top Cabinet officials on 3 August 1990. While MOFA supported Japan's show of solidarity with the US in imposing the sanctions, MITI advocated caution, as it was more concerned about the impact of economic sanctions on the status of the ¥600 billion (US$4.7 billion) in debt payments owed by Iraq to Japanese trading companies (Purrington and A. K. 1991: 308). Japan held this position until a telephone conversation between President George H. Bush and Prime Minister Kaifu on 4 August 1990 that led to Japan's announcement of the four-point package on 5 August, as discussed above.

Japan did not have problems in devising the economic sanctions and condemning Iraq's behaviour, as this approach comprised non-controversial measures (essentially non-military ones that conformed to Japan's minimalist security policy) and complied with Japan's past behaviour against military aggression (namely, Japan's strong reactions directed against Vietnam following its invasion of Cambodia in 1979) (Inoguchi 1993: 98–9). After implementing these non-controversial measures, the Japanese government had hoped for the crisis to be resolved by the 15 January deadline. This would have saved Japan from making tough decisions related to the imposition of controversial military measures (Inoguchi 1993: 99).

However, Japan's refusal to regard Iraq's invasion as a military crisis was short-lived. Japan's political and economic responses failed to appease the US. The US applied immense pressure on Japan through its officials, including President Bush, Vice President Dan Quayle, Secretary (State) James Baker, Secretary (Treasury) Nicholas Brady and US Ambassador to Japan Michael Armacost, as well as members of the Senate and Congress.[4] This pressure against Japan mounted as the US and other countries in the multinational force gathered in Saudi Arabia to enforce the economic sanctions and embargoes. Due to the constitutional constraints on the SDF and the lack of precedence for overseas SDF deployment, Japan was unable to go beyond 'chequebook diplomacy' to provide a 'human contribution' to the resolution of the Gulf Crisis. Japan's actions not only aggravated latent tensions in the relationship between the US and Japan but also reinforced America's perception of Japan as an unreliable ally, unable to play a larger military-strategic role commensurate with its economic power (Armacost 1996: 98).

Within Japan, government officials and high-ranking LDP members who supported Japan's active participation in the Gulf Crisis were displeased with the Japanese government's inability to devise an appropriate response involving an SDF deployment to the Gulf effort. Besides deploying SDF overseas, this group was interested in the preservation of a strong US–Japan security relationship in the post-Cold War period and the restoration of legitimacy to the military as an instrument of state policy (Hook 1996: 81; Yamaguchi 1992: 165). This pro-deployment group (also known as the 'forward-looking' group) asserted their opinions and exerted pressure on the Kaifu leadership. The group included policy elites from MOFA, the LDP executive leadership, members of the LDP's 'defence tribe' (*zoku*) and opinion leaders outside the government. Some of the leading figures included Ozawa Ichiro, Nishioka Takeo, Chairman of the LDP Executive Council, Sakamoto Misoji, Chief Cabinet Secretary, Watanabe Michio, a LDP faction leader who assumed the Foreign Minister position during Miyazawa Kiichi's stint as Prime Minister of Japan, and Kato Mutsuki, LDP's Policy Affairs Research Council leader (George 1993: 565; Hook 1996: 83).

Led by Ozawa, this group perceived the events surrounding the Persian Gulf Crisis as a military crisis for Japan. More importantly, they saw the Gulf Crisis as a policy window for Japan to expand its security policy (Hook 1996: 75; Inoguchi 1993: 99). Their framing of the Persian Gulf Crisis as a crisis was not because of the broad security implications of the crisis on Japan's national security or international security, but rather Japan's lack of contribution to the Gulf effort would have severe ramifications for its international position, especially its bilateral security relationship with the US (USG Department of State 1991). Members of this 'forward-looking group' were responsible for the treatment of the Persian Gulf Crisis as a crisis in Japan's national security discourse, both in economic and military terms. This formed the basis for Japan's security role expansion in the form of the SDF's participation in UNPKOs.

This pro-deployment group faced considerable challenge from the opposition parties, civil society groups and members within the ruling party – all against an overseas dispatch of the SDF based on the principles of Japan's Peace Constitution (Hook 1996: 77, 86). The opposition lines became clear during Diet deliberations on the UNPCC Bill in both the Lower and Upper Houses. Among the opposition parties, the JSP took the lead in opposing the overseas dispatch of the SDF. According to the opposition, Japan should not give in to the American pressure of making a 'human contribution' at the expense of Japan's peace-based legal principle. Doi Takako, JSP's chairwoman, severely criticised the government's Gulf aid policy as being unconstitutional, as the provision of aid was tantamount to direct cooperation in the military operations by the multinational forces. To counter the LDP's proposal, the JSP proposed the creation of a 1,000-member United Nations peace cooperation team restricted to non-military activities in regional conflicts and natural disasters abroad. This proposal did not allow the participation of SDF personnel. Moreover, the personnel should be unarmed and their duties should be compatible with the requirements of the Constitution (*Japan Times*, 16 October 1990; *Jiji Press Ticker Service*, 28 January 1991).

Numerous citizens' groups and pacifist organisations held protest rallies to voice their strong opposition to the UNPCC Bill. Their argument was that the bill breached Article 9 of the Constitution, which renounces Japan's participation in a war and any overseas deployment of Japan's SDF (*Japan Times*, 16 October 1990). Some academics and defence experts also expressed their opposition to the UNPCC Bill, as they argued that Japan's contribution to world peace should preferably be materialised in non-military areas and carried out by civilians instead of SDF personnel (*Japan Times*, 21 September 1991). From within the ruling party, people such as former Chief Cabinet Secretary during Nakasone Yasuhiro's prime ministership, Gotoda Masaharu; former Deputy Prime Minister Kanemaru Shin; former prime ministers Fukuda Takeo and Suzuki Zenko; and Miyazawa Kiichi, who eventually replaced Kaifu Toshiaki as prime minister, expressed a cautious attitude towards the overseas dispatch of the SDF (Hook 1996: 87; Unger 1997: 152).

Despite such widespread opposition, the 'forward-looking' group dominated the national security debates. This group managed to gain acceptance from a reluctant Prime Minister Kaifu and centrist opposition parties to incorporate the SDF's dispatch into the Diet deliberations. When the second version of the government-proposed peacekeeping bill (the IPCL) was introduced in the Diet in June 1992, the pro-deployment group was able to forge alliances with the centrist opposition parties (Komei Party and Democratic Socialist Party (DSP)) to pass the IPCL. The next section illustrates how the pro-deployment group succeeded in incorporating international peacekeeping duties into the SDF's mandate by using the Persian Gulf Crisis.

Threat Construction

During the post-Persian Gulf War period and in the run-up to the eventual passage of the IPCL, the threat construction process was directed not at any state but focused on a variety of elements at the international and national levels. At the international level, the pro-deployment group's threat construction process focused on the fluidity/uncertainty of the post-Cold War security environment caused by the eruption of the Persian Gulf Crisis. The historic changes resulting from the collapse of communism in Eastern Europe and the easing of East–West tensions had ushered in a sense of optimism based on the notion of 'permanent peace' within the Japanese government and the rest of the international community during the early post-Cold War period. However, the Persian Gulf War fractured this mood of optimism. It challenged the much-valued international norm of inter-state sovereignty and exposed the vulnerability of the peace and stability ushered in by the post-Cold War security environment; hence, introducing a renewed sense of uncertainty and fluidity in the security environment.

As Japan's Foreign Minister, Nakayama Taro, said: 'Unlike a year ago, when optimism about the future spread following the fall of communist regimes in

Eastern Europe, the world now greets the New Year wary of the Gulf situation, Soviet domestic politics and changes on the Korean Peninsula' (*Japan Times*, 1 January 1991). In a speech delivered in Singapore in May 1991, Prime Minister Kaifu stressed: 'Iraq's invasion of Kuwait tore the international community's peace and stability asunder and was a direct rejection of the efforts being made to build a new world order' (MOFA Japan 1991). This view was also shared by Kaifu's successor, Miyazawa Kiichi. Urging the opposition parties to enact the IPCL, Prime Minister Miyazawa, in his first policy speech in the Diet in November 1991, said that the international community was in a period of 'tremendous upheaval' that happened once every few centuries in a quest for a new global order (*Japan Times*, 9 November 1991).

The threat construction process at the national level entailed two elements that focused on Japan's vulnerability. First, there was uncertainty related to the future of the US–Japan security relationship in the post-Cold War period. With the collapse of the Soviet Union, some policymakers and academics in Japan were concerned about the ascendancy of isolationists in the US who defended the disentanglement of American security arrangements from Asia, including Japan, and the consequent removal of Japan's much-valued security guarantee (Inoguchi 1998: 86–7). Their fears relating to the breakdown of the US–Japan Security Treaty, which was primarily designed to address the Soviet Union during the Cold War, were exacerbated by the troubled bilateral trade relationship between the two countries, resulting in Japan replacing the Soviet Union as a primary threat (at least in an economic sense) for the American public during the early post-Cold War years. A Deputy Director from Japan's JDA said that the big lesson for Japan during the Persian Gulf Crisis was that if Japan did not contribute troops, the alliance would be in a crisis (Takahashi, personal communication, 2 October 2012). Former Japanese Ambassador to the US Okawara Yoshio supported this view when he stressed that Japan's decision to pass the IPCL was to strengthen its alliance with the US (Okawara, personal communication, 2 October 2012).

The pro-deployment group stressed the negative effects of Japan's lack of contribution to the US-led multinational effort to resolve the Gulf Crisis on the continued US commitment to Japanese national security. To achieve their agenda of allowing SDF to contribute to the Gulf effort and overcome policymaking hurdles, the pro-deployment group relied on pressure from the US government and members of the Senate and Congress (George 1993: 566). This group stressed that Japan's inability to be forthcoming in its contribution to the multinational effort would lead to increased mistrust of Japan amongst American government officials, members of the Senate and Congress, and the American public, exacerbate Japan's 'free-rider' image and eventually lead to a breakdown of Japan–US relations (Hook 1996: 83; Unger 1997: 153). Foreign Minister Nakayama Taro said that Japan should assume greater international responsibilities as called for by the US in order to eliminate rapidly spreading distrust in Japan among the American public (*Jiji Press Ticker Service*, 25 January 1991). Nishihara Masashi, a member of the pro-deployment group, laid down in simple terms the impact of Japan's lack of contribution to the US-led multinational effort when he said: 'If I were an American, I would see Japan as not reliable as a friend' (Weisman 1991).

Second, as the events in the Middle East dominated the security discussions in Japan, another related threat element gained greater prominence at the national level. This was the fear of Japan's international isolation/alienation or the failure of Japan to achieve international acceptance as a result of its much-criticised contribution to the Persian Gulf effort. Ambassador Armacost acknowledged the presence of this international isolation element in Japanese national security discourse in his memorandum to the US State Department analysing the impact of the Gulf War on US–Japan relations. He described this element as an 'opportunity' for the US 'to take advantage of Japan's defensiveness and fear of isolation in the wake of the Gulf Crisis to gain greater GOJ [Government of Japan] cooperation' (USG Department of State 1991, parenthesis added). The fear of international isolation was especially pronounced when Japan was excluded from Kuwait's congratulatory message to the US and members of the United Nations Coalition, which was published in the *New York Times* and *The Washington Post* on 11 March 1991 following the successful conclusion of the crisis. This came as a shock to Japan, especially after its enormous US$13 billion contribution to the war effort. Japan's frustration was accentuated when Germany, a country that had expressed similar hesitation in relation to participation in the Gulf Crisis, was mentioned in the advertisement (Reid 1991).

The fear of international isolation was a genuine concern for the Japanese leadership, but it also served as a useful ground on which the pro-deployment group attempted to gain greater support for Japan's full participation in the US-led multinational effort against Iraq. Kaifu described the announcement of the US$1 billion comprehensive package on 29 August 1990, which included financial aid and offered cooperation in transportation, supplies, and medical treatment, as indispensable and necessary to avoid international isolation. Foreign Minister Nakayama said, 'we have to make up our minds, then, to shoulder our share of the financial burden or face international isolation' (*Japan Times*, 1 January 1991; *Jiji Press Ticker Service*, 25 January 1991). In this same speech before the Lower House plenary session, Nakayama went on to stress the danger related to international isolation in trying to defend the government's decision to dispatch SDF transport planes to the Middle East to help airlift Gulf evacuees from the war zone to their home countries (*Jiji Press Ticker Service*, 25 January 1991). Similarly, Watanabe Michio, a key leader in the LDP, stressed that Japan would become an international 'orphan' if it failed to participate fully in the Gulf (Weisman 1991).

Japan's leadership was cognisant that the fears of international isolation were a result of the idiosyncratic features of Japan's security policymaking process in relation to the overseas dispatch of the SDF. These features refer to the domestic constraints shaping security policy issues and the widespread domestic opposition against the deployment of SDF overseas. According to former ambassador, Yanai Shunji, who was involved in the drafting of the UNPCC and IPCL bills, the Japanese government and LDP were committed to enacting a law that permitted SDF to provide rear-area support during the Persian Gulf Crisis, but this was hindered by the Cold War-based security policy framework (Yanai, personal communication, 24 May 2006). The Japanese security policy-making elite was concerned that the successes of its Cold War security policy had nurtured a feeling that Japan could continue to operate based on the minimalist security policy in the post-Cold War period. Foreign Minister Watanabe Michio said: 'The Japanese people don't want to shed their own blood or sweat themselves. Let's have the foreigners do it – that's what they think' (Weisman 1991). Kosaka Masatake, an academic who was a proponent of security policy expansion, said, 'people in this country often tout the opposite proposition – that national security is not just a function of military power – but their thinking seems generally to be based on the carefree presumption that somebody else will take care of military matters' (Kosaka 1991: 13).

The pro-deployment group was concerned that Japan's failure to review its risk-averse security policy to assist other nations collectively to contribute to the larger peace and stability of the security environment threatened its relations with the international community and exacerbated Japan's isolation from the international community. The pro-deployment group adopted three interrelated approaches in its threat construction process that supported Japan's development of a security policy involving the deployment of the SDF to actively contribute to the regional and international security environment.

The first was to frame Japan's inability to contribute responsibly through its SDF to an international crisis as a threat to Japan's national security. The Middle East was described in the 1990 *Diplomatic Bluebook* as a 'matter of vital national interest' because the nation depended on the region for as much as 70 per cent of its crude oil imports (as cited in *Japan Times*, 17 October 1990). Prime Minister Kaifu's position that the Gulf Crisis did not have an impact on Japan was reversed shortly afterwards. He argued that

> Japan depends on Persian Gulf nations for 70 per cent of its oil needs, and it is in our own national interest to promote regional peace and stability. If Japan does not appear to do its part in the current crisis, it could face an extremely hazardous situation in the future. (*Japan Economic Journal*, 8 September 1990)

The minesweeper mission was not seen as illegal. Instead, it was justified by Kaifu as 'an emergency matter for Japan, which relies on a major portion of crude oil imports from the Persian Gulf region that are indispensable for the country's well-being' (Jimbo 1991). As Nishimura Mutsuyoshi, Director of the Policy Coordination Division at MOFA and involved in the drafting of the IPCL, wrote, 'As with its far-flung economic interests, Japan has a tangible stake in peace all over the world. Warfare almost anywhere can immediately affect us' (Nishimura 1992: 53).

The second approach was to link Japan's security to the threat posed by the Persian Gulf Crisis itself. Kaifu not only tied Japan's security to the crisis but went a step further by linking Japan's security to its ability to contribute to the international security environment. Kaifu said that the crisis posed a 'serious threat' to 'the nation' and the international community, and Japan needed to adopt proactive steps to fulfil its international responsibilities (*Japan Times*, 31 August 1990). In a major policy speech before the National Diet in January 1991, Kaifu described Japan's support of the US and the allied forces fighting Iraq as a 'natural duty'. He added, 'refusal to fulfil this obligation and failure to do so would mean choosing the road to international isolation for Japan' (*Japan Times*, 26 January 1991). This point was repeated in the 1990 *Diplomatic Bluebook* 1990 when it was stated that '[a]t a time when East–West relations are dramatically changing and a new global political order is being sought, it is important for Japan to play an active role in joint efforts to reverse such an illegal act [referring to Iraq's invasion of Kuwait]' (as cited in *Japan Times*, 17 October 1990, parenthesis added).

The third approach was through framing Japan's national security as being determined by its ability to contribute to the formation of the new world order that was being challenged by the Gulf Crisis. The Japanese leadership recognised that the Persian Gulf Crisis had vital significance beyond economics as it served as an important crisis that would determine the international order in the post-Cold War period. Moto Shiina, President of the Policy Group, said,

> The Gulf Crisis has significance far beyond that of any potential economic threat. Of even greater importance in the long run is the fact that certain rules for maintaining global peace and security henceforth will have emerged from the conflict. Japan is involved in this process whether it wants to be or not. (Moto 1991: 15)

Describing the Gulf Crisis as a crisis bringing to light 'the problems which face the world in a post-Cold War era', Kaifu tied the importance of Japan's involvement in the resolution of the crisis to its ability to play a responsible role together with the rest of the international community in addressing other security issues such as poverty and religious and ethnic conflicts (*Japan Times*, 16 November 1990).

SECURITY POLICY DEVELOPMENT

The pro-deployment group used the above threat narrative to justify Japan's participation in the Persian Gulf Crisis, as well as to develop a suitable security role in the post-Cold War period.[5] While the short-term response was to dispatch minesweepers to the Gulf in April 1991 after the armed conflict had ceased, the Japanese leadership had simultaneously also begun debating on Japan's 'international contribution' to the international community through the utilisation of the SDF as part of a long-term measure. The Persian Gulf Crisis was a crucial military crisis that subsequently altered the attitudes of the Japanese people towards an expanded security policy. This was aptly summarised in an editorial published by the *Asahi Shimbun* when it said,

> Never since the end of the World War Two has the nature of Japanese pacifism been so much called to account as at present. Never have the Japanese people begun to think about peace and war as a question so close to themselves as now. (*Asahi Shimbun*, 24 January 1991)

There were two unique features of the Gulf Crisis. The first was the collective way the international community reacted to Saddam Hussein's forceful takeover of Kuwait. The breach of the sovereignty norm made it possible for the US to rapidly assemble a multinational military force made up of twenty-eight states under the auspices of the UN to jointly liberate Kuwait from Iraqi forces. From the outset of the crisis, the international community voiced universal condemnation of Iraq's belligerent behaviour as expressed in various resolutions issued by the UNSC. Second, this collective response involved the use of the military. This informed Japan and the rest of the international community that the military still determined international relations in the post-Cold War era, and the 'use of force' element would remain an inescapable fact of international relations in the post-Cold War period (Green 1998). With the participation of multiple militaries in this effort, it was clear that other states, on top of the US, were willing to put their soldiers in harm's way to resolve the crisis (Mazarr et al. 1993: 3). With the participation and support of the international community the collective security mechanism worked extremely well to quell the first military crisis of the post-Cold War period.

Both features made Japan cognisant that the international environment of the 1990s would not allow Japan to follow the minimalist security policy it had single-mindedly pursued during the Cold War that avoided an active military role in international affairs (Funabashi 1991: 59). The international environment required Japan to drop its traditional strategy of separating economics from politics, which led to the characterisation of Japan as being a 'political pygmy' in external security affairs. Dobson captured these developments when he wrote:

> it was in the aftermath of the Second Gulf War that Japan began the process of political, social and legal soul-searching, while traditional norms came into conflict with newer norms, in an attempt to make 'visible contribution' to the international community's efforts in the Persian Gulf. (Dobson 2003: 60)

The Persian Gulf War illustrated to Japan that any expansion of its international contribution beyond its minimalist economic strategy would come in the area of military contribution to international affairs. As a report released by MOFA observed, 'learning from its experience with the Gulf War, Japan became keenly aware of the need not merely to implement financial and material cooperation, but also to conduct effective manpower cooperation' (MOFA Japan 1995a).

Prime Ministers Kaifu and Miyazawa – Japan's leaders during the Persian Gulf Crisis and who oversaw the eventual passage of the IPCL – were both known to be mainstream conservatives. Both politicians supported the continued application of the minimalist security policy. However, their governments faced considerable pressure from the normal nationalists (or pro-deployment group) within the ruling LDP and the bureaucracy, especially during the Persian Gulf Crisis. This pressure led Kaifu and Miyazawa to change their positions to support Japan's active participation in the Persian Gulf Crisis (Boyd and Samuels 2005: 27). The Kaifu government was open to personnel contributions to the multinational efforts, but outside the military realm. These included deploying ships to the Gulf, supplying transport aircraft to evacuate Japanese residents and foreign refugees, dispatching doctors to Saudi Arabia and dispatching C-130s to Cairo and Amman to evacuate refugees from the Gulf. Even though these proposals involved personnel contribution, Kaifu failed to implement them due to domestic political circumstances related to security matters and widespread domestic opposition influenced by the constitutional constraints against an overseas dispatch of SDF forces.[6]

However, the normal nationalists wanted more. This group argued that Japan should use the SDF to contribute to the 'international peace based on justice and order' so as to occupy 'an honoured place in an international society', as stated in the preamble of the Constitution (Yamaguchi 1992: 165). Ozawa and his supporters were cognisant that the means adopted to resolve the first international crisis of the post-Cold War period would determine the international order in the new security environment; and Japan's lack of contribution (in military terms) to the Gulf effort would have severe ramifications for its international position. Ozawa contended that Japan's war-renouncing constitution allowed for the SDF's overseas deployment, especially for multilateral undertakings formed to punish states challenging the international order. He especially argued that Japan could actively commit itself to military sanctions and other actions, including the deployment of the SDF overseas, if approved by the UN. Yamaguchi Jiro stated that Ozawa's use of the Constitution in the defence of SDF's dispatch overseas led to a situation where, for the first time, the Constitution ceased to be a monopoly of the Socialist Party.[7]

As they began to dominate the national security debate, the normal nationalists managed to gain acceptance from prime ministers Kaifu and Miyazawa, as well as centrist opposition parties, to incorporate the SDF's overseas dispatch into the Diet deliberations. After gaining approval from the Diet for the deployment of minesweepers to the Gulf, Prime Minister Kaifu said, 'For Japan, which is asked to fulfil large responsibilities in international society, I think it is widely understood that we have to make personnel contributions as well as financial (ones)' (Jimbo 1991, parenthesis from original). Prime Minister Miyazawa, Kaifu's successor, who had previously opposed the overseas deployment of the SDF to the Gulf in 1990 even for limited non-combatant roles, also supported this position after being pressured from the normal nationalists within the Takeshita faction when he became a serious prime ministerial candidate (Calder 1992: 40; *Jiji Press Ticker Service*, 16 January 1992; *Mainichi Daily News*, 30 January 1992).

It was clear that Japan's move away from a minimalist security policy towards an expansion of its international security role focused on peaceful initiatives. This was necessary to appease the opposition within Japan as well as to prevent a backlash from Japan's Asian neighbours, who were critical of any expansion in its security role. In a speech at the National Defense Academy in 1991, Kaifu announced that Japan was ready to expand its financial as well as material assistance role by sending the SDF overseas to contribute to international peace and stability in the post-Cold War era (*Mainichi Daily News*, 31 May 1991). In another speech, Kaifu stressed that Japan's international role expansion did not infer a return to its militarist past. He said: 'Such an undertaking will never place Japan on a path towards becoming a military power that will threaten its neighbours' (*Agence France-Presse*, 11 August 1991). Miyazawa asserted this point too. In supporting Japan's international role expansion in security affairs in the form of personnel contribution, he stressed that Japan's international contribution should be carried out without becoming a military threat to other Asian countries (Calder 1992: 40; *Jiji Press Ticker Service*, 16 January 1992; *Mainichi Daily News*, 30 January 1992).

As a result, Tokyo chose the UN-centred multilateral path as the most appropriate avenue for Japan to promote its international security role. The use of the UN to promote Japan's international role was a strategic choice.

First, the UN had been a source of Japan's legitimacy in the international community since its admission in 1956. Just as the UN was a vehicle for Japan's readmission into the international community during the early postwar period, it was again an avenue for Japan to expand its global security responsibilities in the early post-Cold War period. The only difference was the main security policy objective that the Japanese leadership had hoped to achieve. Unlike the 1950s, when Japan used the UN to shield its minimalist security policy from *realpolitik* influences and pressures, the 1990s witnessed the opposite effect. As Ueki argued, 'this time [the 1990s] it [Japan] attempted to use the UN to bring Japan out of its self-imposed constraints to face the realpolitik of the outside world' (Ueki 1993: 350, parentheses added).

Second, the UN was an embodiment of the kind of security goals and principles Japan hoped to achieve in realising and promoting peace (Ueki 1993: 347). Japan was a member of the UN, which meant that it had a responsibility to promote peace in the international environment based on Article 51 of the UN Charter. Article 2 of the UN Charter contains a renunciation of force similar to that in Article 9 of the Japanese Constitution. The pro-deployment group argued that Japan's participation in international efforts to maintain peace under the aegis of the UN was constitutional as the UN provided for similar provisions. As Foreign Minister Nakayama said, 'Japan has obligations as a UN member country. The security treaty mentions the UN Charter. Our Constitution, in its preamble, says that Japan "desires to occupy an honoured place in an international society striving for the preservation of peace"' (*Japan Times*, 1 January 1991). Third, the use of the the UN path also eased the concerns held by Asian countries that suffered at the hands of Japan during World War Two and among Japanese citizens who were eager to maintain the US–Japan security guarantee in the post-Cold War period (Inoguchi 1998: 87).

The value of the UN for the normal nationalists increased as the global institution became more important following the easing of tensions during the Cold War in the late 1980s (Owada 1995). Its value escalated further during the Persian Gulf Crisis as the US-led multinational coalition commenced the process of freeing Kuwait with UNSC resolutions and the US-led multinational force was formed under the aegis of the UN. According to MOFA, by the early 1990s, there was evidence of a growing expectation that the UN would assume the responsibility of implementing collective global security (MOFA Japan as cited in DiFilippo 2002: 26; Pan 2005: 130). According to Tokuchi Hideshi, a high-ranking official from Japan's MOD, the Japanese government deliberately enhanced the UN's positive role following its success in the Persian Gulf War because sole reliance on the US and the US–Japan alliance did not create a legitimate cause for the expansion of Japan's role, especially from a legal standpoint (Tokuchi, personal communication, 14 September 2005). Although Japan had dispatched civilian personnel to UN peacekeeping and electoral missions prior to the Gulf War, the debate took on a different tone during and after the Persian Gulf Crisis in three ways: first, this issue became a national debate within the Japanese state and society; second, Japan's involvement in UNPKOs was associated with Japan's security role and responsibilities in the post-Cold War period; and third, the debate involved the dispatch of the SDF to UNPKOs as part of UN-led international humanitarian relief operations and peacekeeping operations.

In line with the goal of contributing to international peace, the proponents of Japan's security role expansion were cautious to frame Japan's UNPKO contribution in the form of 'international contribution' and not in the traditional category of military contribution. Aurelia George said that this was consistent with Japan's traditional distinction between its international non-military security contribution (such as its Official Development Assistance or ODA policy) and the strictly military concept of security that relates to Japanese defence and the permissible military activities of the SDF associated with that national security objective (George 1993: 565). MOFA defended this position when its spokesman said:

> Peacekeeping operations are not military operations in their traditional sense . . . peacekeeping operations [are] peaceful operations for the maintenance of peace executed by the United Nations and under the authority of the United Nations. So to brand all this with terms like 'military cooperation', 'military action', or 'Japan sending troops into a combat area', or 'Japan sending troops for military actions', is totally erroneous. (As cited in George 1993: 566–7)

A Ministry of Defense official confessed that pursuing the peacekeeping option was simple, as it was for peaceful objectives and there was no use of force (Kurauchi, personal communication, 21 November 2012).

The normal nationalist camp made two attempts to institutionalise peacekeeping duties into Japan's security agenda through a legal framework. The first attempt was the UNPCC Bill (also known as 'Bill Concerning Cooperation with the UN Peace Effort') in October 1990. In this bill, Ozawa and his followers were looking to authorise the deployment of a small group of lightly armed SDF troops to the Gulf to conduct non-military activities (Hirano as cited in Boyd and Samuels 2005: 27). This bill envisaged the UNPCC as consisting of non-SDF government employees, private citizens and members temporarily transferred from the SDF. The non-military activities specified under the UNPCC Bill were overseeing cease-fire agreements, monitoring elections, medical activities, disaster relief measures, transportation, telecommunications and other logistical support. The bill also authorised members of the UNPCC to carry small firearms for protection. Along with the bill, the normal nationalists also proposed a constitutional reinterpretation to allow for the SDF to be deployed under the banner of the UN even if the missions involved the use of force (Boyd and Samuels 2005: 27).

Although the bill failed to pass the National Diet,[8] the lengthy debate within the Diet 'increased awareness in the Diet and among [the] Japanese public that Japan should participate in UN peacekeeping efforts not only by way of financial contributions but also by sending personnel' (Fukushima 1999: 70). This led to the formation of a Special Study Group on Japan's Role in the International Community, LDP, chaired by Ozawa himself, which came to be known as the Ozawa Committee. The committee published a report titled *Kokusai shakai ni okeru Nihon no yakuwari* [Japan's Role in the International Community], which formed the basis of a second bill that was presented by the Japanese government to the National Diet in September 1991 (see Special Study Group on Japan's Role in the International Community, LDP 1992). According to George, the report became the 'vanguard of the party in providing a solid philosophical and policy foundation for the assumption of an international security role by Japan' (George 1993: 565–6).

The findings of this report reflected the importance for Japan to consider burden-sharing and military contribution duties during the early post-Cold War period. The report was very clear in highlighting the importance of Japan joining other countries in the 'construction of a new order' through 'assuming broader responsibilities in the area of security' (Special Study Group on Japan's Role in the International Community, LDP 1992: 52). Not only was sharing the burden insufficient, the report stressed the importance of military contribution to preserve global peace and stability. It stated:

> When military measures have to be devised to handle [. . .] incidents, it is plainly not enough for a major country like Japan, which is supposed to be assisting in the world's leadership, to contribute only financial and material aid. Japan's personnel cooperation should not be confined to tasks like technological and environmental cooperation and disaster relief but should extend to the area of international community's security. (Special Study Group on Japan's Role in the International Community, LDP 1992: 55)

The report strongly recommended that Japan achieve both the above objectives by participation in UN peacekeeping operations. To facilitate this, the committee reported that the Peace Constitution, which had been the main barrier in Japan's participation in 'international contribution', permitted Japan's peaceful cooperation with all nations through the dispatch of the SDF to UN forces under Articles 42 and 43 of the UN Charter – hence, arguing against the need for a constitutional revision (Ishizuka 2004: 140).

Following months of heated domestic debate and maximum resistance from the JSP and JCP, the 'Law Concerning Cooperation for United Nations Peace-keeping Operations and Other Operations' (also known as the IPCL or the 'PKO' Bill) was pushed through the Diet through a trilateral agreement between the LDP, the Komeito and the DSP in 1992. The Law instituted a framework of dispatching personnel overseas, including SDF troops, to participate in inter-national peace and relief efforts (MOFA Japan 1996b). The IPCL differed from the previous UNPCC Bill in several respects. First, the purpose of the IPCL was more clearly defined. With the focus on peacekeeping operations and humani-tarian activities, the IPCL allowed the SDF to make manpower contributions to the UNPKOs and international aid activities (Ishizuka 2004: 140). Second, to avoid any apprehensions about the SDF deployments, the government set the following safeguards on SDF participation in UNPKOs to be in place before and during actual deployment:

(1)   the parties in the armed conflict must have agreed to a cease-fire;
(2)   the parties in the armed conflict and host countries have given con-sent for deployment for the operation and Japan's participation in the operation;
(3)   the operation must ensure strict impartiality;
(4)   the Japanese contingent must withdraw should any of the above requirements cease to be satisfied; and
(5)   the use of weapons is limited to the minimum amount necessary to protect the personnel's lives.[9]
(MOFA Japan 1992: 54)

Under the IPCL, the SDF was allowed to participate only in 'less risky roles', avoiding 'potentially dangerous peacekeeping duties'. These less risky roles included election monitoring; advisory functions involving civil administration; medical care; logistical support; repair and maintenance of roads and bridges; and assistance in environmental restoration (Leitenberg 1996: 41). The frontline activities associated with peacekeeping or 'potentially dangerous peacekeeping duties', such as cease-fire monitoring, patrol in buffer zones, monitoring of arms traffic, collection and disposal of abandoned weapons, relocation and disarma-ment of warring factional forces, assistance in creating cease-fire lines, and assis-tance in the exchange of prisoners of war, were written into the IPCL but 'frozen' pending review of the law in 1995 (Inoguchi 1998: 93–4; C. Rose 2000: 128). The deployment of the SDF required Diet approval to assure civilian authority over the mission and had a maximum duration of two years as stipulated in the law. Any extension of the operation required further Diet approval.

Although the first dispatch under the new law was the UN Angola Verifi-cation Mission II (UNAVEM II), the key development in Japan's UN-centric diplomacy as part of its international security role was Tokyo's active involvement in the Cambodian peace process – SDF's first participation in international security affairs. Instead of just relying on economic aid and indirect support of conflict resolution in Cambodia through the backing of the Association of Southeast Asian Nations (ASEAN) and maintaining dialogue with Vietnam (Dobson 2003: 99; Takeda 1998: 554), Japan's involvement in the resolution of the conflict and the subsequent reconstruction of the nation expanded to include diplomatic measures and manpower contribution (including SDF troops) (Takeda 1998). The promotion of Japan's international role was carried out through Japan's historic deployment of 1300 personnel consisting of two contingents of SDF engineering battalions, military officers as observers, cease-fire and electoral observers, and civilian police as part of a UN-sponsored peacekeeping force in 1992 (known as the UN Transitional Authority in Cambodia (UNTAC) mission). This deployment, according to a MOFA report, was a success and an important contribution to the 'security of the Indochina subregion and the Asia-Pacific region as a whole – and to greater peace and stability in regions throughout the world' (MOFA Japan 1995a).

The year-long mission in Cambodia formed the foundation for subsequent overseas deployments for the SDF in peacekeeping and humanitarian relief operations. The SDF was successfully deployed in various UNPKOs in Mozambique (1993–5), Rwanda (1994), the Golan Heights (1996–2013, 2019–present), East Timor (2002–4, 2010–12), Nepal (2007–11), Sudan/South Sudan (2008–present) and Haiti (2010–13) (Cabinet Office, Secretariat of the International Peace Cooperation Headquarters n.d. (a)). Outside of the UNPKOs, the SDF also increased participation in international humanitarian relief operations to provide assistance to affected people and repair damage caused by conflicts. The SDF was deployed to assist refugees and afflicted persons from Rwanda (1994), East Timor (1999), Afghanistan (2001) and Iraq (2003) (Cabinet Office, Secretariat of the International Peace Cooperation Headquarters n.d. (b)). Based on the revision of the International Disaster Relief Law that was first enacted in 1987 and revised in 1992 when the IPCL was passed, the SDF has participated in disaster relief operations in response to natural disasters such as earthquakes, tsunamis, typhoons and flooding, and even for national emergencies such as airplane and submarine accidents, and epidemics. In terms of disaster relief missions, Japan's SDF was deployed to Ghana (2014), Haiti (2010), Honduras (1998), India (2001), Indonesia (2005, 2006, 2009, 2014 and 2018), Iran (2003), Malaysia (2014), Nepal (2015), New Zealand (2011 and 2016), Pakistan (2005 and 2010), Philippines (2013), Russia (2005), Thailand (2004) and Turkey (1999) (MOFA Japan n.d.).

Since 1992, the SDF peacekeeping missions have increased in frequency, become more complex in terms of duties and spanned over a wider geographical area. This is reflected in the evolution of the IPCL, which has been revised to allow for more flexibility of missions and roles for the SDF in peacekeeping and humanitarian assistance missions. In 1998, the National Diet approved an amendment that dropped the requirement for a cease-fire for those missions involving the UN High Commission for Refugees and permitted the use of weapons by Japanese personnel under the order of the senior officers (Gilson 2007: 33; Katahara 2001: 501, fn. 27). In 2001, the 'frozen' roles in the 1992 bill, as listed earlier, were lifted for the SDF. The revisions allowed the SDF to participate in a wider range of UN activities, removed limits to the use of weapons to protect people 'under their control' and permitted the protection of weapons and weapons stores as part of the SDF responsibility during the mission (Gilson 2007: 33). The SDF's deployment to Iraq, which will be discussed in Chapter 5, was another milestone in Japan's humanitarian assistance policy, as it involved a deployment that was not mandated by the UN and the conflict had not ceased when the SDF was deployed. In 2015, as part of the set of security bills, the National Diet passed a permanent law to authorise the SDF to be deployed for collective international peace missions. The bills also lifted more restrictions and added more roles for the SDF in peacekeeping duties, such as permitting the SDF to protect a specified area and the local population, rescue civilians such as those working for nongovernmental organisations, and even assist soldiers of foreign militaries who are in danger during PKO missions. The legislation also authorised the use of weapons for these new missions (Fujishige 2016; *Japan Times*, 18 September 2015; Mie 2016).

The incorporation of the international peacekeeping role into the SDF's mandate transformed the SDF from a military force designed to only address the Soviet threat into one that was allowed to participate in international peacekeeping operations overseas under the aegis of the UN (Okazaki and Sato 1991: 20–1). This meant that the activities of the SDF were expanded legitimately to include missions on foreign soil to cooperate with other nations to keep the peace and stability in troubled locations. According to Yamaguchi and George, the deployment of SDF forces overseas to make international contribution was not the government's first priority. The main goal was the mobilisation of the SDF on the international stage. This idea of sending the SDF forces overseas had to be 'gift-wrapped' in the guise of international contribution to overcome domestic opposition (George 1993: 565–9; Yamaguchi 1992: 167). As Yamaguchi Jiro succinctly wrote, 'The Self-Defense Forces thus began their transformation from forces devoted strictly to assuring Japan's own defense within the framework of the US–Japan Security Treaty, to ones that could share the tasks of assuring international security' (Yamaguchi 1992: 167). The next three chapters focus on security policy developments within the US–Japan security relationship, starting with the incorporation of regional defence into the SDF's mandate.

NOTES

1. The information for this section is from Mazarr et al. (1993) and Stanwood et al. (1991).
2. The notion of a US–Japan 'global partnership' in the post-Cold War period was discussed when Prime Minister Kaifu met President Bush in Palm Springs, California in March 1990. The main goal was to expand bilateral cooperation beyond the area of economics to include broader international issues. Japan responded positively to this and pursued three initiatives: (1) it expanded the 1990 ODA budget by 10 per cent to extend assistance to Eastern Europe and Latin America; (2) Kaifu went on a nine-day trip to five South Asian countries where he distributed aid and spoke of the new order of global economy, stressing the importance of addressing environmental problems, drugs, terrorism, and population growth; and (3) Foreign Minister Nakayama Taro hosted the Cambodian peace talks on 4–5 June 1991, which set the stage for the eventual resolution of the Cambodian conflict (Calder 1991: 28).
3. There were approximately 500 Japanese trapped in Iraq and Kuwait and 1,400 in the entire Gulf region (*Daily Yomiuri*, 16 January 1991; Unger 1997: 139).
4. President Bush exerted direct pressure on the Japanese leader for assistance in the multinational effort through bilateral meetings and telephone conversations. Ambassador Armacost exerted pressure through public statements directed at Japan to play a larger role in supporting the multinational forces. More importantly, Armacost exerted pressure on Japan through his close relationship with Ozawa Ichiro, who was Secretary-General of the ruling LDP party and a strong proponent of Japan's active contribution to the multinational effort. The pressure from Secretary Brady was also crucial in raising Japan's financial contribution to the multinational effort. It was only after a meeting between Brady and Japan's prime minister, foreign minister and finance minister on 7 September 1990 that Japan increased the package from US$1 billion to US$4 billion on 13 September 1990. Members of the US Congress and Senate, including those that were known as defenders of Japan, expressed high frustration with Japan's slow and ad hoc reactions to the Gulf Crisis. The Senate and Congress threatened to impose restraints on Japanese automobile exports to the US and, more importantly, to review the nature of the security relationship between the two countries. Japan's US$4 billion pledge, announced on 13 September, came two days after the House of Representatives passed an amendment to the National Defense Authorisation Act for fiscal year 1991 requiring Japan to pay all deployment costs for US forces in Japan or face withdrawal of 5,000 US forces from Japan each year (Hook 1996: 82–3; Niksch and Sutter 1991: 5; Unger 1997: 146–55; Weisman 1991).
5. This section is adapted from Singh (2010: 438–42, 2013: 110–17).
6. The deployment of ships was opposed by the Seamen's Union, who refused to man them; the deployment of transport aircraft to evacuate Japanese residents and foreign refugees was opposed by the Japanese airlines, who refused to fly them to dangerous locations such as Amman; the dispatch of doctors to Saudi Arabia failed owing to a lack of volunteers; and the dispatch of C-130s to Cairo and Amman to evacuate refugees from the Gulf never materialised due to the prolonged debate

in the Diet on the constitutional nature of the measure (Calder 1991: 31–4; Fuku-shima 1999: 67; Purrington and A. K. 1991: 307).

7. For Ozawa's statement on Japan's future, including the kind of security role it could adopt in the post-Cold War period, see Ozawa (1994); and for the importance of Ozawa's role in Japanese politics, see Shinoda (2004).

8. Many reasons have been cited to explain the failure of this bill. First, the bill was drawn up in a hasty manner. In the words of Ishihara Nobuo, who was then the Deputy Chief Cabinet Secretary, 'the government submitted the bill to the Diet without fully considering it' (as cited in Shinoda 2004: 48). Second, the speeches by Kaifu, Nakayama and other officials failed to gain support from the public, and the LDP failed to win support from the opposition parties like DSP and Komei Party. The two main points of contention were the legality of deploying SDF troops abroad (especially in combat areas) and whether they could be lightly armed to defend themselves against hostile forces (Inoguchi 1993: 99; Ishizuka 2004: 138; *Japan Times*, 22 October 1990; Purrington and A. K. 1991: 313).

9. The first three conditions are traditional principles of UNPKOs but conditions 4 and 5 are uniquely Japanese and are consistent with Japanese law (Fukushima 1999: 71).

4

REGIONAL DEFENCE

All the optimism of the onset of the post-Cold War period within the Japanese security discourse diminished from the mid-1990s onwards. The occurrences of the North Korean Nuclear Crisis, the Taiwan Strait Crisis and the Taepodong Crisis led the Japanese security policymaking elite to characterise the post-Cold War East Asian security environment as severely uncertain. In response, Japan had to strengthen its defences against these challenges, especially in strengthening the deterrent effect of the US–Japan security alliance. The first milestone in this update occurred during the 1996–9 period with the authorisation for the SDF to adopt a regional defence role within the US–Japan alliance. However, both countries had to wait until the aftermath of the North Korean Nuclear Crisis in 1993–4, the Taiwan Strait Crisis in 1996 and the Taepodong Crisis in 1999 to implement this initiative.

The Crises

North Korean Nuclear Crisis: The North Korean Nuclear Crisis refers to North Korea's declaration on 12 March 1993 that it would become the first member state to withdraw from the Treaty on the Non-Proliferation of Nuclear Weapons (NPT).[1] This came as a shock to many, as Pyongyang had earlier signed the International Atomic Energy Agency (IAEA) Safeguards Agreement in 1992. This agreement led North Korea to declare the existence of thirteen nuclear facilities that had been unknown before, and granted permission to IAEA inspectors to conduct regular inspections of North Korea's Yongbyon complex. However, IAEA inspections conducted in September 1992 revealed a discrepancy between the amount of weapons-grade plutonium North Korea possessed and the amount declared by North Korea. It was inferred from this discrepancy that North Korea had not disclosed all of its nuclear facilities. When the IAEA requested 'special inspections' on two undeclared sites in February 1993, North Korea refused on the grounds that they were restricted non-nuclear facilities. North Korea subsequently announced its withdrawal from the NPT in March 1993, which for many in the international community confirmed its aspirations to produce nuclear weapons, if it had not already done so (Oberdorfer 1999: 280).

Despite conciliatory efforts by the US and South Korea to halt the further escalation of tensions on the Korean Peninsula, North Korea refused the IAEA full access to its nuclear facilities. In response, the Clinton administration ordered the movement of Patriot missile defence batteries to South Korea. It also threatened a blockade and implicitly expressed its willingness to use force against North Korea (Lim 2003: 145). In response, North Korea refuelled the Yongbyon nuclear reactor in April 1994. One month later (in May 1994), North Korea removed the fuel rods from its nuclear reactor, which made it impossible for the IAEA to trace the history of the reactor and gauge how much weapons-grade fissile material North Korea had extracted. This led to the suspension of the ongoing US–DPRK talks and the US began pushing for the implementation of economic sanctions against North Korea through the UNSC. The crisis was only resolved after former US President Jimmy Carter brokered a deal between the US and North Korea during his visit to Pyongyang in June 1994. North Korea granted permission for the IAEA inspections to continue and agreed to freeze its nuclear programme in exchange for the US dropping the threat of sanctions, providing North Korea with light-water nuclear reactors, resuming US–DPRK talks, and declaring the non-use of nuclear weapons against North Korea. The outcome was a four-page 'agreed framework', signed on 21 October 1994, in which North Korea agreed to dismantle its nuclear programme and disclose its past activities. In exchange, the US led efforts to form the Korean Peninsula Energy Development Organization (KEDO), a multilateral initiative involving the US, South Korea, Japan and others to assist in replacing North Korea's graphite-moderated reactors with two light-water reactors, provide five hundred thousand tonnes of heavy oil annually, and work towards the full normalisation of political and economic relations with North Korea.

From the onset of the post-Cold War period, Japan had been active in the North Korean nuclear issue through its normalisation talks with Pyong-yang, which commenced in January 1991. In coordination with the US and South Korea, Japan made North Korea's compliance with nuclear inspections an essential component in the progress of its normalisation talks (Hughes 1999: 84). As tensions on the Korean Peninsula escalated after Pyongyang's announcement of intent to withdraw from the NPT in March 1993 and to refuel the Yongbyon nuclear reactor in May 1994, Japan essentially adopted a cautious approach using diplomacy, limited economic sanctions (such as interrupting the annual flow of remittances from North Korean residents in Japan and cutting financial links between the *Chosen Soren* (General Association of Korean Residents in Japan) and North Korea) (Sanger 1994b), and provision of funds (for example, the Japanese government also contributed US$1 billion (to the total of US$4 billion) to the KEDO project). Though Japan maintained close diplomatic cooperation with the core actors in the crisis, it mainly relied on the US, South Korea, China and the IAEA to assume leadership in the resolution of the issue.

Taiwan Strait Crisis: The tensions on the Taiwan Strait were a result of the growing perception of the Chinese leadership that the independence movement led by President Lee Teng-hui was gaining strength in Taiwan. Beijing abandoned cross-strait diplomacy and deployed ground, air and naval forces to conduct a series of war games, live exercises and missile tests around Taiwan from July 1995 to March 1996.

The exercises were divided into three phases.[2] During the first phase (the second half of 1995), China launched six DF-15 missiles targeting an area some ninety miles off the coast of northern Taiwan. The People's Liberation Army (PLA) vessels and aircraft conducted live-fire tests off the coast of Fujian for ten days. Further military exercises were conducted to the south of the Strait in mid-November 1995, including a joint operation between the PLA's air, land and sea forces. The second phase, which began in March 1996, was the height of the crisis. Beijing policymakers began to seriously consider the likelihood of President Lee's victory in the elections. China announced another round of military exercises known as Strait 961 – a contingency scenario approved by the Chinese Central Military Commission in 1994 to liberate Taiwan (Funabashi 1999: 355). In this phase, the PLA's Second Artillery Division fired three DF-15 missiles armed with dummy warheads at areas off two of Taiwan's main seaports, Kaoshiung and Keelung. Beijing conducted live-fire tests and war games off the coast to the south of the Strait. The PLA mobilised submarines, destroyers, and fighter aircrafts, and they tested various types of missiles (air-to-air, surface-to-air, and surface-to-surface) (Nakai 2000: 73). On 18 March, the third stage of the exercises commenced when the PLA conducted joint exercises of the amphibious forces of the navy, army and air force on Haitan, near Taiwan (Nakai 2000: 73). The aim here was for the army and navy to secure a beachhead on Haitan, which was chosen for its topographical resemblance to Taiwan, with air support and the deployment of helicopters (Funabashi 1999: 356).

The US was closely monitoring the situation on the Taiwan Strait. It paid close attention to China's military exercises, especially when the exercises from

March 1996 were becoming more severe. In order to prevent a further escalation of tensions on the Taiwan Strait and preserve peace and stability in East Asia, the US deployed two aircraft carrier battle groups (centred on USS *Nimitz* and USS *Independence*) to the area near Taiwan – the largest US deployment in Asia for twenty years. This led to the conclusion of the crisis, with China eventually backing down.

The Taiwan Strait Crisis did not catch Japan by surprise. The institutions responsible for Japan's national security, aided by American intelligence, had been closely monitoring the situation. Japan responded in two ways. The first was Japan's official position on the rising tensions in the Taiwan Strait. This was focused on voicing its protests through its MOFA to China's embassy in Japan and exerting pressure on Beijing to exercise restraint on its behaviour. The official protests were significant, as Japan was the only Asian country to lodge official protest against China, joining the US, Australia and Canada. Also, this was the first time that Taiwan had been a subject of Japanese protests since the normalisation of Sino-Japanese relations (Austin and Harris 2001: 140). The Japanese government also supported the deployment of the USS *Independence* from the Yokosuka base, which signalled a show of solidarity with the US on ensuring peace on the Taiwan Strait (Austin and Harris 2001: 140; Green 2001: 90–1).

The second type of response was the 'behind-the-scenes' efforts of the Japanese government during the crisis. While its efforts in the first category were non-crisis-like, Japan's behind-the-scenes efforts under the stewardship of newly appointed Prime Minister Hashimoto Ryutaro adopted a crisis-like approach based on the eventuality that a conflict might break out on the Taiwan Strait. Hashimoto held a series of urgent meetings that led to the mapping out of a contingency plan focusing on the counter-measures Japan could adopt in a conflict situation. The contingency plans focused on a range of possible issues that could surface from an escalation of tension on the Taiwan Strait, such as the rescue of Japanese immigrants in Taiwan as part of a possible large-scale refugee problem, coastal safety measures, and rear-area support for US armed forces (Funabashi 1999: 422–3). Besides drafting a contingency plan, Hashimoto was also closely monitoring events on the Taiwan Strait. He requested regular updates from the US to complement the updates he received from the JDA (Nakai 2000: 77). To closely monitor developments on the Taiwan Strait at close range, the JDA had deployed the Air SDF (ASDF) early warning aircraft (E-2C) and the MSDF's electronic surveillance aircraft (EP-3) to gather as much information as possible. The E-2C was flying daily surveillance missions during the crisis (it usually flew only one mission a week) and the EP-3 was in the air twenty-four hours a day. As part of an early response, Japan also dispatched a Maritime Safety Agency patrol ship to Okinawa before the commencement of the main Strait 961 exercise (Nakai 1999: 17).

1998 Taepodong Crisis: The date 31 August 1998 will stick in the minds of Japanese people for a long time.[3] Without prior warning, North Korea fired what was believed to be a multi-stage rocket, which could have possibly entered Japanese territory and airspace.[4] The first stage of the rocket was a propulsion device, which separated one or two minutes after the launch and fell into the Sea of Japan. While the missile continued flight, another object was separated. This was the second-stage propulsion device that flew about 60km over Misawa, Aomori Prefecture, before plunging into the Pacific Ocean beyond the Sanriku coast. On 4 September 1998, North Korean authorities announced that the rocket fired was a peaceful attempt that successfully launched a satellite, Kwangmyongsong, into orbit (*Nikkei Weekly*, 7 September 1998). Immediately after the launch, the US, South Korea and Japan could not confirm the presence of a satellite in orbit. However, the US later confirmed that North Korea had tried and failed to place a satellite in orbit, as the satellite broke into pieces seconds before reaching orbit. What was initially thought to be a two-stage Taepodong-1 missile with a range of 1600km was subsequently believed to have had a solid-fuel third stage with a potential range of between 3800km and 5900km (Center for Nonproliferation Studies n.d.).

According to reports, the Japanese government was not surprised by the ballistic missile test, as officials had received prior information from American intelligence in early August 1998 that the North Koreans were preparing such a test. In response, the MSDF dispatched P-3Cs and mobilised its Aegis-class ship (*Miyoko*) in the Sea of Japan to collect information. The MSDF mission of gathering information was supported by the dispatch of the E-2Cs and other ASDF aircrafts (*Daily Yomiuri*, 31 August 1998; Federation of American Scientists n.d.). Considering the information that supported the claim that a missile test was imminent, the Japanese government used diplomatic means to urge North Korea to refrain from conducting the missile test (*Daily Yomiuri*, 31 August 1998, 3 September 1998). However, Pyongyang ignored the request.

Despite possessing prior knowledge of the missile test, the Japanese government was shocked at the flight of the ballistic missile, which flew over Japan's landmass with parts of it landing in the Sea of Japan. Its shock was also related to the advanced stage of North Korea's missile programme. The 'shock' attitude triggered the Japanese government's adoption of a hardline posture against North Korea's belligerent behaviour by imposing unilateral measures, even obstructing the US-led multilateral approach taken to resolve North Korea's nuclear issue. The Japanese government filed a protest to the North Korean permanent representative at the UN, saying that the launch was extremely regrettable (*Daily Yomiuri*, 31 August 1998). The Japanese government suspended normalisation talks with North Korea, banned chartered flights from Japan to North Korea, and halted food aid that was meant to alleviate North Korea's food shortage. Japan also delayed its contribution of US$1 billion for the light-water reactor project as part of the KEDO multilateral project in coordination with South Korea and the US (Tanaka 1999: 23). In the hope of attaining more specific information about the ballistic missile, the JDA dispatched its ships and aircraft to the waters where the objects were thought to have possibly fallen; they conducted searches, but no fallen debris was found.

The Japanese government also unilaterally raised the profile of the Taepodong Crisis internationally through diplomatic means. It submitted a letter to the president of the UNSC and the UN General Assembly denouncing North Korea's actions as being outside accepted international norms. It stressed the negative impact of North Korea's belligerent act on the issue of WMD proliferation and the overall stability of the East Asian region (*Daily Yomiuri*, 4 September 1998, 10 September 1998). Also, Foreign Minister Komura Masahiko took the initiative to include a warning to North Korea in the ASEAN Regional Forum (ARF) meeting's official statement in July 1999. Komura urged North Korea to stop its provocative behaviour and he also sought the support of other ARF members to pressure North Korea to end the development, production, deployment and export of missiles (Castellano 1999; Yamamoto 1999). To complement the unilateral measures, Japan increased bilateral and trilateral cooperation with the US and South Korea to come up with counter-measures against North Korea's missile threat and to exert diplomatic pressure on North Korea to resolve the missile issue. These included ministerial meetings, continued cooperation in the KEDO project, and conducting a joint study with South Korea on North Korea's missile development programme.

The 'Crisis' in the Crises

North Korean Nuclear Crisis: Following a general principle of Japanese security policy, the Japanese government expressed serious concerns related to the possibility of nuclear weapons being introduced on the Korean Peninsula. It pressured North Korea to accept nuclear inspections by the IAEA through several avenues, including its own normalisation talks with Pyongyang. When North Korea decided to withdraw from the NPT in March 1993, the Japanese government expressed alarm even though, for Japan, this move was potentially North Korea's bargaining tactic.

However, the Japanese government did not adopt a crisis approach during the North Korean Nuclear Crisis. In fact, according to Ishihara Nobuo, Deputy Chief Cabinet Secretary, North Korea's withdrawal from the NPT in March 1993, along with the Rodong-1 missile test in May 1993, did not receive adequate attention from the Japanese Diet because the members were debating on the IPCL, especially on the issue of whether SDF officials could carry weapons during their UNTAC mission in Cambodia (Ishihara 1995: 49). Despite North Korea's refusal to permit inspection of its nuclear facilities, Japan continued to emphasise dialogue and expressed caution on the use of economic sanctions against North Korea (*Nikkei Top Articles*, 2 April 1993). Hata Tsu-tomu, Japan's Foreign Minister, said, 'Applying economic sanctions alone is not a good method. Dialogue with North Korea is crucial' (*Nikkei Top Articles*, 13 November 1993). Japan played a marginal role in the diplomatic negotiations with Pyongyang, especially after normalisation talks broke down in November 1992. It did, however, carefully monitor the progress of negotiations between the US and North Korea, and between the two Koreas (Mizuno 1993).

As tensions on the Korean Peninsula escalated with North Korea's removal of fuel rods from its nuclear reactor in May 1994, the Japanese leadership started to review the economic sanctions option more seriously, including the possibility of a naval blockade. This alarm coincided with the introduction by Washington of a draft plan of economic sanctions in June 1994 (*Nikkei Top Articles*, 13 November 1993). The draft plan outlined three stages for the incre-mental implementation of sanctions: first, the cessation of all economic and technical assistance; second, the halting of all remittances and scheduled flights to North Korea; and if the first two stages failed to produce desired results, the final stage would be the interception and blockade of all North Korean ships (*Asahi Shimbun Yukan* as cited in Hughes 1996: 89). At this point, the Hata government (August 1993–April 1994) thought it was necessary to prepare for an emergency on the Korean Peninsula (*Daily Yomiuri*, 17 April 1994, 2 May 1994). For Japan, an economic blockade, including a naval blockade, or even limited attacks on North Korean nuclear facilities with or without a UN resolu-tion, was the worst-case scenario (*Daily Yomiuri*, 17 March 1993). Hata said, 'Japan has to prepare for an emergency' (Radlin 1994). During this stage, the debate within the government focused on the kind of role Japan could play in enforcing sanctions and dealing with an emergency on the Korean Peninsula. This was a pressing issue at the time, as the Japanese government lacked a legal framework that would permit Japan to implement the sanctions and respond rapidly to an emergency.

The Japanese government made significant progress in several areas. The first was related to rescuing Japanese citizens stranded in emergencies over-seas. The Diet introduced a bill to support the dispatch of an SDF aircraft to rescue Japanese citizens from emergencies overseas (Yoshida 1994). The second area of progress was in formulating a list of draft sanctions against North Korea. These included: a prohibition on Japanese and North Korean officials travelling between the two countries, as well as any contact between their diplomats in a third country; the blocking of chartered flights between the two countries; the toughening of immigration checks for private North Korean citizens entering Japan; the restriction of academic and cultural exchanges; and the restriction of bilateral trade and capital flows, including investment and loans, and flow of money from Japan to North Korea (*Daily Yomiuri*, 4 June 1994).

However, the debate on what Japan could do during a contingency remained mired in uncertainty. The Japanese government was reluctant to clarify its position towards how it could assist the US military even when tensions surrounding the North Korea nuclear issue had escalated. In mid-1994, the Japanese government informed its American counterparts that in the event of a Korean conflict it was unable to provide logistical support, participate in a naval blockade or conduct a minesweeping operation (Hughes 1999: 95). While the Japanese government repeatedly stressed that it would support UN-imposed economic sanctions against North Korea (*Japan Times*, 15 June 1994; *Nihon Keizai Shimbun*, 17 June 1994), the dominant approach preferred by the Hata government and the subsequent government made up of an alliance between the LDP, SDPJ, and New Party Sakigake was centred on dialogue and the hope that the crisis would be resolved through negotiations (*Japan Times*, 1 June 1994; *Nihon Keizai Shimbun*, 14 June 1994; *Nikkei Weekly*, 18 April 1994).

Despite the existence of a 'clear and present danger', Japan's failure to adopt a crisis approach to the 1993–4 North Korean Nuclear Crisis was striking. There were three reasons for this. First, as Hughes notes, most Japanese policymakers were cautious about US assessments of North Korea's nuclear bomb. For example, Hatakeyama Shigeru, Vice Minister at the JDA, said that Secretary William Perry's assessment that North Korea had already acquired two nuclear bombs could not be confirmed (*Asahi Shimbun* as cited in Hughes 1996: 83). Prime Minister Hata said that he believed that North Korea did not have the bomb, albeit it was probably diverting material to manufacture one (*Nikkei Shimbun* as cited in Hughes 1996: 83). Although Japan's policymakers agreed that North Korea was in the process of manufacturing a nuclear bomb, they believed North Korea's nuclear threat was more of a long-term issue that posed no short-term military danger (Hughes 1996: 83). According to Hughes, Japan's main concern in relation to the 1994 North Korean Nuclear Crisis was not the nuclear threat, but a political-security one; namely, North Korea's ability to disrupt the US security system in the region, especially US security relationships with South Korea and Japan (Hughes 1996: 88).

Japanese policymakers also feared that the imposition of sanctions would lead to a backlash from the North Korean community in Japan. It was thought that this could occur in the form of exerting financial influence over Japanese political parties through the links of the North Korean community to organised crime, promoting civil disorder or even carrying out terrorist attacks (Hughes 1996: 92; Nakamoto 1994; Sanger 1994a). According to a secret government report leaked to the media, the Japanese government highlighted the possibility of the *Chosen Soren* holding large demonstrations at Japanese government buildings, the US Embassy in Tokyo and US military installations in Japan. There could also be increased violence directed at the police by certain sections of the *Chosen Soren* and conflict between the North

Korean community and right-wing extremist Japanese organisations (Asou as cited in Hughes 1996: 92).

Second, the Japanese government was of the view that economic sanctions against North Korea should be designed to extract concessions rather than have a punitive effect. A senior Japanese official said: 'We are in agreement [with the US] on the overall goal of bringing the North Koreans back to the negotiating table. But stopping the remittances of funds [from Japan] is a very heavy sanction. Our differences are over the weight of the sanctions and the timing' (Sanger 1994c, parentheses added). The Japanese government concurred with the statement of South Korea's Foreign Minister, Han Sung Joo, that 'Pressure will not work' (Oberdorfer 1999: 282). It had hoped that North Korea would react positively to Tokyo's and Seoul's soft stances against sanctions (*Nihon Keizai Shimbun*, 14 June 1994). The Japanese government feared that a naval blockade could result in North Korea becoming more isolated from the international community and even turning to violent moves, such as an armed attack on South Korea (*Daily Yomiuri*, 13 March 1993; Isaka 1993). Moreover, the Japanese government believed that China held the key to defusing tension with North Korea over its suspected nuclear programme (Ishihara 1995: 54). It held talks with Chinese officials to inform them of the importance of dialogue to the resolution of this issue and urged China to force North Korea back to the negotiating table (Isaka 1994).

Third, the debate on what Japan could do in the event of a conflict on the Korean Peninsula touched on sensitive constitutional issues related to the SDF's participation in efforts to resolve the crisis. As the nuclear crisis escalated, the US requested Japan's assistance in the provision of rear-end logistical support such as supply of fuel and other goods, permit the use of facilities for the repair of US warships in Japan, permit the use of Japanese civilian harbours and airports by the US military, the SDF's participation in a naval blockade of North Korea to aid in enforcement measures in the event of the UN-imposed economic sanctions, and the dispatch of SDF minesweepers to Korean waters (*Daily Yomiuri*, 9 June 1994; Mulgan as cited in Hughes 1999: 93–4). As in the 1991 Persian Gulf Crisis, Japan demonstrated indecisiveness in responding to US requests and adopted a cautious stance (R. P. Cronin 1994; Hughes 1999: 94). This was because the debate touched on the constitutional interpretation related to collective self-defence if punitive measures were to be supported or adopted by Japan. For Japan to fulfil this role, it would first have to introduce new laws and revise existing ones, such as the SDF Law to permit the MSDF to provide rear-end military support to the US troops, and the Goods Control Law so that national property could have been freely offered to US military ships (*Daily Yomiuri*, 9 June 1994).

This was certainly not a task suited to the nature of the Japanese political system during the North Korean Nuclear Crisis. This period saw the breakdown of the LDP's dominance of the Japanese political system and the ascendancy of the Hosokawa, Hata and Murayama governments. The SDPJ was a core member of the aforementioned coalition governments. Their presence contributed to Japan's failure to regard the North Korean Nuclear Crisis as a military crisis and to consider legal revisions to support an expanded SDF role in a contingency on the Korean Peninsula alongside the US military. The SDPJ had a historically close and friendly relationship with North Korea and constantly rejected a punitive approach against North Korea. The SDPJ stressed the importance of an UN-centred approach in addressing the North Korean nuclear problem, fearing any enactment of emergency legislation would lead to unconstitutional military action (*Mainichi Daily News*, 23 April 1994; Ina 1994).

This division of opinion surrounding Japan's support for economic sanctions and its role during a military crisis was at its most intense during the Hata government. Within the coalition, the Shinseito, led by Ozawa, was in support of Japan's active security role alongside the US and South Korea in the event of a military crisis on the Korean Peninsula. Ozawa had a negative perception of North Korea. He believed that North Korea possessed nuclear weapons and that Japan needed to strengthen its crisis management procedures in case of a conflict on the Korean Peninsula. Ozawa also favoured active Japanese participation in enforcing sanctions against North Korea if the UNSC voted to impose such sanctions. Hata's Foreign Minister, Kakizawa Koji, supported the move to revise legislative measures to permit the SDF's active response to the crisis. He said that, in addition to diplomatic efforts to maintain a dialogue with North Korea, 'Japan needs to discuss what legislative arrangements are needed' to prepare for an emergency arising from the rising tensions on the Korean Peninsula that could have involved Japanese participation in a naval blockade of North Korea and active support to the US military (Kato and Naka 1994). Kakizawa continued, 'It is understood that Japan is permitted the right of self-defense but is not allowed the right of collective defense. Can this be left intact? I hope there will be national debate on the matter without preoccupation' (*Daily Yomiuri*, 21 May 1994). After strong opposition from the SDPJ and some LDP members, Kakizawa retracted his remarks, saying they were 'inappropriate' (*Daily Yomiuri*, 21 May 1994). Chief Cabinet Secretary Kumagai Hiroshi was also in favour of making legislative arrangements, including revisions to the SDF Law, so that Japan could deal with emergencies as a result of the escalated tensions on the Korean Peninsula. He said, '(Legislative arrangements) can naturally be possible' (*Daily Yomiuri*, 2 May 1994, parenthesis from original).

The other two important actors in this crisis were South Korea and the US. Operating within the US–ROK alliance, both states had perceived the North Korean Crisis as more of a crisis compared to Japan. On the one hand, South Korea adopted a conciliatory approach towards the North, as it saw North Korea as a partner in the reunification efforts and avoided measures that could trigger a conflict on the Korean Peninsula (Greenhouse 1994). On the other hand, the South displayed crisis perceptions and saw the North as an enemy state that could threaten the South with nuclear weapons and challenge the peace-based reunification efforts pursued by Seoul (Park 1994: 86).[5] If South Korea developed a nuclear capability, Japan would most likely follow suit – an outcome that would worsen the security situation for South Korea. Overall, North Korea's belligerent behaviour accentuated Seoul's perception of the high likelihood of war exacerbated by the North's larger and more powerful armed forces.

The South Korean government implemented defensive measures that included intensifying civil defence exercises (Kihl 1997: 182). At one point, South Korean President Kim Young-sam placed the country's military forces on alert against a possible attack from North Korea, activating all the emergency consultative procedures with the US, and South Koreans began storing food in preparation for a possible conflict (Burton 1994; Burton and Graham 1994; Mazarr 1995: 96). Maintaining the view that the most likely response from North Korea to the UN sanctions would be terrorist activity, South Korea placed its police force on emergency alert.

Crisis perceptions during the North Korean Nuclear Crisis were highest among US officials. The crisis threatened its primacy in the post-Cold War world order and threatened regional stability of Northeast Asia. North Korea's nuclear weapons programme constituted a threat to American troops in South Korea and, if left unchecked, would trigger a nuclear arms race in Northeast Asia (Park 1994: 85). On a global scale, North Korea's nuclear ambitions was a direct challenge to America's nuclear non-proliferation efforts, as it could trigger other states to acquire a similar capability, which could be supported by North Korea's exporting its nuclear weapons technology and missile delivery systems (Mazarr 1995: 94; Park 1994: 86).

The North Korean nuclear issue led to intense debates in the US, in which the possibility of 'preemptive strikes' against North Korea's nuclear facilities was raised (Manning 2002: 75). In recognition of the threat escalation on the Korean Peninsula, the US and South Korea resumed the *Team Spirit* military exercises in South Korea and deployed the Patriot anti-missile batteries in South Korea. The US air force built up its supply of munitions and spare parts in South Korea, the US army replaced its older helicopters in South Korea with new Apache helicopters, and the US threatened to seek UN resolution to impose sanctions, including a naval blockade, against North Korea (Gordon 1994; Park 1994: 87). Although the view was that a war was unlikely on the Korean Peninsula,[6] the US Command in Korea did prepare for the possibility of hostilities with the North (Green 2001: 120).

According to an official who was at the Planning Staff Office at the Pentagon during the 1994 North Korean Nuclear Crisis, the US was making plans for a regional contingency on the Korean Peninsula and assessing the type of support Japan could provide (Przystup, personal communication, 16 June 2015). Although MOFA and JDA officials held a series of meetings with officials from the US State Department, Defense Department, and the US Forces in Japan (USFJ), it was clear to the US that Japan was unable to support the US in a regional contingency without new legislation permitting such support from the SDF. At this stage, the Japanese government recognised the emergence of political problems between Japan and the US resulting from asymmetrical approaches between the two countries on how to resolve military crises in East Asia (Hughes 1999: 95). Though the North Korean Nuclear Crisis was not a crisis for the Japanese government when it occurred, it did subsequently become a crisis when the Japanese government was looking to upgrade its security relationship with the US in the mid-1990s.

Taiwan Strait Crisis: When Prime Minister Hashimoto was preparing Japan's response to the Taiwan Strait Crisis in March 1996, he was presented with two sets of possible conclusions on how the crisis could unfold. The first was MOFA's non-crisis perspective, which became the Japanese government's official response. MOFA officials were confident that based on American information, the missile exercises would not escalate into a contingency.[7] On 12 March 1996, for instance, MOFA's spokesman stressed, 'The Japanese Government does not foresee military conflict in that region. We do not expect that military conflict will be imminent' (MOFA Japan 1996c). Hence, according to MOFA, the Japanese government should approach the crisis in a calm and cautious manner (Funabashi 1999: 390).

Also, Tokyo recognised that an outburst would have severe political and security ramifications on Sino-Japanese relations. Omori Yoshio, Director of the Cabinet Research and Information Office (CRIO), confirmed this when he said

> The Japanese government couldn't say it [seriousness of the Taiwan Strait Crisis], nor did the United States use that turn of phrase. Especially if the Japanese government said, this is big trouble, it could be used as an excuse for the mainland attacking or the Taiwanese attacking, or it could trigger something like that, so we couldn't say anything. (As cited in Funabashi 1999: 401, parenthesis added)

The Hashimoto government refused to deploy MSDF to the waters near the westernmost tip of Yonaguni Islands, near China's missile exercises. Prime Minister Hashimoto said 'it would stand out too much if we sent the Maritime SDF' (as cited in Funabashi 1999: 394). Hashimoto also rejected a call by a LDP member from the National Diet's Lower House on cancelling China's Foreign Minister Qian Qichen's visit to Japan on 31 March 1996, arguing that the visit could open a bilateral dialogue on the Taiwan Strait Crisis ('Response to the Standing Committee on Foreign Affairs, House of Representatives' as cited in Funabashi 1999: 394). Moreover, like the North Korean Nuclear Crisis, the cautious approach also served Japan's interests, as it allowed the government to delay making decisions on certain controversial issues, such as whether Japan would fulfil the role of a good ally of the US or seek to maintain good bilateral relations with China, and what kind of a role Japan would play alongside the US during a conflict on the Taiwan Strait (see MOFA Japan 1996c).

The second perspective presented to Prime Minister Hashimoto was the crisis perspective formulated by officials from the CRIO and JDA. This perspective argued for the possibility of an escalation of the military exercises into an armed conflict on the Taiwan Strait. As China's intentions in relation to the military exercises remained unclear, an invasion of Taiwan could not be ruled out. Such a scenario would trigger a response from the US military that could have a direct impact on Japan's national security and its role within the US–Japan security alliance. This perspective caught Hashimoto's attention. According to Funabashi, Hashimoto was particularly 'impressed by the sharp political sense' displayed by CRIO Director Omori during these presentations (Funabashi 1999: 389). This resulted in the Prime Minister perceiving the activities on the Taiwan Strait in terms no less than a crisis, which shaped Japan's behind-the-scenes attitude and discourse towards the Taiwan Strait Crisis.

Even though this perspective contrasted with America's official assessments, the Japanese government saw this as an opportunity to develop a more active security role within the US–Japan security relationship. Prime Minister Hashimoto was concerned not only about the economic and strategic impact of the Taiwan Strait Crisis, but also about the kind of role Japan could constitutionally play alongside US military forces if the crisis escalated into a conflict (see Funabashi 1999: 386–419). Although the military exercises did not escalate into a conflict, the situation still led to the deployment of the two US aircraft carrier battle groups – an indication that the US was willing to risk war against Beijing to ensure that the latter did not use force to settle the China–Taiwan dispute (B. Lee 1999: 9). The involvement of the US in a conflict on the Taiwan Strait would invariably involve applying pressure on Japan to contribute to the resolution of the conflict. The Japanese government was aware that non-involvement or a neutral stance in the event of a conflict on the Taiwan Strait could endanger the US–Japan alliance not only in the short term but also in the long term (Mochizuki 1997: 24). To prevent another 'shameful' experience, such as the first Persian Gulf War and the 1994 North Korean nuclear crisis, Hashimoto was willing to 'push for maximum measures to provide logistical support (but not for combat support) to the United States, even if that meant adopting extrajudicial procedures' (as cited in Funabashi 1999: 416, fn. 8).[8]

The Japanese security policymaking elite recognised that a revision of its role within the bilateral security guidelines was only possible when society's attitudes towards security issues and the presence of the US troops in Japan become more favourable. The Japanese government was hoping that a crisis approach towards the Taiwan Strait Crisis could be a policy window to produce this shift. This was crucial, as a national consensus was rapidly consolidating in Japan for the reduction of US forces following the rape of a twelve-year-old girl by three American military servicemen in Okinawa in September 1995 (Nakai 1999: 17). For the Japanese government, a crisis approach was important in deflecting attention away from the situation in Okinawa and emphasising the strategic importance of the American presence there. A Foreign Ministry official revealed that 'If [Beijing's military demonstration] has any effect on Japan, it would be a good one.' The official further revealed that the Japanese people should discuss national security issues more openly and that the Chinese military threat to Taiwan 'will be a good opportunity for the people to do so' (Inose 1996, parenthesis added). In appreciating the long-term impact of Japan's crisis approach towards the Taiwan Strait Crisis, an official serving on the Japan–US committee working to reduce US military bases in Okinawa commented that 'It will possibly have some favourable effects on the Japan–US security relationship in that it might change Japanese attitudes towards the security issue' (Inose 1996).

Taepodong Crisis: The Taepodong Crisis was a bigger crisis for Japan than for the US or South Korea. Though all three countries expressed serious concerns about the rocket launch, the US and South Korea were the first to reopen contact with North Korea soon after the incident in the hope of resuming dialogue with Pyongyang. Japan, on the other hand, maintained its hardline stance towards North Korea. This subsequently became a stumbling block for trilateral policy coordination on the North Korea issue, reversed only when Tokyo resumed its financial contribution to the KEDO project in October 1998.

The US expressed vehement opposition to North Korea's suspected missile test immediately after the launch. While the American government seemed certain at the beginning that North Korea had launched a Taepodong missile, it did not rule out the possibility of a satellite launch, as claimed by North Korea (Priest 1998; *Reuters*, 31 August 1998). In fact, the Clinton administration subsequently softened its approach towards North Korea following successful US–North Korea talks in early September 1998. Being the preferred negotiating partner for North Korea, the US was able to gain important commitments from North Korea on a range of issues, such as Pyongyang's return to the US–North Korea nuclear talks and the four-party talks scheduled to resolve security issues on the Korean Peninsula. North Korea also agreed to suspend its nuclear programme and allow the US to visit a suspected underground nuclear facility. In return, the US agreed to remove North Korea from its list of states that sponsor terrorism, completed the delivery of the remaining heavy oil due that year, commenced the construction of the two light-water nuclear reactors in North Korea in November 1998, and declared additional humanitarian assistance in terms of food aid to North Korea (*Korea Times*, 12 September 1998; Sanger 1998; *USIA Transcript*, 10 September 1998). On 14 September 1998, both the US State and Defense departments announced that North Korea's 31 August 1998 launch had been a failed attempt to launch a satellite into orbit (*Asahi Shimbun*, 21 September 1998).

South Korea's tone of response was similar to that of the US. The South Korean government expressed serious concerns immediately after North Korea's rocket launch. The South Korean Foreign Ministry spokesman said: 'Whether it's a satellite or a missile, it shows North Korea has acquired an ability to deliver a missile. This is a serious threat to the region' (Choe 1998; *Reuters*, 10 September 1998). Despite their concerns, South Korea did not adopt a crisis approach towards the Taepodong Crisis. For South Korea, the North Korean threat was not new. Although they were concerned about North Korea's firing of the missile, according to Kang In-duk, South Korea's Unification Minister, they were 'not very surprised' (*Associated Press*, 8 September 1998). Also, South Korea's position was shaped by the preference of President Kim Dae-Jung's government for pursuing the sunshine policy of reconciliation with North Korea. The Kim government was keen to resume dialogue with its northern neighbour, as officials were optimistic that a new leadership under Kim Jong Il would be more accommodative to peaceful efforts. Based on this approach, South Korea urged both the US and Japanese governments to avoid adopting a confrontational approach towards North Korea. After conducting independent analyses supplemented by consultations with the US, South Korea came to a similar conclusion with the US that the missile launch was a failed satellite attempt (*Associated Press*, 18 September 1998; *Reuters*, 7 September 1998, 10 September 1998).

Contrary to the US and South Korea, Japan adopted a crisis attitude towards the Taepodong Crisis. Even though Japan had faced previous ballistic missile crises, including more damaging ones, such as the 1993 Rodong-1 missile test (Akutsu, personal communication, 14 November 2012; Kurauchi, personal communication, 21 November 2012; Michishita, personal communication, 21 September 2015), the 31 August 1998 incident assumed a unique place in Japanese national security discourse for three reasons.

First, the Taepodong Crisis was perceived as a direct threat to Japan's national security. It was the first time in the postwar period that the Japanese people had felt their country and lives were immediately threatened by a military power of a foreign country (Kamiya 2001). The multi-stage Taepodong missile was perceived to have flown over Japan's landmass, possibly even entering Japan's airspace before one part plunged into the Sea of Japan and another into the Pacific Ocean just off Japan's east coast. Tanaka Akihiko wrote that, for the average Japanese, the missile test was 'probably the most vivid and forceful reminder of the threat North Korea poses to Japan's security' (Tanaka 1999: 23). Mori Yoshiro, LDP Secretary-General, warned that 'a war could have broken out' and the Japanese journal *Foresight* wrote that the Taepodong launch was the first time there was 'the real possibility of direct attack on Japan' by North Korea (*Foresight* and Chang as cited in Green 2001: 124). A senior Japanese official told *Newsweek*: 'This could have been taken as a declaration of war if it involved anyone but North Korea' (Emerson and Takayama 1998). Kamiya Matake likened the Taepodong launch to the Soviet launch of Sputnik in October 1957 for the Americans, and one Japanese defence analyst claimed that 'the Taepodong came as almost as much a shock [to Japan] as Commander Perry's black ships' (*Jakarta Post* as cited in Hickey 2000: 57, parenthesis added; Kamiya 2001).

Second, the Taepodong Crisis was a showcase of a clear escalation of the North Korean missile threat to Japan's national security. The launch demonstrated a significant advancement in North Korea's missile programme in a short time span, and the Japanese state and society became aware that the intermediate-range Taepodong missile could strike any part of Japan. This accounted for the difference in Japan's reactions to the May 1993 Rodong-1 missile test and the August 1998 Taepodong Crisis. The Rodong-1 missile test made a strong impression in Japan; however, the missiles landed in the waters off Noto Peninsula and did not reach the Japanese mainland. Hence, there were doubts as to whether the missile could damage Japan (Kamiya 2001). Also, according to a high-ranking official from the MOD, the Taepodong launch occurred when the issue of North Korea becoming a nuclear state was increasingly becoming a concern for Japan. This was not the case during the 1993 Rodong-1 test (Kurauchi, personal communication, 21 November 2012).

Third, the Taepodong Crisis raised widespread doubts about the Japanese government's ability to defend the country and its citizens from external threats. The government was unable to collect and analyse the information as swiftly as required during the crisis. Although the JDA was able to collect information through its own means, it was unable to analyse the information in the shortest possible time and promptly communicate it to relevant agencies and to the public (Hisada 1999). Japan's lack of reconnaissance satellites meant that the JDA was unable to collect the required information and relied extensively on the US for intelligence and information on the missile test (Federation of American Scientists n.d.). Due to these problems, Japanese government did not know the exact nature of the object that had plunged into the Pacific Ocean off the Sanriku coast of Japan. Using the Japan–US early warning information system, the US first made public to Japan that the nose cone was expected to fall in the Sea of Japan only eight minutes after the launch. But it then took more than two hours for the US to confirm that the nose cone had in fact fallen into the Pacific Ocean (*Daily Yomiuri*, 8 December 1998). The public was not informed of the missile launch for eleven hours (Morimoto 1999: 28).

Moreover, the Japanese government was slow in implementing national emergency measures, as there were no detailed prepared procedures for responding to such a contingency (*Daily Yomiuri*, 7 March 1999). When the Japanese authorities received news about the missile launch from the US, the ASDF's sixth air defence missile group, the Patriot group, at Misawa Air Base did not take any special action and continued its routine drills, such as radar contact and mock firings. Even after being told on 14 August 1998 about a US intelligence report on missile construction in North Korea, no special instructions were given to the ASDF's Patriot groups located at six different bases in the country to adopt an emergency posture (*Daily Yomiuri*, 9 December 1998).

Considering these problems, the Japanese government immediately adopted a crisis approach to the Taepodong Crisis and refused to accommodate the engagement strategy pursued by the US and South Korea. Japan refused to resume its share of funding for the construction of the light-water nuclear reactors in North Korea, which was frozen after the Taepodong Crisis. Japan did not budge from its position even in response to pressure from the US. Foreign Minister Komura Masahiko defended the government's decision, saying that inaction would send North Korea a misleading message (*Daily Yomiuri*, 22 September 1998).

The Japanese government eventually resumed the funding for the KEDO project in October 1998, as the government recognised that the maintenance of KEDO to prevent North Korea from developing nuclear weapons was in Japan's long-term interests. According to Chief Cabinet Secretary Nonaka Hiromu, 'KEDO is the most realistic and effective framework to prevent North Korea from developing nuclear weapons. Other than the already agreed framework (under the auspices of KEDO), there is no realistic choice for Japan to prevent North Korea from taking such attempts' (*Japan Times*, 22 October 1998). Japan also suspended food aid to the famine-hit state and cancelled chartered flights between the two countries. When America announced that it was considering providing an additional 300,000 tonnes of food relief after the US–North Korea talks in New York in September 1998, Japan did not show support for this initiative (Sanger 1998). Chief Cabinet Secretary Nonaka said that Japan had no intention of following the US or other nations in providing food aid to North Korea (*Japan Times*, 22 October 1998). Unlike the US and South Korea, the Japanese government maintained the position that the rocket launch was not an attempt to launch a satellite but a test for North Korea's Taepodong missile. Though a JDA report did not rule out an unsuccessful satellite launch, it concluded that the small object inside the rocket's final stage was probably not a satellite, but a test firing of a ballistic missile. This was based on information gathered by its naval monitoring ships, Japan's own research on rocket technology, and consultations with US experts (*Daily Yomiuri*, 31 October 1998; *Mainichi Daily News*, 31 October 1998).

Japan's 'overreaction' towards the incidents was noted by others. Although the US and South Korea expressed understanding of Japan's response, their frustrations incrementally increased when Japan's attitude, especially its suspension of funds to the KEDO project, prevented progress in the North Korean issue. The divergence in Japan's stance from the US was noteworthy, as both were traditionally regarded to share common security values and threat perceptions. Morimoto Satoshi said, 'while the United States detected preparations for a missile launch in North Korea, it does not seem to have anticipated the force of Japan's reaction' (Morimoto 1999: 26). Also, the statement issued by the UNSC in criticising North Korea's behaviour exposed Japan's 'overreaction' to the missile test, as it fell short of calling the rocket launch a missile test, as Japan hoped (*Nihon Keizai Shimbun*, 16 September 1998).

However, Japan's attitude somewhat softened subsequently. Apart from agreeing to resume its share of the financial contribution to the construction of the light-water reactors, Japan lifted the charter flight ban in November 1999, announced one month later (in December 1999) that it would resume diplomatic ties with North Korea, and lifted the freeze on food aid to the North. It also decided to sign a contract for building a nuclear power plant in North Korea. However, Japan's adoption of a crisis approach had been important to achieve two goals for the security policymaking elite. The first was to implement policies that would allow Japan to respond effectively to contingencies that directly affect Japanese state and society. Second, the crisis-based approach was crucial in strengthening Japan's security contribution to the US–Japan security alliance, especially in adopting a regional defence role to maintain peace and stability in the East Asian security environment.

THREAT CONSTRUCTION

North Korean Nuclear Crisis: North Korea replaced the former Soviet Union as Japan's primary security threat following the North Korean Nuclear Crisis (*Japan Times*, 16 July 1994). Japan's threat construction process surrounding this crisis focused on the negative impact of North Korea's suspected nuclear weapon and ballistic missile programmes, as well as its 'unpredictable behaviour', on Japan's national security and the regional and international environment.

At the national level, the rapid advancement of North Korea's ballistic missile programme was a serious concern for the Japanese security policymaking elite. Japan became aware of North Korea's strengthening ballistic missile development programme after Pyongyang first tested a medium-range Rodong-1 missile over the Sea of Japan in May 1993. This development was perceived as a 'serious threat' to national security. The 1993 *Defense of Japan* wrote 'If North Korea succeeds in developing its new Rodong-1 missile, a greater part of the Japanese territory may come within its range, depending on where the missiles are deployed' (as cited in *Japan Times*, 31 July 1993). At the same time, the security policymaking elite was also concerned about the negative impact of North Korea's nuclear capability on Japan's national security. Kono Yohei, Japanese Foreign Minister, directly linked North Korea's potential nuclear capability to Japanese national security when he explained that Japan's readiness to offer funds to the KEDO project was 'a question of Japan's own security' (*Daily Yomiuri*, 12 January 1995).

Moreover, the threat construction process highlighted the danger from the combined effects of North Korea's missile development programme, in the form of the Rodong-1 and its successor Rodong-2, and its nuclear weapons programme. Japan recognised that if such a weapon was used, it would be the primary target (Green 2001: 120). In recognising the severity of the threat, Suzuki Masataka, a JDA official who oversaw the compilation of the 1993 *Defense of Japan* report, said: 'Combine nuclear weapons with missile development and we have a source of strong concern' (*Japan Times*, 31 July 1993). Since North Korea possessed a considerable stockpile of chemical weapons, the Japanese security policymaking elite was also concerned about North Korea's ability to attach chemical and biological warheads to its ballistic missiles (*Asahi Shimbun*, 5 April 1994; *Japan Times* as cited in Hughes 1996: 84).

Apart from its nuclear weapons and ballistic missile programmes, North Korea's unpredictable behaviour was also evinced by Japan's threat construction process. North Korea's constant show of belligerent behaviour raised questions about its predictability. The 1993 *Diplomatic Bluebook* (published by MOFA) wrote, 'It is hoped that North Korea will take positive steps, but it is hard to predict North Korea's behaviour' (MOFA Japan 1993). During the announcement of the 1997 *Defense of Japan*, the JDA spokesman said, 'North Korea continues to maintain a closed system. Developments are not clear, and therefore continuing caution is required with regard to the situation there' (Kwan 1997).

The threat elements at the international level focused on the same elements as the national level. The security policymaking elite's attempt to highlight the negative impact of North Korea's behaviour to the international level was quite straightforward. The was because an international consensus surrounding Pyongyang's destabilising behaviour formed quite quickly following its repeated refusals to allow IAEA inspections of its suspected nuclear facilities, its decision to withdraw from the NPT, and its removal of the fuel rods from its nuclear reactor. In Japan's threat construction process, North Korea's attempt to arm itself with WMD was a serious challenge not only to the security of Japan but also to world stability (*Japan Times*, 31 July 1993). Moreover, North Korea was also seen as a threat to the entire East

Asian region. The 1996 *Defense of Japan* described North Korea as a serious unstable factor in East Asia because of its reported development of nuclear weapons and long-range ballistic missiles (as cited in *Japan Times*, 20 July 1996; *Nikkei Weekly*, 29 July 1996).

Taiwan Strait Crisis: Japan's threat construction process was based on both Japan's official response (where a conflict was not imminent) and the behind-the-scenes response (where a conflict might erupt on the Taiwan Strait). The main defining feature of the threat construction process surrounding the Taiwan Strait Crisis was the notion of 'uncertainty' reflected in two aspects – uncertainty in China's behaviour and uncertainty surrounding the unintended consequences from China's military exercises, especially when live ammunition was used. These elements were expressed at both the national and international levels of the threat construction process.

The most significant feature to characterise the uncertainty surrounding China's behaviour during the Taiwan Strait Crisis was Beijing's openness to the use of force option in response to either a declaration of independence by the Taiwanese authorities, or foreign interference in what China regarded as a domestic issue. For the Japanese security policymaking elite, reliance on the 'use of force' option was evidence of China's willingness to project military power in pursuit of its national interests at the expense of causing instability in the East Asian environment (Hughes and Fukushima 2003: 68–9). Ambassador Yanai confirmed this when he said Japan was concerned about China's use of force option against Taiwan, as it would affect the security of the region (Yanai, personal communication, 24 May 2006). The spokesperson from MOFA said,

> What I can tell you about the Japanese position is that we understand that the People's Republic of China has not abandoned the right to use force against a plot – say, a possible interference by a foreign force on the unification of Taiwan; and that the Japanese Government is naturally interested in the situation between the People's Republic of China and Taiwan. (MOFA Japan 1996d)

Second, the uncertainty element was tied to China's undeclared intentions during the crisis. According to officials from the CRIO and JDA, China's uncertain intentions did not rule out the possibility (though they admitted it was unlikely) of a Chinese invasion of Taiwan. They raised a scenario wherein small-scale Chinese forces would land on the Taiwanese islands in the vicinity of Quemoy and Matsu (Funabashi 1999: 388). According to CRIO's Omori, China was using missile intimidation and possibly even an attack on smaller islands in Taiwan to force Taiwan to declare martial law, which would destroy the legitimacy of the elections (Funabashi 1999: 389). Besides the possibility of Chinese forces landing in Quemoy and Matsu, JDA officials argued that there were 10,000 other islands in the vicinity which China could use for its invasion (Funabashi 1999: 389).

The threat construction process also evinced a sense of urgency towards unplanned developments in China's military exercises that could significantly raise tension on the Taiwan Strait and challenge Japan's national security. Japanese officials stressed Japan's vulnerability, especially during the second phase when live ammunition was used, as the exercises were conducted close to Japanese territories. The military exercises were only 60km from Japan's Yonaguni Island and forced the redirecting of Japanese commercial planes flying on the Okinawa–Taipei route. These concerns were expressed in MOFA's protests to China. Kato Ryozo, Director-General of the Asian Affairs Bureau at MOFA, shared with the Chinese Counsellor from China's Embassy in Japan, Zheng Xianglin, that Tokyo was worried that 'something unexpected' might happen as the missile tests were being conducted near Japanese waters and territory (MOFA Japan 1996e).

The behind-the-scenes threat construction process indicated a more blatant impact on Japanese national security. The JDA highlighted the possible danger to national security triggered by US involvement in the response to a Chinese invasion of Taiwan. One MSDF officer expressed that in the event of China's invasion of Taiwan, US involvement in the conflict could force China to invade the Yaeyama islands – the southernmost islands that are part of Okinawa Prefecture (*Tokyo Shimbun* cited in Funabashi 1999: 416, fn. 8). Moreover, the security policymaking elite doubted the accuracy of Chinese missiles. During an interview with Funabashi Yoichi, Prime Minister Hashimoto said he told the bureaucrats

> If the exercises go according to plan, no crisis should occur. We don't know how accurate their missiles are. If they miss their target and something happens, how will Taiwan react? It's why accidental factors might come into play on this side too. That's what's scary. (As cited in Funabashi 1999: 387)

The Japanese security policymaking elite made it clear to the US that Japan was more vulnerable as it was forced to rely on the US to detect Chinese missiles. This was regarded as a serious concern by the Japanese government because of Tokyo's inability to detect a missile that was fired at Taiwan but veered off to head towards Japan (Austin and Harris 2001: 139).

The uncertainty feature from Japan's threat construction process was not only directed against Japan but also at the peace and stability of the East Asia or Asia-Pacific region. This was important for Japan's security policy expansion, which involved taking greater ownership of the regional security environment through a regional defence role. During Japan's protests to the Chinese embassy in Japan, Director-General Kato said that Japan did not think that the heightening of tensions in the Taiwan Strait was desirable for peace and stability in East Asia, and he called upon China to exercise restraint (MOFA Japan 1996e).

The uncertainty surrounding China's behaviour and intentions in Japan's threat construction process was not only confined to the period during the Taiwan Strait Crisis, but assumed a permanent place in Japan's security discourse. China became both an existential threat and a reason for the security policymaking elite to justify the continuous development and strengthening of Japan's security policy, including expanding US–Japan defence cooperation. Due to the Taiwan Strait Crisis, Japan became more vigilant in its monitoring of China's military exercises from 1996 onwards. The defence white papers wrote about China's 'frequent' large-scale military exercises, including combined drills between the army, navy and air force and landing exercises (Japan Defense Agency [JDA] 1996: 44, 1997: 50, 1998: 50, 1999: 37–8). The Japanese government also paid close attention to China's inventory of nuclear-capable ballistic missiles. The defence white papers from 1997 provided detailed accounts of Chinese missile inventory and the missile development programmes in China, and linked China's missile development with the possibility of war on the Taiwan Strait. These defence documents highlighted China's construction of military bases on the shore across the Strait from Taiwan that could serve as launching pads for short-range ballistic missiles against Taiwan (JDA 2000: 47, 2001: 52). The 2002 and 2003 reports went further by stating the means through which China could enhance its operational mobility and readiness for using force against Taiwan (JDA 2002: 61, 2003: 65). Finally, China's behaviour during the Taiwan Strait Crisis had a direct impact on Japan's policy on the disputed territorial claim over the Senkaku/Diaoyu Islands. In Japan's general election in October 1996, the LDP took a tough stance on the territorial dispute when it publicly announced, 'the Senkakus and Takeshima are Japanese territories' (*Daily Yomiuri* as cited in Funabashi 1999: 408). The Japanese security policymaking elite became more sensitive to China's activities in the East China Sea, especially near the disputed islands. Foreign Minister Kono Yohei, usually known for this dovish stance on security issues, declared, 'Since [Chinese ships] secretly entered our exclusive economic waters, we cannot put up with such action' (*Agence Presse* as cited in Armacost and Pyle 2001).

Taepodong Crisis: Unlike the other crises discussed here, the key feature of the Taepodong Crisis' threat construction process was the *direct* nature of the threat to Japanese national security and people. The 1999 defence white paper described the Taepodong Crisis as a 'grave' situation with *direct* effects on the security of Japan (JDA 1999: 202, emphasis added). In a letter submitted to the president of the UNSC on 4 September 1998, the Japanese government denounced North Korea's test firing of a missile, asserting that it directly affected Japan's national security (*Daily Yomiuri*, 10 September 1998). Leading security expert Morimoto Satoshi (1999: 25) said, 'Our nation has passed through a number of crises over the past fifty years, but never has it encountered so direct and immediate [a] threat as it [was] presented by the North Korean missile launch'. The direct nature of the threat led the Japanese government to emphasise the vulnerability of the Japanese territorial state and its people to external threats, in this case, North Korea's ballistic missiles. Okuyama Jiro, MOFA's Assistant Deputy Press Secretary, said,

> Strategically speaking, there is a real threat to Japan's security and other countries in the region because many countries are within the range of North Korea's long-range missiles. We would be happier if there were more defense capabilities against possible incoming missiles from territories other than Japan. That is not limited only to North Korea, but the real danger that we feel now is from them. (MOFA Japan 2002a)

The direct feature of the Taepodong Crisis took precedence over the identification of the rocket launched on 31 August 1998 or the purpose of North Korea's launch. Prior to establishing whether the rocket that flew across Japan was a failed attempt to launch a satellite into orbit or a missile test, the Japanese government took a hardline stance based on North Korea's lack of prior warning about the missile test; hence exacerbating Japan's vulnerability. Japan's Chief Cabinet Secretary, Nonaka Hiromu, said at a news conference that North Korea's act, which was made without any advance notice to Japan or any other nations, was extremely dangerous and regrettable no matter which it was (*Japan Times*, 8 September 1998; *Nikkei Weekly*, 7 September 1998). As one MOFA official said, 'Nevertheless, we cannot underestimate the significance of the fact that a neighbouring country launched a missile *over our heads* without notifying us in advance' (*Daily Yomiuri*, 2 December 1998, emphasis added). Nukaga Fukushiro, JDA's chief, stressed that whether the test involved a ballistic missile or a satellite, 'the fact is that North Korea launched something over Japan into the Pacific Ocean without any advance notification.' He added, 'From a security standpoint, we take this very seriously' (*Nihon Keizai Shimbun*, 15 September 1998). An official from Japan's MOFA further repeated this concern when he said 'the problem is not whether the test involved a ballistic missile or a satellite, but that North Korea launched something over Japan into the Pacific Ocean without any advance notification' (*Nihon Keizai Shimbun*, 16 September 1998). Moreover, Pyongyang displayed insincere and irresponsible behaviour. Not only did it not notify Japan in advance, but according to the Japanese government, North Korea was insincere because it failed to admit to having conducted a missile launch (*Japan Times*, 22 October 1998).[9]

Contrary to the position taken by South Korea and the US (as well China and Russia), the Japanese security policymaking elite remained adamant in labelling the incident as a missile test. Japan's official documents, such as MOFA's *Diplomatic Bluebook* (since 1999) and JDA's *Defense of Japan* (since 1998) both persisted in referring to the crisis as a ballistic missile launch. Some Japanese government sources said that it was a two-stage ballistic missile whose warhead passed over Japan before plunging into the Pacific Ocean (*Nihon Keizai Shimbun*, 31 August 1998). Others, such as the JDA report, stated that the rocket was a three-stage missile, based on the Taepodong-1 missile. The report said the rocket's nose cone may have entered Japanese airspace at an altitude of about 60km before falling into the sea about 60km off the Sanriku coast – inferring a direct hit on Japan's territory and, in turn, its national security (*Daily Yomiuri*, 31 October 1998). When Prime Minister Obuchi Keizo met South Korean Foreign Minister Hoon Soon Yung during the latter's visit to Japan in September 1998, he said that North Korea's missile launch had been a great shock to the Japanese people and that they had concerns over it (*Japan Times*, 5 September 1998).

Japan's threat construction process also had a distinct focus on North Korea's rapid development of its ballistic missile programme from Rodong-1 to Taepodong-1. The 1999 defence white paper wrote: 'the North's missile development is becoming a more and more serious destabilising factor for the East Asian region, including Japan' (as cited in *Daily Yomiuri*, 28 July 1999; Yamamoto 1999). When the JDA received information about a possible test in July 1998, it took precautionary measures that included the deployment of ships with high-tech missile-detecting equipment to the Sea of Japan. In expressing shock at the range of the rocket that was fired, one JDA official said, 'We did not expect one of its missiles to reach the Pacific Ocean' (*Daily Yomiuri*, 9 September 1998). Japan's defence white paper predicted, 'It is extremely likely the development of a Rodong missile with a range of 1,300 km has been completed, and that some have already been deployed. . . . It is possible that most parts of Japan are now within the missile's range.' The white paper also pointed to the possibility that a Taepodong-2 missile with a range of between 3,500 and 6,000 km was being developed at a rapid pace (as cited in *Daily Yomiuri*, 28 July 1999; Yamamoto 1999).

Due to North Korea's advanced missile programme, Japan was concerned that the North Korean ballistic missile could be attached with a nuclear warhead. Such concerns were based on continuing suspicion over the North's development of nuclear weapons since the 1994 North Korean Nuclear Crisis. Both concerns were expressed by the JDA's Director-General Nukaga in his final report of the Taepodong incident, presented to the Cabinet in 1998. He said North Korea's development of long-range ballistic missiles constituted a threat to Japan, as the entire nation would fall within the range of such missiles and these missiles could be armed with nuclear warheads (*Daily Yomiuri*, 31 October 1998). Although JDA officials were of the view that North Korea's rockets were not yet capable of carrying a nuclear warhead, they were cautious not to underestimate the situation. One senior JDA official said,

> By modifying part of their rocket design, it would be possible for the rocket to carry a nuclear warhead. Simulations by the JDA show that North Korea may have developed a rocket that can deliver a warhead in excess of the range of 1600 km that the Taepodong-1 has. (*Daily Yomiuri*, 11 December 1998)

To justify Japan's hardline stance as a result of the Taepodong Crisis, Japan's threat construction process also had an international dimension. This was important for Japan, as it did not want to stand out in its criticisms against North Korea's belligerent behaviour and risk inviting criticisms from neighbouring countries. Also, the international dimension in Japan's threat construction was critical for gaining legitimacy in Japan's security policy expansion, including strengthening US–Japan defence cooperation. In similar fashion to the three previous crises, Japan's threat construction process associated with the Taepodong Crisis evinced the linkage between Japan's national security and the peace and stability of the regional and international security environment. The threat posed by North Korea's missile testing, its advanced missile programme and the associated risks (namely North Korea's possession of WMD and missile proliferation) was framed by the Japanese government as a threat to regional and international security.

Chief Cabinet Secretary Nonaka criticised North Korea's behaviour, stressing that its action was completely unacceptable and had grave consequences for the political situation in Northeast Asia (*Nihon Keizai Shimbun*, 31 August 1998). In a letter submitted to the president of the UNSC, the government not only said that the launch directly affected Japan's national security but also stressed the impact of the missile test on the peace and stability of the whole of Northeast Asia (*Daily Yomiuri*, 10 September 1998). This letter also highlighted how North Korea had disregarded international law, as the missile had passed near routes used by commercial aircraft and landed in waters crossed by major shipping routes. This behaviour ignored the basic principles of the Convention on International Civil Aviation and the UN Convention on the Law of the Sea, of which North Korea was a member (*Daily Yomiuri*, 10 September 1998). When Prime Minister Obuchi Keizo addressed the fifty-third session of the UN General Assembly, he said: 'The recent missile launch by North Korea, even if it was an attempt to launch a satellite into orbit, poses a serious problem, which directly concerns both Japan's national security and peace and stability in Northeast Asia' (MOFA Japan 1998).

The Japanese government linked the threat from the Taepodong Crisis to possible WMD proliferation and North Korea's growing capability to use them in the Asia-Pacific region (*Daily Yomiuri*, 10 September 1998). In raising the possibility that such missiles could be armed with nuclear warheads, JDA's chief Nukaga told a Cabinet meeting: 'It (the 31 August launch) is a matter of vital importance to Japan and Northeast Asia. It is also an issue that the international community must urgently confront' (*Daily Yomiuri*, 31 October 1998, parenthesis from original). The Japanese security policymaking elite in their speeches repeatedly stressed the serious concern of North Korea's 'secret nuclear facilities' to the international community. Numata Sadaaki, MOFA's spokesman, said:

> We are seriously concerned about this [31 August 1998 missile launch] because the deployment of missiles by North Korea does affect Japanese security and it also affects peace and stability in Northeast Asia. It is also of serious global concern, in terms of the proliferation of weapons of mass destruction. (WuDunn 1998, parenthesis added)

Foreign Minister Komura articulated the connection between North Korea's insincere behaviour (referring to its secret nuclear facilities) and the threat to the international community, when he said at a speech during the 145th Diet session: 'The recent missile launch, recent suspicions about secret nuclear facilities, and other matters represent a major source of concern not only for Japan, but the entire international community' (MOFA Japan 1999c).

The threat posed by North Korea's advanced ballistic missile programme was extended to concerns of ballistic missiles proliferation, which became one of the main security concerns for the international community in the post-Cold War period. Japan argued that North Korea's dire economic situation could steer North Korea to export its missile technology to Asian and Middle Eastern countries in exchange for financial support for its missile programme (MOFA Japan 1999d). Morimoto Satoshi wrote, 'The August 1998 launch was possibly in part Pyongyang's way of advertising its new technology to potential customers in the Middle East and elsewhere' (Morimoto 1999: 25).

SECURITY POLICY DEVELOPMENT

While the North Korean Nuclear Crisis, Taiwan Strait Crisis, and Taepodong Crisis informed Japan that the East Asian neighbourhood was fraught with uncertainty, these incidents provided the Japanese security policymaking elite with a policy window to expand its security role in regional and international affairs.[10] Apart from national defence measures, the focus was on addressing the imbalance in Japan's burden-sharing responsibilities within the US–Japan security alliance. Though the US–Japan alliance faced several challenging issues (namely, the troubled economic and trade bilateral relationship and the

American fatigue to stay engaged in East Asia following the end of the Cold War), the US and Japan were committed to reaffirming the security alliance from the onset of the post-Cold War period. Both agreed that the alliance was 'indispensable' to the stability of post-Cold War East Asia, but it had to be revised in response to the new security challenges in two ways.

First, the purpose of the alliance had to expand beyond solely defending Japan's national security. At the thirtieth anniversary of the signing of the Mutual Defense Treaty in 1990, US Defense Secretary Dick Cheney and Japanese Foreign Minister Nakayama Taro agreed that the US–Japan security alliance should no longer solely be to defend Japan, but to contribute to the peace and stability of the Asia-Pacific region (*Japan Times*, 22 February 1990). Second, Japan's role within the security alliance had to expand, especially in terms of assisting the US military in maintaining the peace and stability of the Asia-Pacific region. The bilateral summit between President Bush and Prime Minister Miyazawa in January 1992 declared that Japan and the US should form a 'global partnership' that could contribute to world peace and prosperity. This partnership meant that both states would work closely on global issues, such as nuclear and conventional arms proliferation, regional tensions, the refugee crisis and drug trafficking (Nishihara 2000: 9). However, it was clear that a global partnership to maintain peace and stability required the world's first and second largest economies to not only cooperate in economic terms but also to strengthen defence cooperation, especially in the form of widening Japan's share of the common defence burden within the alliance (*Mainichi Daily News*, 11 January 1992). The latter issue was pressing for the US and Japanese governments, as America faced budgetary constraints that had a direct impact on the American forward presence and Japan's security guarantee provided by the US military.

The reaffirmation of the US–Japan relationship commenced on a positive note. Both governments agreed to upgrade the bilateral Security Consultative Committee (SCC) to a ministerial-level meeting in 1990. Instead of a meeting with the US ambassador to Japan and the commander of the USFJ, this upgrade meant that the Japanese foreign minister and director-general of JDA met the US secretaries of Defense and State. This was followed by a repeated push by the American government to build a stronger bilateral defence relationship through the widening of Japan's share of the defence burden within the US–Japan Security Treaty. This first occurred during the meeting of the defence chiefs of both countries, Secretary Cheney and Director-General Ikeda Yoshihiko, in April 1991. To incorporate Japan as an integral part of US grand strategy for the Asia-Pacific region, Secretary Cheney advocated the signing of an Acquisition Cross Service Agreement (ACSA), which meant developing a mechanism for the exchange of materials such as fuel and services between the American and Japanese militaries. For Washington, an ACSA was important for the effective operation of the alliance, and it had pressured Japan to conclude this government-to-government accord since 1988 (*Daily Yomiuri*, 25 July 1994).

The Japanese government responded to the American pressure by enhancing its technological and financial contribution in terms of host-nation support to the alliance but did not alter the foundation of Japan's defence policy, especially in terms of incorporating a wider security role in regional defence. This was because Tokyo encountered difficulties in convincing its domestic constituents, who preferred the continuation of the minimalist security policy centred on antimilitarism. However, the North Korean Nuclear Crisis, Taiwan Strait Crisis and Taepodong Crisis changed this situation.

The tensions on the Korean Peninsula caused by the North Korean Nuclear Crisis became the basis on which the US requested Japan's participation in US military operations in the event of armed conflicts in the 'Far East'. The US submitted its first such demand in April 1994 and resubmitted this request in December 1995 (*Mainichi Daily News*, 17 May 1997). In May 1994, Washington pressured Tokyo to sign the bilateral ACSA so that the security alliance would be ready to address a possible contingency on the Korean Peninsula caused by Pyongyang's belligerent behaviour. Even though the Japanese government was concerned about a possible contingency on the Korean Peninsula and its severe implications, such as a refugee crisis on Japanese shores, it failed to respond positively on possible measures it could offer to the US military in the event of a regional contingency (Kurauchi, personal communication, 21 November 2012).

Nevertheless, the North Korean Nuclear Crisis made it clear to the Japanese security policymaking elite that its security role alongside the US in the bilateral security relationship could not remain as it was. Much more was expected from Japan in resolving military crises in the Asia-Pacific region. Tokyo conducted a study on the possibility of expanding Japan's security role in three areas: evacuating Japanese citizens based overseas; coping with a large wave of refugees fleeing a conflict; and enforcing UN sanctions, which included the possibility of a sea/naval blockade if a conflict or other emergency erupted in the Far East (*Japan Times*, 4 May 1996). More importantly, the 1994 North Korean Nuclear Crisis triggered strategic thinking on ways for the SDF to assist the US military in times of a regional contingency (Kano, personal communication, 29 November 2012; Kurauchi, personal communication, 21 November 2012; Soeya, personal communication, 22 September 2005). It introduced the possibility for both the US and Japan to prepare for a conflict in the Far East – an urgent matter, especially because up till this point, according to Tanaka Hitoshi, Japan had no operational plans for a contingency in the region (H. Tanaka, personal communication, 8 September 2012). Discussions focused on how Japan could respond to US requests for military assistance, such as assistance in the refuelling of US warships. It became clear at this point that the purpose of the alliance and Japan's role in it had shifted from being a member of the Western camp during the Cold War to assuming the role of regional defence in the post-Cold War period (Serizawa, personal communication, 29 November 2012).

The instability on the Taiwan Strait added urgency within the Japanese security policymaking elite to incorporate a regional defence role within the US–Japan security relationship. Although Tokyo and Washington had commenced negotiations to review the security alliance after the announcement of the East Asia Strategic Review (EASR) (also known as the Nye initiative in 1995) (USG Department of Defense 1995), it was only after the Taiwan Strait Crisis that the Japanese security policymaking elite was able to shore up the confidence of the Japanese people to support not only the US–Japan security framework, but also a regional defence role involving the Japanese military assisting US troops to maintain peace and stability in the Japanese neighbourhood and the larger Asia-Pacific region (Kojima, personal communication, 14 September 2005; Morimoto 1997: 138; Samuels, personal communication, 16 September 2005; A. Tanaka, personal communication, 6 September 2005; Tokuchi, personal communication, 14 September 2005).

While the connection between the North Korean Nuclear Crisis and the strengthening of the US–Japan security relationship is widely accepted, the impact of the Taiwan Strait Crisis on this development is contested (Kojima, personal communication, 14 September 2005; Soeya, personal communication, 22 September 2005; A. Tanaka, personal communication, 6 September 2005; Tokuchi, personal communication, 14 September 2005). It is widely argued that the 1994 North Korean Nuclear Crisis sparked discussions related to the revisions to the 1978 Guidelines for Japan–US Defense Cooperation that would include a provision for the SDF to adopt a regional defence role within the alliance. Moreover, the signing of the Clinton–Hashimoto Declaration, which set the foundation of the review of the US–Japan security relationship, was originally planned for November 1995. However, this did not happen, as President Clinton had to postpone his Tokyo trip due to domestic political reasons. Moreover, the 1995 rape incident in Okinawa had caused a significant drop in Japanese support towards the US bases in Japan, resulting in Clinton's decision to postpone the visit to Japan (Green 2001: 90; Mochizuki 1997: 14).

However, the Taiwan Strait Crisis contributed to Japan's adoption of a regional defence role in the bilateral alliance in three ways. First, the Taiwan Strait Crisis raised the importance of the US–Japan Joint Security Declaration for both governments by several notches. Takamizawa, a high-ranking defence official, mentioned that the Taiwan Strait Crisis was most important for Japan to understand what the US would do in a crisis. Despite Tokyo's attempts to reach out, Washington did not share appropriate information on what it was planning to do during the Taiwan Strait Crisis. This experience led Japan and the US to recognise that both countries needed to share information on procedures and operations and formulate mechanisms that facilitated logistical support in a maritime interdiction (Takamizawa, personal communication, 28 September 2012). In turn, this created a context for the revitalisation of the alliance during the April summit between President Clinton and Prime Minister Hashimoto in 1996 (Mochizuki 1997: 5). According to Winston Lord, while the US–Japan Joint Declaration was already strong, the Taiwan Strait Crisis 'served to strengthen the document even more' (as cited in Funabashi 1999: 425).

Second, the Taiwan Strait Crisis did not change the text of the joint declaration, but added urgency to the strengthening of US–Japan defence cooperation and led Japan to become concerned about China (Bush, personal communication, 30 April 2015). As one White House official that was involved in the Taiwan Strait Crisis said,

> Had it not been for Taiwan, I am not convinced that what occurred in April [announcement of the US–Japan Joint Security Declaration] would have been possible. . . . The Taiwan question solidified views on both sides for the viability of the future, at least in the near term, of the relationship. (As cited in Funabashi 1999: 425, parenthesis added)

Also, Japan and the US used the Taiwan Strait Crisis to garner support for the strengthening of the alliance at home in response to China's assertive behaviour. According to a MOFA official, Japan first realised the aggressive behaviour of China during the Taiwan Strait Crisis, and it was an important catalyst for the revisions of the defence guidelines in 1997 (Asari, personal communication, 25 September 2012).

Third, two critical items that signalled the expansion of Japan's security role within the US–Japan security arrangement were included in the joint declaration only after the Taiwan Strait Crisis. The first was the ACSA, which both countries had failed to agree on previously (*Japan Times*, 16 April 1996). The ACSA was signed just before the Hashimoto–Clinton summit on 15 April 1996. Second, Tokyo and Washington decided to insert an agreement to review the 1978 Guidelines for Japan–US Defense Cooperation into the joint declaration in early April 1996 (after the Taiwan Strait Crisis) (*Japan Times*, 7 April 1996; Mochizuki 1997: 15). The main aim of the guidelines review was to improve bilateral policy coordination and military cooperation to handle 'situations that may emerge in the areas surrounding Japan and which will have an important influence on the peace and stability of Japan' (Mochizuki 1997: 15–16). Also, it was only after the Taiwan Strait Crisis that the Japanese government announced it would not apply the three principles against arms exports in support of military cooperation with the

US (*Japan Times*, 10 April 1996). The move did not stir any controversy (*Japan Times*, 10 April 1996; Mochizuki 1997: 15).

Although the expansion of the SDF's regional defence role alongside the US military was first outlined in the new 1995 NDPO (*Taiko*) (MOFA Japan 1995b), this crucial development only became a defining feature of the US–Japan security alliance at the 1996 Hashimoto–Clinton summit in Tokyo – described by the Secretary of Defense, William Perry, as 'the most significant summit since the end of the Cold War' (*Japan Times*, 16 April 1996). Both leaders signed the 'Japan–US Joint Declaration on Security – Alliance for the 21st Century', which outlined a new direction of the bilateral relationship for the post-Cold War period (MOFA Japan 1996a). A key point in the Joint Declaration was the decision to revise, for the first time, the 1978 Guidelines for US–Japan Defense Cooperation. The review of the guidelines, completed in September 1997, enhanced Japan's responsibility in the context of US–Japan defence cooperation in all three of the areas that had been outlined in the original guidelines – under normal circumstances, during a direct attack against Japan, and in 'situations in areas surrounding Japan that will have an important influence on Japan's peace and security'. The first and second areas led to increased cooperation between Japan and the US in more specific and detailed terms compared to the 1978 guidelines (see Akaha 1998; MOFA Japan 1997; Mulgan 2004; Murata 2000; Soeya 1998a, 1998b; Stokes and Shinn 1998). However, the momentous development in the US–Japan defence cooperation was the security policymaking elite's commitment to authorise the SDF to cooperate with the US military in the third area – Article 6 contingencies – in specific ways. Though the Article 6 contingencies were present in the 1978 version, the discussion was brief, with the focus mainly on consultation between the two parties and the provision of Japanese facilities to the US military during a regional contingency (Mulgan 2004: 157). As Mulgan (2004: 163) wrote, '[b]y far the most significant aspect of the new Guidelines is that they provide[d] a bridge for Japan's transition from an exclusively defence-oriented posture to that of a regional alliance partner'.

To meet its new obligations as stipulated in the revised defence guidelines, Prime Minister Hashimoto submitted three legislative bills to the National Diet in April 1998: the Law to Ensure the Security Situation in Surrounding Areas (*Shuhen Jitai Anzen Kakuhoho*); a bill to revise the SDF law (*Jietaiho*); and a bill to revise the 1996 ACSA between Japan and the US (Akaha 1998: 474). However, these bills did not receive the deserved attention in the National Diet until the Taepodong Crisis. The Taepodong Crisis and its related threat discourse hastened the process that led to the passage of the security bills that were stalled in the National Diet. Their passage after thirteen months of debate in the Diet provided the first legal framework that legitimised the SDF's regional defence role during both times of peace and crises. The Diet passed the three bills in April 1999 (eight months after the Taepodong Crisis), and they came into effect in August 1999.

The first bill, also known as the Regional Contingency Law, authorised the SDF to provide active support to US forces not only during a direct attack on Japan but also during security crises in the Asia-Pacific region that have an important influence on Japan's peace and security. In the past, Japan could only provide permission to the American forces for the use of the bases during a direct attack on Japan. The new bill instead provided a legal framework for Japan's SDF to assist the US military in terms of rear-area logistical and material support during a regional contingency. More specifically, Japan was authorised to participate in a range of activities in new areas, such as in relief activities and measures to deal with a refugees crisis, search and rescue missions,[11] non-combatant evacuation operations,[12] activities that ensured the effectiveness of economic sanctions[13] and support from Japan for US forces' activities – including providing access to the US military for the use of SDF facilities, such as civilian airports and ports, and providing of services, such as rear-area supplies (except for arms and ammunition) during a regional contingency (Hughes 2004: 102–4; Mulgan 2004: 154–5). Moreover, this bill also authorised close operational cooperation during a regional contingency that would involve the SDF participation in a range of activities including intelligence-gathering, surveillance and minesweeping, protection of lives and property, and to ensure navigational safety (Mulgan 2004: 155).

The second bill, the SDF Law, was amended to allow SDF ships and helicopters to evacuate Japanese citizens during military emergencies. Prior to this amendment, such missions usually involved the use of cargo ships because the deployment of MSDF ships was unauthorised (Mulgan 2004: 158). In addition, the revision to the SDF Law authorised SDF personnel to use weapons for self-defence when providing rear-area support and engaging in search and rescue operations for US military personnel (Aoki 1999). The third bill, related to the revision of the ACSA, expanded the SDF's support to the US military during peacetime and contingency operations. For peacetime operations, this mandated the SDF to provide logistical support for US forces during training, joint exercises, peacekeeping operations and humanitarian missions. This support included the supply of fuel, spare parts, military components as well as food, water and clothing to the US military. Apart from peacetime operations, the bill expanded bilateral cooperation to include the supply of fuel and other emergency goods during regional contingencies near Japan as well (Mochizuki 1997: 15).

The other significant development triggered by the Taepodong Crisis was the security policymaking elite's decision to participate in the US-led Theater Missile Defense (TMD) project (referred to in Japan as the Ballistic Missile Defense (BMD)). Having expressed interest in this programme in the 1980s, it was only after the Taepodong Crisis that the Japanese government fully committed itself to the BMD project.[14] Though the primary purpose was to strengthen its national defence capabilities against incoming missiles, Japan's decision to jointly participate in this project also widened its regional defence role, namely protecting the Asia-Pacific security environment from the threat of ballistic missiles. Not only through research and financial means, Japan operationalised BMD monitoring systems and equipped its Aegis destroyers with the BMD systems, along with strengthening its tactical, operational and strategic coordination with the US (Calder 2009: 146; MOFA Japan 2007).

Even though Japan countered any reference to the relationship between collective self-defence and the BMD system,[15] the integrated nature of the anti-missile systems support the argument of widened regional defence for the SDF. First, the SDF could respond to a request by the US to provide cover against missile attacks on the perimeter of the US combat zone and in Japanese territorial waters during a regional crisis, such as on the Taiwan Strait (Hughes 2002: 77). Second, the nature of the system made it difficult for Japan to distinguish whether or not incoming missiles were targeting Japan's national security, especially with the large presence of US troops centred on bases and facilities across Japan. Finally, the literature on missile defence argues that the nature of the anti-missile system inevitably subsumes Japan into US military operations in deterring the threat posed by ballistic missiles in Northeast Asia. Japan's participation in the anti-missile system made it susceptible to a heavy reliance on the US for technology and information and building compatibility with US BMD systems. Such a condition necessitated close US–Japan military cooperation to maintain peace and stability in the Asia-Pacific region against missile attacks (P. M. Cronin et al. 1999: 181; Hughes 2002: 77). Cronin, Giarra and Green wrote,

> TMD has the same implications for bilateral integration at the operational and support level as does the Defense Guidelines, with even more tangible definition and consequences for the bilateral alliance and the way that the United States and Japan must plan, procure, consult, and operate in the future. (P. M. Cronin et al. 1999: 170–1)

It is important to note that the acceptance of enhanced burden-sharing responsibilities by Japan had been in non-combat areas, rear-area functions and a clear avoidance of collective self-defence missions. Nevertheless, the adoption of the regional defence role for the SDF in the US–Japan security alliance was a critical milestone in Japanese post-Cold War security policy. It shifted the purpose of the alliance from solely defending Japan's national security to protecting the Asia-Pacific strategic environment, and it widened the SDF's military support to the US military not only during peacetimes, but in a regional contingency as well. This development led to the further institutionalisation of US–Japan defence cooperation through the alignment of procedures and operational plans to counter regional contingencies, introduced a greater sense of flexibility during deployment of the SDF in time of a contingency, and finally, strengthened Japan's missile defence system to protect Japan and possibly the region from threats posed by ballistic missiles and nuclear capabilities. These new roles for the SDF inculcated greater mutual trust between the two allies and strengthened Japan's role as a reliable ally within the US–Japan security relationship. They also formed the foundation of the SDF's deployment overseas to missions in Afghanistan and Iraq (H. Tanaka, personal communication, 8 September 2012), which are discussed in the following chapter.

Notes

1. For detailed and comprehensive accounts of the background of the North Korean nuclear issue, see Manning (2002); Oberdorfer (1999).
2. For information on the PLA's exercises, see Scobell (2003: 176–7).
3. The details of this incident were taken from *Daily Yomiuri* (28 July 1999, 4 September 1998); Federation of American Scientists (n.d.).
4. Some reports cited Japanese officials saying that the suspected missile did not violate Japanese airspace and territorial sovereignty, as its altitude was more than 100km over Japan (*Nikkei Weekly*, 7 September 1998).
5. South Korea's concerns about the Korean Peninsula were accentuated by the reduced American presence at home during the early post-Cold War period. Under pressure to reduce the American military presence in East Asia, the Bush administration released a report entitled 'A Strategic Framework for the Asian Pacific Rim: Looking Toward the 21st Century', which stipulated changing the US forces' role in East Asia from a 'leading' to a 'supporting' role. This meant a reduction of US troops in South Korea, which involved a reduction of 7,000 troops by the end of 1992 and a second withdrawal of 6,000 troops between 1993 and 1995. However, the second withdrawal was suspended owing to tensions on the Korean Peninsula (Lee as cited in Park 1994: 79).
6. US Secretary of Defence William Perry said: 'This [the North Korean Nuclear Crisis] is not an imminent crisis' (*St Louis Post*, 4 April 1994).
7. Winston Lord, US Assistant Secretary of Defence, told the House of Representatives International Relations Sub-Committee that although the present situation was 'serious', Washington did not believe Taiwan was in imminent danger of an attack (*Daily Yomiuri*, 16 March 1996).
8. In fact, the ruling LDP party was already looking at ways to enhance security cooperation with the US. Yamasaki Taku, a senior LDP lawmaker and Chairman of the Party's Policy Research Council, had asked the party's Security Research Commission (meant to look into emergency defence legislation and ways to strengthen US–Japan defence cooperation) to work out guidelines to address threats to national security during the early stage of China's missile exercises in March 1996 (Inose 1996).

9. Pyongyang's insincerity was also made evident to the Japanese government during the ship intrusions into Japanese territorial waters in March 1999. Press Secretary Okada Masaki referred to North Korea as being insincere because North Korea claimed they had nothing to do with the intrusions. He said, 'We very much regret that there is no sincere response from the North Korean side' (MOFA Japan 1999b).
10. This section is adapted from Singh (2013: 117–22).
11. Japan's search and rescue operations were limited to Japanese territory and 'at sea around Japan, as distinguished from area where combat operations are being conducted' (Akaha 1998: 472).
12. Though the revised guidelines stated that each government was responsible for the evacuation of its own citizens, they left open the possibility for Japan to contribute to the evacuation of non-Japanese and non-US civilians (Akaha 1998: 473). The areas of cooperation included information sharing, transportation for the evacuation of non-combatants, customs and immigration for non-combatants, and provision of temporary accommodation, transportation and medical services to non-combatants in Japan (Hughes 2004: 102).
13. The revised guidelines stated that both Japan and the US would cooperate in areas of information sharing and inspection of ships, as authorised by UNSC resolutions to ensure effectiveness of economic sanctions (Akaha 1998: 473). However, the ship inspection bill that would have authorised the SDF troops to conduct such inspections was removed following a disagreement between two members of the LDP-led coalition government (the Liberal Party (Jiyuto) and the New Komei Party) on SDF's ability to use weapons and fire warning shots during such missions (*Daily Yomiuri*, 27 May 1999).
14. The National Security Council of Japan approved this joint research project in December 1998 and the official exchange of notes related to the joint technological research between the two governments occurred in August 1999 (*Asahi Shimbun*, 25 December 1998).
15. Tokyo's participation in the BMD project raised concerns related to Japan breaching the collective self-defence ban. However, the Japanese leadership repeatedly challenged this notion. When Japan deployed the BMD system in 2003, Fukuda Yasuo, Chief Cabinet Secretary, defended the move by saying that the BMD system was intended solely to defend Japan and would never be used to defend another country. This meant that the participation in the BMD system did not create problems with the right to collective self-defense (Nabeshima 2007). Officials from the defence establishment further supported this position. JDA argued that the system Japan was introducing using the sea-based Standard-3 interceptor missile was unable to shoot down missiles aimed at US territory because they would be flying much higher in space than those on the way to Japanese territory. A key senior Defense Agency official said: 'Our system won't be capable of shooting down missiles at such a high altitude. It's impossible' (Yoshida 2006a).

5

GLOBAL MISSIONS

The start of the twenty-first century coincided with the further strengthening of the US–Japan security alliance. The Japanese government authorised the SDF to offer military assistance to the US military not only for regional contingencies, but for global missions as well. To understand this development, the September 11th attacks on the US proved to be a crucial policy window. These attacks gave the security policymaking elite an opportunity to expand the SDF's geographical and operational scope in assisting the US military by means of active participation in the US-led war on terrorism through the OEF and OIF campaigns, which set a favourable context for the expansion of the SDF's mandate to include global security roles.

THE CRISIS

On September 11th, 2001, four teams of nineteen suspected Islamic terrorists hijacked four commercial planes and conducted a series of coordinated terrorist attacks against the US. Two airliners rammed into the two iconic World Trade Center (WTC) towers in New York, the third plane crashed into the Pentagon building, and the fourth crashed in western Pennsylvania after a reported struggle between the passengers and the hijackers. The terrorists targeted the economic and military nerve centres of the world's strongest power using low-tech and unconventional means. With the death toll at close to 3,000 people, these attacks were the worst terrorist attacks against the US in its entire history.

The US declared 'war' against the perpetrators. It identified the Al-Qaeda organisation and its leader, Osama bin Laden, as prime suspects who had taken refuge in Afghanistan under protection of the Taliban regime. As the Taliban refused to cooperate, the US led an international military coalition into Afghanistan one month after the attacks. The operation, known as OEF, was targeted at capturing Osama bin Laden and dismantling the Al-Qaeda network and the Taliban regime. The American-led war against terrorism was controversially extended to Iraq. This was on the basis that Iraq's President Saddam Hussein had links with Al-Qaeda and was willing to sell WMD to the terrorists. The operation, known as OIF, commenced on March 2003 and was officially declared won by President George W. Bush on May 2003 following the overthrow of Saddam Hussein's regime. While successful in capturing and executing Saddam Hussein, the US-led 'coalition of the willing' remained mired in a protracted armed conflict in Iraq until 2011.

When Prime Minister Koizumi Junichiro and his government were preparing Japan's response to the September 11th attacks, two important points influenced their decision-making process. The first was to avoid the mistakes of the first Persian Gulf War, and the second was to provide substantial assistance to the American efforts in addressing this crisis. The Koizumi government was swift in its response.[1] Not only did it issue an instantaneous condemnation of the attacks, the Koizumi government also established a liaison office at the Crisis Management Centre of the prime minister's residence (later upgraded to the Emergency Anti-Terrorism Headquarters) forty-five minutes after the attacks (Shinoda 2002, 2003: 28). Koizumi called for a Cabinet-level meeting of the National Security Council on the morning of 12 September – the first such meeting since the 1998 Taepodong Crisis (Shinoda 2002, 2003: 28). Within a week of the attacks, Japan devised a seven-point plan that highlighted its firm determination to 'strongly support' the US and actively engage in efforts to combat terrorism (MOFA Japan 2001a; *Nihon Keizai Shimbun*, 21 September 2001). In expressing Japan's support, closeness and sympathy, Koizumi visited the US to hold summit talks with President Bush on 24–5 September 2001. Koizumi presented Japan's seven-point plan, which included a US$10 million contribution to the families of the victims in the attacks (MOFA Japan 2001b).

The Koizumi government initiated a massive diplomatic effort that involved the deployment of high-level envoys to meet leaders and prominent government officials of countries that have significant influence over Islamic states (see MOFA Japan 2001c). These visits not only displayed Japan's commitment and solidarity with the international community but were also means of lobbying support from the Muslim countries affected by the terrorist threat for the US-led anti-terrorism campaign. Japan also embarked on a massive assistance programme, especially in refugee assistance and reconstruction of post-Taliban

Afghanistan. In the area of refugee assistance, Japan extended funds and relief materials to international agencies and countries hosting the large displaced population from Afghanistan resulting from the OEF campaign. Contributing to the peaceful reconstruction of Afghanistan, Tokyo hosted the International Conference Assistance for Afghanistan on 21–2 January 2002. At this gathering, sixty-one countries and twenty-one organisations pledged support to build peace, stability and prosperity in Afghanistan. Japan contributed US$500 million, as part of the US$4.5 billion pledged by the international community (*Daily Yomiuri*, 29 January 2002).

Besides diplomatic and financial assistance efforts, the Japanese government also announced military initiatives, an action that was a significant departure from the 1991 Gulf War Crisis. One of the most important developments was the passage by the National Diet on 29 October 2001 of the Anti-Terrorism Special Measures Law, which allowed the SDF to support US troops in the international fight against terrorism. This involved the dispatch of six MSDF ships with 1,200-member crew to the Indian Ocean to assist the US troops in November 2001 (MOFA Japan 2001d). Three ships – two destroyers (*Kurama* and *Kirisame*) and one supply ship (*Hamana*) – were sent to waters near Diego Garcia in the Indian Ocean for purposes of information gathering, provision of supplies and logistics assistance. Three other ships – a supply ship (*Towada*), a minesweeper (*Uraga*) and a helicopter-carrying destroyer (*Sawagiri*) – were sent to the Indian Ocean to provide relief supplies to Afghan refugees and logistics support to US and UK ships and other allied nations. For the first time in history, Japanese destroyers and minesweepers also escorted the aircraft carrier Kitty Hawk from Yokosuka Naval Base to the Indian Ocean for a military operation (*Asahi Shimbun*, 26 November 2001; *Daily Yomiuri*, 14 May 2005). Despite strong opposition from within the LDP and the New Komei Party,[2] the Japanese government dispatched the Aegis-equipped destroyer to the Indian Ocean to aid in the intelligence-gathering activities in December 2002. The Basic Plan, which was a document that outlined the SDF's activities during OEF, was revised several times, keeping the SDF troops deployed in the Indian Ocean until January 2010 when the DPJ-led government came to power.

The Koizumi government showed unreserved support for America's military campaign in Iraq, pledging up to a total of US$5 billion in financial assistance to Iraq. It provided humanitarian assistance to the affected people in countries neighbouring Iraq, such as Jordan and the Palestinian Authority, by supplying humanitarian relief materials and dispatching civilian medical teams (MOFA Japan 2003a). More importantly, Japan provided physical support to Iraq's reconstruction efforts through its historic deployment of SDF forces. On 26 July 2003, the National Diet passed a Law Concerning Special Measures on Humanitarian and Reconstruction Assistance, which enabled the deployment of the SDF to Samawah in al-Muthana province. After an investigative team declared that Samawah had minimal security problems, a 600-strong SDF unit started its humanitarian duties in January 2004 and withdrew from Iraq by July 2006.

THE 'CRISIS' IN THE CRISIS

The September 11th attacks created a furore that amounted to an international crisis. The international community became cognisant of the severity of the threat posed by terrorism to global security and showed strong support to the US-led military campaign in Afghanistan. Due to the strong international support and UN mandate, the Japanese security policymaking elite faced no problems in embracing the threat posed by international terrorism to justify the SDF's participation in the OEF. There was consensus within Japanese state and society that the SDF's participation in the US-led international effort was necessary, both as a responsible ally of the US and as a member of the international community. A poll conducted by *Nihon Keizai Shimbun* showed that 70 per cent of respondents supported the SDF providing logistical support to the US-led military campaign, while only 23 per cent were opposed to it (*Nihon Keizai Shimbun*, 25 September 2001). Japan's SDF participation in the OEF had a significant impact on Japan's security policy, setting the stage for its contribution to counter-terrorism measures and its military role in global security (Tokuchi, personal communication, 14 September 2005).

However, the situation surrounding the SDF's participation in OIF was different, as international opinion was visibly divided surrounding the use of force option against Iraq. There were essentially two main opinions. The leaders of the US and UK-led 'coalition of the willing' viewed the military campaign as a 'preventive war'. This was necessary to overthrow Saddam Hussein's regime, which was regarded as the antithesis of the dominant US-led normative structure and the peace and stability of the international community. To garner as much support as possible from the international community, the US (and the UK) intermittently changed their justifications to gain a UN resolution that would authorise the use of force option. It used four main arguments: (1) Deterrence was no longer feasible against Saddam Hussein. He was an evil 'madman' bent on the destruction of the US regardless of the risks to himself or his country; (2) Saddam Hussein was associated with Al-Qaeda and had assisted in the carrying out of the September 11th terrorist attacks; (3) Saddam Hussein was close to acquiring nuclear weapons, which posed a serious threat to the stability of the Middle East and the international community; and (4) Besides nuclear weapons, Saddam Hussein also possessed chemical and biological weapons that could be used to devastating effect against American civilians at home or US troops in the Middle East (Kaufman 2004: 6).

The countries in the coalition of the willing faced a mammoth challenge in gaining an international consensus (through the UN) to launch a preventive war against Iraq. The debate commenced on a positive note when there was unanimous support for UNSC Resolution 1441, passed in November 2002, which called for Iraq to comply with the disarmament obligations and to allow for the return of weapons inspectors to Iraq. As Iraq failed to cooperate and meet the obligations set out in this resolution, the US and UK attempted to introduce another resolution for the UNSC to consider. At this stage the US and UK, along with Spain, saw the military option as inevitable. According to these countries, a preventive war against Iraq was justified legally based on Resolution 1441 and the previous resolutions passed by the UNSC since 1990 onwards, namely Resolution 678 (which permitted a multinational coalition led by the US and UK to force Iraq's withdrawal from Kuwait during the first Persian Gulf War) and Resolution 687 (which demanded Iraq to declare that it had eliminated all WMD). Although the draft second resolution failed to pass at the UNSC, the US and UK issued a final ultimatum to Saddam Hussein that the price of failing to disarm was a military invasion. After announcing that diplomacy had failed, a combination of American and British troops commenced the invasion of Iraq on 19 March 2003.

France, Germany, Russia and China held the other view towards the war in Iraq. While concurring with the US and UK that regime change in Iraq was preferable and all attempts by Saddam Hussein to possess WMD and chemical weapons must be halted, these countries diverged on the means of achieving these objectives. They contested the evidence presented by the US and UK on Iraq's connection to Al-Qaeda and the presence of WMD in Iraq. Even if Saddam Hussein was hiding WMD, these countries held the view that the weapons inspectors should be given more time and resources. For these countries, the Iraq issue had to be resolved peacefully. War was only an option after everything possible was pursued to disarm Iraq peacefully. Moreover, the military campaign had to be authorised by the UN. For these states, none of the resolutions up till then authorised the use of force option against Iraq. Hence, only the passage of the second resolution by the UNSC could authorise a military campaign against Iraq. Due to these arguments, these countries viewed the war launched by the US-led coalition of the willing as illegal.

In Japan, the division in viewpoints towards the use of military force against Iraq resembled the divided international opinion. The debate was between the security policymaking elite, led by Prime Minister Koizumi, who supported the use of the military option against Iraq, and those who vehemently opposed it, comprising members of the opposition parties, some prominent members from the LDP, members of NGOs and civil society groups, and the majority of Japanese society.

From the beginning, the Japanese security policymaking elite took a proactive stance on the Iraq issue. Japan had close and high-level consultations with the US and other members of the UNSC. It stressed the importance of a unified diplomatic approach towards the Iraq issue under the auspices of the UN for a peaceful solution. Not only did Japan directly call on Iraq to comply with the relevant UNSC resolutions, but it also took every possible opportunity to persuade countries in the Middle East, especially those close to Iraq, to urge Saddam Hussein to comply with the resolutions. A peaceful solution was important for Japan due to the controversial ramifications of Japan's outright support of the use of the military option against Iraq, which was viewed by the security policymaking elite as an inevitable outcome. When Richard Armitage, US Deputy Secretary of State, visited Japan in August 2002 for a vice-ministerial security meeting, he made it clear that the US did not need a second UNSC resolution to use the military option against Iraq – suggesting that there was a high likelihood of this option becoming a reality (*Mainichi Daily News*, 28 August 2002). Nukaga Fukushiro, chief of the JDA, made this sentiment known when he said: 'The US is serious (about attacking Iraq),' following his meeting with Christopher LaFleur, US Acting Assistant Secretary of State for East Asian and Pacific Affairs, on 28 August 2002. He added that Japan faced a tough decision on this matter (*Daily Yomiuri*, 12 September 2002, parenthesis from original).

Similar to OEF, the Japanese security policymaking elite was clear that Japan had to show strong support to the US-led operation in Iraq, which would involve a SDF deployment. As the government recognised that it would face serious difficulties in dispatching the SDF to Iraq, either under the Anti-Terrorism Bill that authorised SDF's involvement in the OEF or the 1997 US–Japan defence guidelines, it debated introducing a new law that would authorise the SDF's provision of logistical support in the event of a US attack on Iraq in January 2003 (*Mainichi Daily News*, 1 January 2003; *Nihon Keizai Shimbun*, 1 September 2002).

Despite the Japanese government's decision to support the US-led initiative, Koizumi remained vague on Japan's position until an international consensus on the use of the military option became stronger. The Japanese government worked hard in the hope of mustering greater support for the second UN resolution on Iraq in February 2003 (one month before the deadline). Japan embarked on an active diplomatic effort to convince non-permanent UNSC members, such as Angola, Cameroon and Guinea, to support a new resolution authorising military action against Iraq. For Japan, a second UNSC resolution was important because it would signal a strong international consensus that would justify Japan's support for the US attack against Iraq, as well as its eventual participation in the reconstruction of Iraq in the aftermath of the war (*Nihon Keizai Shimbun*, 29 January 2003). In late February 2003, Japan voiced its support for a new resolution on Iraq submitted by the US, the UK and Spain with the strong hope that France would support it (*Mainichi Daily News*, 25 February 2003). However, the second resolution was not submitted to the UNSC, as France had declared that it would use its veto.

As the diplomatic means showed no sign of succeeding, Koizumi declared his official support for a military campaign hours after the US, UK, and Spain had set the deadline for Iraq to comply with all the UN resolutions as 17 March 2003. Instead of the traditional reliance on UN-based diplomacy, Koizumi supported the use of force option against Iraq without a new UN resolution on the basis that existing UNSC resolutions, namely resolutions 678, 687 and 1441, authorised the use of force option. Foreign Minister Kawaguchi Yoriko explained this position at the Budget Committee session of the National Diet's Lower House on 6 February 2003. She said that the Japanese government did not see Resolution 1441 itself as legally justifying war. However, Kawaguchi continued to justify the government's support in the following way: Resolution 1441 clarified that Iraq had not complied with Resolution 687; the truce from the first Persian Gulf War would only come into effect when Iraq complied fully with Resolution 687; and finally, if Iraq was in violation of Resolution 687, the truce was not effective and the use of force was theoretically possible under Resolution 678 (*Daily Yomiuri*, 15 February 2003).

From the onset, all the opposition parties (DPJ, Liberal Party, JCP, and SDP/SDPJ) and some members of the LDP were against the use of a military option against Iraq. They expressed vehement and continuous opposition at various stages starting from the Koizumi government's show of support for the use of military force to disarm Iraq to the eventual dispatch of SDF troops at the beginning of 2003. The domestic opposition gradually mounted, and it was the strongest when the Japanese government debated the introduction of bills to authorise the SDF's participation in the reconstruction phase of Iraq. This came in the wake of the deaths of two Japanese diplomats killed in Northern Iraq in November 2003. Although the two members of the ruling coalition with the LDP (New Komeito and the New Conservative Party) were against the war during the early discussions, both declared their support as the deadline of 17 March drew closer. The New Komeito leader, Kanzaki Takenori, said: 'Japan has no choice but to support the US' (*Nihon Keizai Shimbun*, 18 March 2003).

Like those states who opposed the war in Iraq, the opposition against the Japanese government's position focused on the legality of the preventive war to disarm Iraq and the subsequent occupation of Iraq without UN authorisation. Their main source of opposition was that the decision to use force in Iraq undermined the UN process and Japan's show of support to the illegal war undermined its traditional reliance on the UN process. They questioned Japan's support of the war in Iraq based on the grounds of tying Iraq to Al-Qaeda and the presence of WMD in Iraq – both positions clearly lacked evidence. The opposition urged the Japanese government to oppose the use of military force as it undermined the UNSC's authority as key to maintaining global peace and stability. Instead of adopting the use of force option, members of the opposition supported the continuation of arms inspections in Iraq. They stressed the importance of gaining an international consensus achieved through the UN framework for a peaceful resolution of the Iraq issue. For this group, the use of force option should only be a last resort after all peaceful means had been exhausted and should be sanctioned by the UN through a resolution that signalled an international consensus.

The opposition parties accused the Koizumi government of the following (from *Japan Times*, 19 March 2003, 21 March 2003; *Mainichi Daily News*, 21 March 2003; *Nihon Keizai Shimbun*, 21 March 2003): (1) failing to provide a convincing explanation for why the government supported the US attacks in the absence of a new resolution; (2) failing to explain the reasons for the sudden change in the government's position to argue that previous UN resolutions provided a legal basis for the use of force option; (3) failing to explain the long-standing refusal to clearly state before the legislature its position regarding the increasing likelihood of a US war against Iraq; (4) putting SDF personnel in danger because, first, they could only use their weapons for self-defence purposes (or when faced with life-threatening situations or bodily harm to themselves, other SDF personnel or anybody under their protection), and second, it was difficult to distinguish between combat and non-combat zones given the unstable nature of Iraq (*Japan Times*, 18 June 2003; *Nikkei Weekly*, 16 June 2003); and (5) for the JCP and SDP, failing to convincingly explain how the government's support and participation in the US-led war was within the confines of the Constitution of Japan (*Japan Times*, 14 June 2003).

The main opposition party, the DPJ, submitted a resolution to the Diet calling for more inspections, instead of the use of force. It submitted its own version of the Iraq reconstruction bill to the Diet that called for the dispatch of non-military personnel with limited roles and deployed for a shorter period (*Japan Times*, 2 July 2003; *Mainichi Daily News*, 4 July 2003). However, this was rejected by the LDP-led ruling coalition. The opposition also submitted a no-confidence vote on 25 July (the day before the Iraq reconstruction bill was scheduled to pass) against the Cabinet led by Prime Minister Koizumi to prevent SDF's participation in the controversial OIF campaign. However, this was also voted down by the ruling coalition (*Nikkei Weekly*, 28 July 2003).

Certain prominent members within the LDP distanced themselves from Prime Minister Koizumi's support of the US-led war against Iraq. Former LDP Secretary-General Koga Makoto argued against Japan's support of the war based on Japan's own history. He said: 'Because Japan suffered much in World War Two, it should fulfil its responsibility and mission to avert war.' Another former chief of the ruling party, Nonaka Hiromu, argued for the continuation of inspections. He said, 'I'm glad to hear that many countries at the UNSC said UN arms inspections in

Iraq should continue' (*Daily Yomiuri*, 17 February 2003). According to Kyuma Fumio, a high-ranking member of the LDP and former JDA chief, 'Japan does not have to, and should not, send the SDF to support US military action on Iraq just because Washington claims Iraq is a dangerous country producing weapons of mass destruction' (Takahashi 2002).

The NGOs and members of civil society also protested against the Koizumi government's support of the US-led war against Iraq and decision to dispatch SDF troops to Iraq. In a *Kyodo News* poll conducted in February 2003, 79 per cent of respondents opposed the US-led invasion when asked whether the government should support a military strike (*Japan Times*, 14 February 2002). A poll carried out by *Mainichi Daily News* in March 2003 accounted for 84 per cent of the respondents opposed to an attack on Iraq (*Mainichi Daily News*, 31 March 2003). Thousands of anti-war protestors took to the streets in Tokyo, Osaka, Nagoya, Okinawa and Hokkaido to voice their opposition. The protest, which attracted around 40,000 people in Tokyo, was part of a nationwide joint action against the war organised by a network of forty-seven Japanese civic groups and NGOs (*Mainichi Daily News*, 9 March 2003).

Threat Construction

The September 11th attacks raised the level of threat from international terrorism for the entire international community. Most advanced democracies, including Japan, reacted in a similar way. Japan's responses to the threat were milestones in its security policy practice. Compared to its minimal contribution to the 1991 Persian Gulf Crisis, Japan's contribution to the US-led 'war on terror' – referred to by the Japanese government as a 'fight against terrorism' – was distinctly different. Despite having a Peace Constitution that restricted Japan from using 'war' as a tool to resolve a military conflict and engaging in collective defence efforts, the SDF participated in the OEF and OIF campaigns. Moreover, the Japanese government supported the US-led preventive war against Iraq and subsequently dispatched SDF troops to provide humanitarian assistance for Iraq's reconstruction efforts even though there was no clear UN support for this military operation and there was vehement opposition at home. The threat construction processes for both OEF and OIF explain how the security policymaking elite was able to justify its military contribution to both campaigns.

OEF

The Japanese security policymaking elite internationalised the threat posed by terrorism in three ways. First, Japan's threat construction process emphasised the 'new' nature of the international terrorism threat caused by the September 11th attacks. Although the threat posed was not new, the nature and scale of the terrorist attacks in New York and Washington meant they were perceived as a 'new' challenge to international security affairs. Foreign Minister Kawaguchi highlighted this when she referred to the series of terrorist attacks in the US as having 'renewed our perception of the *new* threats to our security' (MOFA Japan 2002c, emphasis added). The severity of this 'new' threat was underscored by Prime Minister Koizumi when he said, 'We cannot silently ignore terrorism' (*Nihon Keizai Shimbun*, 12 September 2001). The *Diplomatic Bluebook* 2003 expressed similar concerns, stating that the terrorist attacks 'raised strong awareness that terrorism poses a grave threat to the peace and stability of the entire international community' (MOFA Japan 2003b).

Second, the security policymaking elite stressed that the September 11th attacks affected not only the US, but the entire human population. Koizumi said, 'The terrorist attacks are not only on the United States. They represent a despicable attack on all humankind' (MOFA Japan 2001e). Third, and related to the previous point, the threat posed by international terrorism attacked the widely accepted values that governed the international community. The Prime Minister made this point on several occasions. During the ceremony for all victims of terrorist attacks in the US, Koizumi said: 'These terrorist attacks are a serious challenge not only to the United States, but to the freedom, peace and democracy of the world' (MOFA Japan 2001b). During his meeting with President Bush in Washington on 25 September 2001, Koizumi remarked, 'The latest terrorist attack is a renewed challenge to freedom and democracy' – referring to values that are seen to be widely shared by the international community, especially by Japan and the US (*Nihon Keizai Shimbun*, 26 September 2001). In a speech at the Council for Foreign Relations in September 2002, the Japanese leader said, 'September 11th destroyed families, and it destroyed our assumptions about how the world operated' (MOFA Japan 2002d).

At the national level, the Japanese security policymaking elite regarded the attacks against the US as attacks on itself and the fight against terrorism as its own challenge. This represented an 'imagined' direct connection between US national security and Japan's national security. Japan's national security was threatened by the attacks in two ways. First, the attacks were a direct hit on Japan's national security in terms of the human and material damage that they caused. Many Japanese banks, life insurance companies and brokerages had offices in the WTC towers, and more than twenty Japanese citizens were killed in the attacks. Nakatani Gen, JDA's Director-General, said: 'Many Japanese victims were involved in the attacks, so we can hardly look on unconcernedly like last time [referring to Japan's contribution to the 1991 Persian Gulf War]. We are under threat' (*Nikkei Weekly*, 24 September 2001, parenthesis added).

At a ceremony dedicated to the victims of the terrorist attacks, Koizumi said, 'Many people fell victim to these attacks. The damage was inflicted, of course, on Americans, but also on people throughout the world, including *Japanese*'

(MOFA Japan 2001b, italics added). While Koizumi may have been referring to the Japanese people killed in the attacks, he was also indirectly highlighting the 'damage' inflicted on Japan's national security by the attacks. In his New Year Reflections speech in January 2002, Koizumi mentioned that the September 11th attacks were a core issue with major implications for Japan's national security. In showing this link, the *Diplomatic Bluebook* 2003 wrote, 'Japan considers terrorism as a threat to its own national security' (MOFA Japan 2003b; also see JDA 2003: 241; MOFA Japan 2002e).

Second, the national security discourse exposed the vulnerability of the Japanese state to similar terrorist attacks. At a press conference, Japan's JDA chief announced that terrorist incidents could also occur in Japan (*Nihon Keizai Shimbun*, 12 September 2001). Uruma Iwao, National Police Agency (NPA) Security Bureau chief, repeated this concern when he revealed information from foreign intelligence sources that members of a radical fundamentalist Islamist group had entered Japan before the terrorist attacks in the US. Although the possibility of Japan being a terrorist hideout remained low, Uruma told the National Diet's Lower House Foreign Affairs Committee that the launch of a terror campaign in Japan could not be dismissed. Uruma said, 'If members of such groups are already in Japan, it is possible that they will carry out terrorist attacks here' (*Mainichi Daily News*, 18 September 2001). NPA's white paper, released in September 2001, repeated similar vulnerabilities to the Japanese state. The report warned that Japan's status as an economic power had attracted terrorist organisations to use Japan as a financial base to support their operations.[3] The rise of terrorist bombings in Asia led the Japanese Foreign Minister to write the following in an article published in the *Japan Echo*. Kawaguchi Yoriko said:

> Recent bombings on Bali in Indonesia and in the Philippines show that the terrorists are stepping up their activities in Southeast Asia, and we cannot discount the possibility that the wave of violence will come to Japan, which has deep human and economic ties with the region. (Kawaguchi 2003: 27)

OIF

Compared to the OEF, the threat construction process for the SDF's deployment to OIF was more complex. The was due to the difficulty the security policymaking elite faced in gaining legitimacy for Japan's show of outright support for the US-led military campaign against Iraq and the subsequent dispatch of the SDF to this campaign. Due to widespread opposition within Japan, the security policymaking elite inflated the threat posed by the instability in Iraq, including linking the Iraq situation with the North Korean threat. This threat discourse facilitated Japan's show of support to the US-led mission in Iraq, as well as SDF's deployment to participate in this campaign.

Japan's threat construction process at the international level had a complex set of sub-elements. First, the Japanese government argued that the threat had escalated after the September 11th attacks due to the relationship between international terrorism and Iraq's secret possession of WMD. At the Munich Conference on Security Policy entitled 'The Global Challenge of International Terrorism' in February 2003, Motegi Toshimitsu, Senior Vice Minister for Foreign Affairs, said:

> Iraq has continued to be a threat to the international community. The problem of Iraq's development of WMDs has been recognised once again as a serious threat to the international community, together with the recognition of the heightened risk of terrorists' acquiring WMDs. (MOFA Japan 2003c)

Relatedly, Prime Minister Koizumi also warned that Iraq's 'toxic gas and other chemical weapons, or anthrax and other biological weapons' posed a serious threat to the international community. The Japanese leader said, 'if they fall in the hands of dictators and terrorists, it would not be [a] matter of tens or hundreds of lives but would be of thousands and tens of thousands of lives being threatened' (MOFA Japan 2003d).

Second, Iraq's insincere behaviour was particularly prevalent in Japan's official threat construction discourse. It was perceived as a challenge to the peace and stability of the international community. Iraq's insincerity was represented by its repeated refusals to abide by the international norms that challenged the proliferation of WMD and comply with a series of UNSC resolutions. Referring to the lack of improvement in Iraq's behaviour since the first Persian Gulf War, Prime Minister Koizumi said,

> The way things have elapsed since then, however, during this period Iraq has unfortunately ignored, or has not taken seriously, or even ridiculed the United Nations resolutions. I do not believe that Iraq has acted with sufficient sincerity. (MOFA Japan 2003e)

The *Diplomatic Bluebook* 2004 wrote:

> Iraq had continued to refuse and obstruct inspections by international organizations that were based on a series of United Nations Security Council resolutions while suspicions were raised even after the Gulf War about Iraq's possession and development of weapons of mass destruction (WMD). (MOFA Japan 2004a)

Third, Japan's threat construction process revealed to the international community the dangers of the collapse of the Iraqi state. The notion of Iraq as a 'failed state' became an important element of the threat construction process after the military invasion ended and the US-led coalition of the willing, including Japan, was trying to garner increased international support for Iraq's reconstruction efforts. Japan drew clear connections between the scenario of Iraq as a 'failed' state and the concomitant perilous nature of international terrorism. Here, an analogy was drawn between Iraq and Afghanistan: that Iraq as a 'failed' state could become a base for terrorist activities, as Afghanistan was in the past. Foreign Minister Kawaguchi said in her policy speech to the Diet in January 2004 that:

> The reconstruction of Iraq is an urgent issue to be tackled by the international community. If Iraq should become a 'failed state' as well as a base for terrorist activities like Afghanistan in the past, it would be a great threat not only to the Middle East but also to Japan and the international community. (MOFA Japan 2004b)

Moreover, Iraq's status as a failed state also magnified the threat posed by international terrorism to the international community, as it increased the chances of terrorists acquiring WMD from Iraq. The *Diplomatic Bluebook* 2004 pointed out that if Iraq became a failed state:

> It could serve as a base for terrorist activities or a source of proliferation of WMD, then it will pose a grave threat in terms of security for the whole international community including Japan. Should Iraq, which possesses abundant oil resources in particular, becomes a nest of terrorists and obtain WMD, then its threat will further increase. (MOFA Japan 2004a)

Fourth, Japan's threat construction process for OIF displayed a distinct relationship between Iraq as a WMD-armed country and the September 11th attacks. This relationship was an important one, as the terror attacks on the US had become a popular source of legitimacy for the international community to justify the use of military force to counter the threat from international terrorism. The *Diplomatic Bluebook* 2004 wrote:

> Particularly, the terrorist attacks in the US on September 11, 2001 made the international community clearly understand the threat by the possession and use of WMD and missiles by so-called states of concern known to be involved in the assistance of terrorist organizations and proliferation of WMD and missiles. Consequently, it became an urgent task to tackle the Iraq issue, which threatens the peace and stability of the international community. (MOFA Japan 2004a)

Although Japan's official threat construction process was largely international, as discussed above, it also discussed the impact of the Iraq issue on Japan's national security. The *Diplomatic Bluebook* 2004 wrote: 'Japan is vigorously tackling the Iraq issue, understanding that it is a critical issue directly related to Japan's national interests' (MOFA Japan 2004a). The impact on Japan's national security was related to the threat from WMD falling into the hands of international terrorists. Prime Minister Koizumi stressed the links between WMD, international terrorism, and Japan's national security when he said:

> What would be the consequences were dangerous weapons of mass destruction to fall into the hands of a dangerous dictator? Any consequences would certainly not be limited to the people of the United States. This is not a matter without implications for Japan. (MOFA Japan 2003f)

Moreover, the instability in Iraq would have a direct impact on Japan due to its extensive reliance on the Middle East for 90 per cent of its crude oil and energy. The *Diplomatic Bluebook* recognised this relationship when it wrote, 'Based on such recognition, Japan has been actively making efforts toward ensuring the peace and stability of this region' (MOFA Japan 2004a).

Another source of a threat element used by Prime Minister Koizumi during the Iraq crisis was related to North Korea (Mizumoto, personal communication, 26 August 2005). As the deadline drew closer and the international and domestic opposition remained strong, the Japanese security policymaking elite began to rely more on the negative impact of North Korea's nuclear development programme on Japan's national security. Koizumi utilised the North Korean threat to underscore the importance of the American military support in protecting Japan from the North Korea nuclear threat. Prime Minister Koizumi said, 'If you think about North Korea, we have to say the Japan–US security alliance has been a great deterrence' (*Mainichi Daily News*, 3 March 2003). This element proved to be useful for the security policymaking elite. It allowed Koizumi to regain the popularity lost during debates on the Iraq crisis. This was because the Japanese people believed his focus on maintaining the Japan–US alliance made sense amid heightening tensions over North Korea (*Nikkei Weekly*, 24 March 2003). In the *Daily Yomiuri* poll, 70 per cent of the respondents found the government's support for the US-led war in Iraq 'reasonable and unavoidable' for the sake of national interests (*Daily Yomiuri*, 25 March 2003).

Threat Deflation

Due to the controversial nature of the Iraq mission, the security policymaking elite also engaged in threat deflation to justify the SDF's participation in the OIF.

This was essential due to the lack of international and domestic consensus on the use of the military option by the US, and to mitigate criticism of Japan as being too close to the US. The threat deflation was carried out through underscoring the humanitarian dimension to rationalise SDF's deployment to Iraq.

As a responsible actor in the international community, the security policy-making elite argued that Japan had to assist in the humanitarian efforts in Iraq. Although the construction of the threat of Iraq was based on strategic-military factors (WMD) as discussed above, the security policymaking elite also framed Iraq as a humanitarian issue. It required intervention from the international community, including Japan, to restore peace and stability through reconstruction efforts. When the Japanese Cabinet approved the SDF's deployment to Iraq for the reconstruction mission, Prime Minister Koizumi said,

> It is important that the international community should extend assistance for Iraqi rehabilitation and reconstruction so that the country would be rebuilt as quickly as possible and its people would be able to live in a free and prosperous society. (MOFA Japan 2003e)

In another statement, he added

> We [Japan] won't have fulfilled our responsibility as a member of the international community if we contribute materially and leave the man-power contribution up to other countries. (As cited in Richardson 2004, parenthesis added)

The security policymaking elite argued that it was Japan's responsibility to aid Iraq, as it had been in a similar position before. Iraq's situation was compared to Japan's situation immediately after its defeat at the end of World War Two. According to the security policymaking elite, Japan's past made the contribution to the humanitarian crisis in Iraq a necessity. Since Japan had experienced a similar devastating situation and yet had successfully overcome it, Japan had a responsibility to share its experience. The *Diplomatic Bluebook* said:

> Considering Japan has achieved its present prosperity from the ruins of WW2, Japan has a responsibility to make contribution appropriate to its level of national power to Iraq, which has been striving to reconstruct itself amidst the confusion. (MOFA Japan 2004a)

As a result, the Japanese Prime Minister appealed to citizens to support Tokyo's extension of financial, material and personnel assistance, including the SDF deployment to aid Iraq in the reconstruction phase. When the decision was made by the Cabinet to dispatch SDF troops to Iraq as part of the Law Concerning Special Measures on Humanitarian and Reconstruction Assistance in Iraq, Koizumi said:

> I believe that, as a responsible member of the international community, Japan must also fulfil its responsibility in the creation of an environment that will allow the people of Iraq to work to rebuild their own country with optimism. For that purpose, I have decided that there is a need for Japan to provide not only financial assistance, but also material assistance and personnel assistance, including the despatch of SDF. (MOFA Japan 2003g)

The security policymaking elite used the Constitution to legitimise Japan's support to aid Iraq. According to Koizumi, the preface of the Japanese Constitution required Japan to behave responsibly to defend the peace and stability of the international environment.[4] He said, 'Indeed, I believe that the international community is calling upon Japan, and the people of Japan to act in accordance with the ideals of our Constitution' (MOFA Japan 2003g). It was important for Japan to bring peace and stability to Iraq and create conditions for Iraq to be governed by the norms and values held by the international community. The statement made by Prime Minister Koizumi after the Cabinet's approval of the SDF's deployment to Iraq read: 'Japan will be actively engaged, recognising that recovery of peace and stability in Iraq and its neighbouring areas is important for Japan' (MOFA Japan 2003f).

SECURITY POLICY DEVELOPMENT

Fully aware that its much-criticised involvement in the 1991 Persian Gulf War could not be repeated, the Koizumi-led government showed unequivocal support to the US-led military initiative to combat international terrorism and contributed in the most active way permitted by the Constitution, including in the form of human contribution.[5] This was necessary to show Japan's commitment to its most important ally, the US (*Daily Yomiuri*, 17 September 2001).[6] Underscoring the importance of the US and Japan's contribution, Prime Minister Koizumi said, 'The US plays a critical role for peace and security in the region surrounding our nation. It is our duty and a matter of course to provide as much assistance as possible when that country is about to make great sacrifices for a noble cause of the international community' (*Nikkei Weekly*, 24 March 2003). In a policy speech to the 153rd Session of the Diet, Koizumi announced, 'I conveyed to President Bush that Japan strongly supports the United States and that Japan will implement all possible measures in response to these acts of terrorism' (MOFA Japan 2001e). This approach formed the foundation for Japan's active military contribution to both the OEF and OIF missions, and the incorporation of a global focus in the US–Japan defence cooperation.

The incorporation of a global focus in the US–Japan defence cooperation occurred in two ways. The first was through an expanded geographical scope. The 'areas surrounding Japan' provision incorporated in the 1997 revised defence guidelines authorised the SDF to engage in collaborative efforts with the US military outside Japanese territory in peacetime, as well as during a regional contingency. As discussed in Chapter 4, this inferred an expansion of Japan's conception of national security from simply focusing on Japan's territory to covering the Asia-Pacific as well. Although both governments had remained ambiguous on the geographical scope of the 'area surrounding Japan', Japanese policymakers understood that this provision 'strictly limited the area to Japan's territory and the high seas (and its airspace) surrounding Japan' (Shinoda 2002), not envisaging the Indian Ocean to be part of the revised guidelines (Hughes 2004: 127).

Japan's contribution to the US-led war on terror changed this. The ATSML expanded the geographical limit of Japan–US defence cooperation during a military crisis. The Basic Plan, which outlined the measures and the geographical scope of the SDF's activities during OEF, stated that the SDF was legitimised to undertake supply and transportation activities in the following areas: the territory of Japan; the Indian Ocean, which includes Diego Garcia, Australia, and the territories of countries located on the coast of the Indian Ocean; and the territories of countries along the routes from the territory of Japan to the coast of the Indian Ocean containing points of passage or points where fuel and other supplies will be loaded and/or unloaded (MOFA Japan 2001d). Hence, the ATSML added a wider geographical area, the Middle East in this instance, to the SDF's activities.

The second area was the expansion of the operational scope of the SDF's contribution to US–Japan defence cooperation. The first instance of this was Japan's participation in the OEF with the passage of the ATSML on 29 October 2001 by the National Diet. The enactment of the ATSML led to the SDF's deployment to Afghanistan, to assist in US-led anti-terrorism efforts. Despite designating all SDF's support services in 'non-combat' areas, this was essentially the first SDF dispatch to a conflict area since its formation in 1954. The Japanese military was engaged in a range of activities from November 2001 until Japan's withdrawal in January 2010. The MSDF deployed destroyers and supply ships to replenish military vessels of the multinational force engaged in anti-terrorist measures with water and fuel for both ships and helicopters (MOD Japan 2010b: 345). Even though the MSDF mission was originally to supply fuel to American and British naval vessels only, its mandate broadened from November 2002 when Japan began providing fuel to Germany, France, Italy, the Netherlands, Spain, Greece, Canada and Pakistan (Calder 2009: 137;

Hughes 2004: 126). Japan also deployed MSDF flotillas (comprising a supply ship, a minesweeper and a helicopter-carrying destroyer) to Karachi, Pakistan, to provide relief supplies to Afghan refugees, and to the Indian Ocean to provide relief supplies to Afghan refugees and logistics support to ships from the US and UK and other allied nations (*Asahi Shimbun*, 26 November 2001). Despite much controversy, the Japanese government deployed its Aegis destroyer (*Kirishima*) to the Indian Ocean in December 2002 to protect Japanese vessels that were conducting refuelling duties and carrying out surveillance activities as part of the anti-terrorism campaign.

Moreover, the SDF's role was not only to assist but also to protect. The ATSML authorised SDF members to use their weapons to protect themselves and anyone under their care, such as refugees, while performing their duties (Shinoda 2002). This was a significant development in relation to the SDF's duties, as the troops were previously only authorised to use weapons for self-defence and to protect others in the same mission, as stated in the PKO Law – and additionally to protect their property, as stated in the revised defence guidelines (Shinoda 2002). Apart from transportation and replenishment activities, *Asahi Shimbun* (2006) reported that MSDF ships intercepted 'suspicious' vessels for inspections. In support of the US deployment, Japanese destroyers and minesweepers also escorted the aircraft carrier *Kitty Hawk* from Yokosuka Naval Base to the Indian Ocean. This was the first time MSDF ships had escorted a US aircraft carrier heading for a military operation. Along with the MSDF, Japan's ASDF was deployed to support the campaign in Afghanistan, namely in refuelling, transportation of supplies, and medical and maintenance support to the US and other militaries deployed in the Indian Ocean and Arabian Sea (Hughes 2004: 126).

The SDF's involvement in the OEF was a milestone in Japanese security policy. The ATSML expanded the functions of the mutual defence cooperation between the American and Japanese militaries, and also between the SDF and other militaries engaged in OEF. The SDF was, for the first time, engaged in a large-scale international military effort to aid in the resolution of a global military crisis and jointly address the threat posed by international terrorism. Along with the US and other militaries, the SDF adopted international military responsibilities in line with being a responsible member of the international community and contributing to global peace and stability.

The SDF's participation in the reconstruction efforts in Iraq further strengthened the global focus in the US–Japan defence cooperation. This mission was important for Japan to fulfil the requirements of being an effective and reliable ally of the US in addressing a global security challenge. Japan passed the 'Law Concerning Special Measures on Humanitarian and Reconstruction Assistance in Iraq' in July 2003 and introduced a Basic Plan, which authorised the deployment of 600 Ground Self-Defense Force (GSDF) troops in January 2004 to provide humanitarian and reconstruction assistance. The SDF's duties covered the provision of medical services, purification of the water supply, and the repair and reconstruction of public facilities such as schools and hospitals (National Institute for Defense Studies 2005: 227–8). The GSDF deployment was supplemented by the presence of around 200 ASDF personnel that were engaged in the transportation of humanitarian and reconstruction supplies from Kuwait into Iraq beginning in February 2004. After Japan's GSDF withdrew from Iraq in July 2006, the ASDF personnel not only stayed but broadened their mission to provide direct support to other allied forces (MOD Japan as cited in Calder 2009: 138; Hughes 2004: 130–1).

SDF's participation in OIF reconfigured the kind of missions for which the Japanese military could be deployed and the roles it could assume. Prior to OIF, the SDF's overseas deployment was permitted only when there was a UN or international mandate for involvement, and in areas where the conflict had ended. SDF's participation in OIF challenged both these conditions. There was no UN mandate for the US-led war in Iraq, as no second resolution was either tabled at or passed by the UNSC. There was also controversy on whether Samawah, SDF's operational area in Iraq, was a 'safe' area. Prime Minister Koizumi admitted this when he answered 'How do I know?' to a question that asked where the 'safe areas' were in Iraq during a parliament session (Tamamoto 2004: 11). Moreover, at a press conference, Koizumi stated, 'I am well aware that the current conditions in Iraq are severe ones and the situation cannot always be described as being safe' (MOFA Japan 2003g). The actual participation of the SDF in OIF, which was largely seen as a risky mission that challenged the boundaries of Japan's Peace Constitution, set a precedent for future possible SDF deployments.

Apart from SDF's participation in the reconstruction efforts in Iraq, Japan agreed to participate in a US initiative known as the Proliferation Security Initiative (PSI). Japan showed active support to this initiative based on its nonproliferation policy and strong relationship with the US. The PSI allowed the US and its allies to search planes and ships carrying suspicious cargo and seize illegal weapons or missile technologies. In a show of its commitment, Japan hosted the first PSI maritime exercise in East Asia in October 2004 – called Team Samurai – with support from the US, Australia, France and observers from eighteen other countries. Due to legal restrictions, the role of the MSDF in the PSI initiative was still limited to patrolling the seas and providing information to other members of the PSI. The main duties of interdicting and inspecting suspicious ships, as well as searching and confiscating suspicious materials that could be used for manufacturing WMD, were carried out by the JCG (*Daily Yomiuri*, 29 October 2004).

The Japanese government's push to show strong support to the US-led military campaigns in Afghanistan and Iraq laid the foundation for further strengthening of the alliance for global security. The main outcome was the deepening of the bilateral strategic relationship, namely in terms of the alignment of strategic objectives of the two states and the strengthened interoperability of the two militaries for normal times and military contingencies. The upgrading of the US–Japan defence cooperation reinforced the shift from a regional to a global focus over a wider range of activities/missions. This update started with the upgrading of the ACSA in 2004, which authorised the reciprocal provision of supplies and services between the US and Japanese militaries over a wider range of activities aimed at contributing to global security. Before the 2004 revision, the ACSA applied to bilateral exercises and training, UNPKOs, humanitarian international relief operations and operations in response to situations in areas surrounding Japan. The revised ACSA incorporated operations in armed attack situations or situations in which an armed attack was expected, and operations to further the efforts of the international community to contribute to global security (MOFA Japan 2004c).

The 2005 SCC meeting between the foreign and defence ministers of Japan and the US resulted in the setting of common bilateral strategic objectives for global security challenges, such as international terrorism, proliferation of WMD, US policy to the war on terror and even seeking a peaceful resolution on the Taiwan issue (Hughes 2007; Pempel 2005: 11). As part of the efforts to study roles, missions and capabilities of the SDF and the US military in achieving those objectives, the SCC released a document entitled 'Transformation and Realignment for the Future' in October 2005 to strengthen the cooperative relationship in response to diverse security challenges in global affairs. This report laid out areas for greater integration in military cooperation in a range of critical areas, such as policy and operational coordination during both peace times and crisis periods, information sharing and intelligence cooperation, and BMD (MOFA Japan 2005).

The institutionalisation of bilateral interoperability to address both regional and global military contingencies progressed further when Japan and the US undertook a Defense Policy Review Initiative in May 2006 (Hughes and Krauss 2007: 158). As part of this review, the US Army Corps I was relocated from Washington to Army Camp Zama in the Kanagawa Prefecture to facilitate the geographical coverage of the 'arc of instability' stretching from Northeast Asia to the Middle East. According to Hughes (2007: 331), the consequence of this shift was that 'Japan would serve as a frontline command post for US global power projection to as far away as the Middle East.' Moreover, as the GSDF rapid-reaction force was stationed alongside the US I Army Corps at Camp Zama, it operationally tied it to the global deployments of the US military (Hughes 2007: 335). The consolidation of the two rapid-reaction forces, according to Calder (2009: 149), enhanced operational coordination, mobility and readiness – not only making the two militaries more integrated but also facilitating a more integrated response to military contingencies in the regional and global security environment.

Apart from the bilateral agreements, Japanese policy statements such as the National Defense Program Guidelines (NDPG) 2004 and the 2004 Mid-Term Defense Program (MTDP) also stressed the strengthening of the global dimension in the US–Japan security relationship. The NDPG 2004 (MOD Japan 2004a) stressed that a strong bilateral relationship was important in facilitating international efforts to deal with global security challenges – such as the proliferation of WMD and ballistic missiles – as well as international terrorist activities that threatened international peace and stability in an age of 'increased interdependence and growing globalization'. The MTDP 2004 (MOD Japan 2004b) supplemented Japan's objectives as stated in the NDPG. In strengthening US–Japan security cooperation to address global security challenges collectively, the document outlined strengthened cooperation in a range of areas that included intelligence sharing on international situations, policy consultations, role-sharing in international efforts, cooperation in BMD, and exchanges in equipment and technology. The incorporation of a global dimension into the US–Japan defence cooperation set the stage for another milestone in the following decade, discussed in the following chapter: the addition of collective self-defence missions to the SDF's mandate and US–Japan defence cooperation.

NOTES

1. For a detailed list of the measures taken by Japan, see MOFA Japan (2002b).
2. Their argument was that the intelligence provided by the Aegis vessel to the US fleet could be used in operational military plans in the US-led military mission against Iraq. This meant Japan was involved in a collective self-defence mission, which was banned in Japanese security policy practice (*Japan Times*, 16 December 2002; *Mainichi Daily News*, 4 December 2002).
3. The white paper reported that six Sri Lankan nationals were arrested in Ichikawa and Funabashi in Chiba Prefecture in June 2000 on suspicion of illegally staying in Japan. The police confiscated videotapes and documents describing terrorist acts by the Liberation Tigers of Tamil Eelam (LTTE), a terrorist organisation in Sri Lanka. Investigators discovered that a total of 45 million yen had been transferred to the group in Sri Lanka over the preceding decade and the six arrested in Chiba admitted it was for the purpose of supporting the LTTE. The LTTE was believed to have received weapons from the Taliban, the Islamist fundamentalist regime of Afghanistan that was said to offer protection to Osama bin Laden (*Daily Yomiuri*, 22 September 2001).
4. The preface of the constitution reads,

> We recognise that all peoples of the world have the right to live in peace, free from fear and want. We believe that no nation is responsible to itself alone, but that laws of political morality are universal; and that obedience to such laws is incumbent upon all nations who would sustain their own sovereignty and justify

their sovereign relationship with other nations. We, the Japanese people, pledge our national honour to accomplish these high ideals and purposes with all our resources. (Prime Minister of Japan and His Cabinet 1946)

5. This section is adapted from Singh (2013: 122–9).
6. Unlike the Persian Gulf War in 1991, the US did not pressure Japan for a human contribution to the OEF. The request for support came from Richard Armitage, Deputy Secretary of State, who told Japan's Ambassador to the US, Yanai Shunji, during a meeting in Washington in September 2001 that Japan should 'show the flag' in the US-led war against terrorism. However, he stopped short of specifying what kind of support Japan should contribute. In October 2001, Armitage repeated his request, but this time he was more specific about the type of support Tokyo could provide. He suggested the gathering of information about terrorist groups, adopting of rules prohibiting funds from reaching these terrorist groups, authorising the SDF to provide logistical support and extending humanitarian aid to refugees fleeing Afghanistan (*Mainichi Daily News*, 18 September 2001, 6 October 2001; *Nihon Keizai Shimbun*, 6 October 2001).

6

COLLECTIVE SELF-DEFENCE

The final policy development that signalled Japanese security policy expansion was the incorporation of collective self-defence missions into the SDF's mandate. This chapter illustrates how Prime Minister Abe Shinzo and his government utilised the China threat emanating from the series of China-related maritime incidents during 2010–15 to successfully achieve this milestone in Japanese security policy. This threat narrative centred on China's assertive maritime behaviour and its implications set the context for the official reinterpretation of Article 9 by the Japanese Cabinet in July 2014 and the signing of the Guidelines for Japan–US Defense Cooperation in April 2015. While the threat narrative surrounding China was central to the signing of the defence guidelines in 2015, this narrative was deflated by the Abe-led security policymaking elite during the approximately four-month-long debate (May–Sept 2015) on the security bills in the National Diet to authorise the SDF to adopt collective self-defence missions.

The Crisis

Though the maritime military competition between Japan and China appeared from the late 1990s (Patalano 2014: 39), the period 2010–13 was a historical peak.[1] It started with the fishing trawler incident in September 2010, which 'marked the beginning of a new contentious phase in their handling of the disputed Senkaku Islands' (Smith 2015: 188). The Chinese trawler *Minjinyu 5179* allegedly rammed into two JCG ships (*Yonakuni* and *Mizuki*) after it was caught fishing in Japanese controlled waters. When the Chinese captain resisted the JCG's efforts to inspect the vessel, the JCG officials boarded the trawler and arrested the captain and his crew. The crew were released almost a week later, but the Japanese government detained the captain for ten days, His detention was extended as the officials explored options to prosecute the captain on the account that he was causing danger and interfering with the duties of the JCG. The captain was finally released three weeks after the incident.

Chinese state and society reacted strongly against Japan's decision to detain the Chinese captain and his crew. The Chinese government repeatedly summoned the Japanese ambassador to China, even during the early hours, and cancelled bilateral meetings and cultural exchange initiatives subsequently. When the Japanese government announced that the captain's detention would be extended, the Chinese government arrested four Japanese citizens in Hebei province in China, accusing them of entering a restricted military zone. Beijing ceased all rare-earth exports bound to Japan, which was an important element for Japanese companies producing high-quality electronics goods, and inflicted lengthier custom clearance on Japanese goods at Chinese ports. More alarming for Japan was the increase in the presence of Chinese vessels and aircrafts near or inside the Japanese claimed waters and airspace in the East China Sea. These were deployed not only for surveillance activities, but according to the Japanese government, also to challenge Japan's administrative control of the disputed islands.

The temperature around the Senkaku/Diaoyu Island territorial dispute saw another peak in September 2012 when the DPJ-led government decided to purchase three out of the five islets of the Senkaku/Diaoyu Islands from their private owners. The origins of this decision lay in the aftermath of the fishing trawler incident. Due to the heightened nationalism and activism within Japan against China following the September 2010 incident, conservative groups pressured the DPJ government to adopt a stronger posture against China to assert Japan's sovereignty over the disputed islands. Tokyo Governor Ishihara Shintaro went a step further when he controversially initiated fundraising to facilitate the Tokyo Metropolitan Government's purchase of the islets. Concerned that Ishihara's proposal would lead to a serious deterioration of Sino-Japanese relations, the DPJ's Noda government decided that a safer option would be for the Japanese government to purchase the islets. However, the Chinese government perceived this move as an attempt to nationalise the disputed islands and change the status quo in the East China Sea.

The Chinese state and society expressed vehement opposition towards this move. There were widespread demonstrations across China, some of them leading to serious damage of Japanese properties and products. A more serious implication of the 2012 incident was an increase in the Chinese military's involvement in the East China Sea, especially in terms of military vessels entering the disputed areas to assert Chinese control and weaken Japan's administrative control over the islands. The Chinese government also deployed paramilitary ships to the disputed waters to conduct regular patrols, along with the deployment of surveillance planes that were accompanied by fighter jets in territorial waters and airspace of the islands (Smith 2015: 2). Tensions escalated in 2013 when the Chinese naval vessel locked its radar on a MSDF ship and MSDF helicopter, which was understood as a step before actually launching a military strike. In November 2013, Tokyo became concerned when Beijing announced a new Air Defense Identification Zone (ADIZ) in the East China Sea. For Tokyo, this was a serious development because China's ADIZ overlapped with Japan's ADIZ, and included the disputed Senkaku/Diaoyu islands.

Compared to previous Chinese maritime incursions, Japan's responses to the above incidents displayed more alarm. Japan protested strongly against China's egregious behaviour in a Japanese-controlled maritime area. To gain international support, Japan utilised as many bilateral and multilateral platforms as possible to highlight China's assertiveness and how its actions did not conform to accepted international conventions. Tokyo increased sea and air patrols using its military in the area surrounding Japan. It conducted round-the-clock air surveillance to monitor Chinese maritime activities and maintain a state of readiness in the event of a contingency in areas surrounding Japan (MOD Japan 2016).

However, the more significant impact of the maritime incidents was on Japan's security policy, which underwent 'the most comprehensive phase of its security policy reform' (Grønning 2014: 1). Repeated Chinese attempts to militarise the maritime domain led Japan to adopt a stronger security policy against China (Hornung 2014: 104). The 2010 NDPG issued by the DPJ-led government announced that a new defence strategy known as the 'Dynamic Defense Force' (DDF) would replace the passive 'Basic Defense Force Concept' that had defined Japanese security policy since the onset of the postwar period. The new defence strategy inferred strengthened deterrence against contingencies, as well as a proactive response to ensure stability of the regional and international environment (MOD Japan 2010a: 7). Instead of focusing on Japan's north, the NDPG shifted its defence focus to the south-west of the country, reflecting the emergence of the East China Sea as a new frontline for Japan. To strengthen the south-western region, the Japanese government augmented its naval capability through expanding its submarine fleet and destroyer-class ships, including additional Aegis destroyers; strengthened air patrol and surveillance capabilities through early warning aircraft and Global Hawk unmanned aerial vehicles; strengthened aerial refuelling and transport aircraft; strengthened the country's air force capabilities with F-35A Joint Strike Fighters; and acquired an amphibious island defence force. To support this, Abe increased defence spending for the first time in eleven years when he came to power in 2012 ('Beyond Abenomics' 2013).

Apart from military capability, Japan addressed its military readiness in response to maritime incidents. This was visible in four ways. First, the MSDF was reorganised from five regional fleets to four, as well as adding destroyers with a flexible, high-alert response capability to the fleet (Smith 2015: 198). Second, Japan strengthened the inter-service cooperation between the army, navy and air force in defending the islands (Smith 2015: 200). In the 2013 NDPG, the Abe government retained the DPJ's DDF concept but incorporated the 'jointness' component (Hornung 2014: 105). Third, Japan augmented its crisis management efforts. A revised law was passed to expand JCG's authority to deal with individuals landing illegally on Japanese islands or with ships that behaved suspiciously in Japanese territorial waters (Smith 2015: 223). Fourth, the role of the Japanese military expanded in addressing maritime incidents alongside the JCG. Rather than just routine deployment to chase away intrusions, Japanese fighter jets were engaged in dangerous encounters with Chinese aircrafts (Smith, personal communication, 13 May 2015).

To complement efforts to strengthen Japan's military preparedness to counter China's assertive behaviour in the maritime domain, both the DPJ and LDP governments strengthened the US–Japan security alliance. The measures, especially the ones taken by the LDP, ensured a robust American engagement and presence in East Asia, and elevated Japan's role as a strategic actor to address the escalated unpredictability caused by China's assertive behaviour.

DPJ's strengthening of the alliance coincided with Washington's implementation of the rebalancing towards Asia initiative implemented by the Obama administration. The alliance underscored the importance of cultivating 'jointness' between the two militaries. This occurred in the formation of 'joint air defence headquarters at Yokota Air Base, a joint headquarters for the US army and GSDF at Camp Zama, joint/shared use of facilities, and joint training and exercises' (Hornung 2014: 106). Japan also purchased several amphibious landing ships for its GSDF and conducted joint training and exercises in enhancing amphibious capability (Smith 2015: 224). Abe worked harder to strengthen the US–Japan security relationship when he returned to power in December 2012. His objectives were to resolve outstanding bilateral issues that were causing problems for the alliance, such as the transfer of the Futenma Base within the Okinawa prefecture, and to strengthen a range of bilateral capabilities to counter China. The Abe government also pushed towards changing the legal framework that prevented the SDF from engaging in collective self-defence missions alongside the US military. The rest of this chapter illustrates how Abe and his government successfully achieved this milestone in Japanese security policy.

The 'Crisis' in the Crisis

Though constitutional revision has been on the LDP's agenda since 1955, it experienced a boost when Abe succeeded Koizumi as Japan's prime minister in 2006. Strongly influenced by his grandfather and former Prime Minister Kishi, Abe was committed to revising the postwar regime that he viewed as restricting Japan's security policy. In his first policy speech to the Diet in 2006, Abe declared: 'The time has come to boldly review the postwar regime by going back to its starting point and sail out anew.' He added that it was his 'duty to depict a new national picture that can endure rough waves in the next 50 or 100 years.' These changes were critical for Japan to become a 'beautiful country', as envisioned by Abe (*Japan Times*, 28 January 2007).

To achieve the 'beautiful country' characterisation in terms of security policy, Abe argued that Japan must move on from its past misdeeds and take pride in its national strength (Abe 2006; Estéves-Abe 2014: 166). Japan must address the strategic challenges it faced head on. This could only be carried out through restoring economic strength, augmenting Japan's military preparedness, strengthening the US–Japan security relationship and pursuing a proactive security policy in global affairs. To achieve this, it was important for Japan to undo the domestic legal constraints that limited the practice of an expanded security policy, as well as being a reliable and effective ally to the US. Abe focused on lifting the long-standing ban on the SDF to use force in collective self-defence missions, especially in aiding the US when attacked in a contingency (Pugliese 2017: 157).

In his first foreign policy speech in 2006, Abe said his government would identify contingencies characterised as exercising the right of collective self-defence that were prohibited by the Constitution (*Japan Times*, 1 October 2006). He controversially defended his Chief Cabinet Secretary, Shiozaki Yasuhisa, who overturned Japan's official position that was used to defend the acquisition of a ballistic missile system. Instead of being 'aimed solely at defending our country' as outlined by Chief Cabinet Secretary Fukuda Yasuo in December 2003 (Yoshida 2006a), Shiozaki argued that it was permissible for the Japanese government to reinterpret Article 9 so that Japan was able to intercept a North Korean ballistic missile bound for the US. His comment was in response to growing frustration within the Bush administration towards Japan's inability to intercept a rogue missile heading to the US, due to the ban on the right to collective self-defence (Nabeshima 2007). Although JDA officials questioned Shiozaki's remarks,[2] Abe defended Shiozaki by stating that '(The government) is obliged to defend the lives and property of the people. We have to study (the issue) to ensure national security efficiently' (Yoshida 2006a, parentheses from original source). To his end, the Abe government commissioned a blue-ribbon panel led by Ambassador Yanai Shunji to assess the legality of Japan's right to participate in collective self-defence missions. The panel's conclusion was that Japan had the right to engage in collective self-defence missions, namely in four situations: (a) when a ballistic missile is fired at the US; (b) when the SDF is in international waters near a ship from an allied nation that is under attack; (c) when other forces in the same peacekeeping missions come under attack; and (d) when forces of other countries fighting overseas ask for logistics support (Yoshida 2007). Despite the panel's conclusion, the Abe government was unable to make any headway in collective self-defence issue until his second stint as Prime Minister.

That second stint came at a unique juncture. Abe took over a DPJ-led government that made history in 2009 by ending the LDP's dominance of Japanese politics since 1955. From the time he was running to displace the DPJ in the national election, Abe saw the DPJ governments as being in crisis. The DPJ government's crisis management efforts during the triple disasters (a massive earthquake, a powerful tsunami, and a nuclear meltdown at the Fukushima No. 1 nuclear power plant – collectively known as the Great East Japan Earthquake) were unsatisfactory and displayed weak leadership. The Abe-led opposition also strongly challenged the DPJ's handling of the China-related 2010 and 2012 maritime crises and accused the DPJ-led governments of ill-preparedness in terms of policy coordination and weakness in dealing with China (Smith 2015: 220–1). This led to the decline of Japan–China relations to their lowest point in the postwar period. Moreover, the US–Japan alliance had suffered a decline in credibility under the DPJ government. This started with Prime Minister Hatoyama Yukio's decision to readjust Japan's security policy so as to correct Japan's overdependence on the US and, instead, develop a stronger Asia focus in Japanese security policy. To make matters worse, his government stalled the realignment of US troops in Okinawa, which had been agreed in 2006.

To be sure, the DPJ's security policy looked very similar to the LDP's by the time the third DPJ government, led by Prime Minister Noda, took office. It lifted the four-decade-long ban to allow joint development and export of military technology with other states, implemented a responsive security policy to the regional strategic environment (as outlined in the 2010 NDPG), and worked to strengthen the US–Japan alliance through the resumption of the Two-plus-Two bilateral meeting after a four-year hiatus, as well as proposing to revise the bilateral defence guidelines (*Daily Yomiuri*, 10 January 2013). In fact, the DPJ's problems with the US–Japan alliance had existed before the DPJ government, and even during Abe's first stint as Prime Minister (see Ogawa 2009; Swaine 2013: 70). However, it was clear that Abe was going to make the DPJ responsible for the deterioration of Japan's security guarantee from the US to push his reform agenda.

This was not only a view held by Abe and other LDP politicians, but was supported by the American side too. Though the Obama administration showed firm commitment to the alliance and security guarantee towards Japan, Washington was frustrated with the DPJ government. In fact, President Barack Obama's visit to Japan in November 2009 did not resolve the problems within the US–Japan alliance caused by Hatoyama's ambiguous policy towards the alliance and refusal to transfer the US Marine Corps' Futenma Air Station in the Okinawa Prefecture. Such a sentiment was expressed by a National Bureau of Asian Research report, which argued that core expectations of Tokyo and Washington were unmet (Finnegan 2009). A bipartisan report published by the Center for Strategic and International Studies (CSIS) in August 2012 stated that there was 'idiosyncratic political discord' during the DPJ's time in government (Armitage and Nye 2012: 15). It stated:

> It is our view that Japan is at a critical juncture. Japan has the power to decide between complacency and leadership at a time of strategic importance. With the dynamic changes taking place throughout the Asia-Pacific region, Japan will likely never have the same opportunity to help guide the fate of the region. In choosing leadership, Japan can secure her status as a tier-one nation and her necessary role as an equal partner in the alliance. (Armitage and Nye 2012: 15)

Also, the US became more vocal in its criticism of Japan's inability to perform collective self-defence missions. In his farewell press conference, US Ambassador to Japan Thomas Schieffer called on Japan to reinterpret the Constitution to allow for the SDF to jointly engage in such missions (*Kyodo* as cited in Liff 2017: 158). The Armitage and Nye report also called for stronger alliance cooperation and lifting of restrictions on collective self-defence missions. It stated: 'It would be a responsible authorization to allow our forces to respond in full cooperation throughout the security spectrum of peacetime, tension, crisis, and war' (Armitage and Nye 2012: 15).

Such calls were in line with Abe's views. On his return to office in 2012, Abe endeavoured to lift the internal limitations that prevented Japan from adequately defending itself from rising tensions in the maritime space, as well as to restore strength in the US–Japan alliance to placate the abandonment fears that were prevalent during the DPJ's time in government. The Abe government immediately resumed work on the transfer of Futenma Base and was committed to widening Japan's roles within the alliance. Abe focused on identifying gaps in the legal system that would authorise Japan to adopt the security roles required to defend its national security, as well as to exercise a robust security policy to address regional and global challenges (Hosoya 2014). One of the major gaps was the lifting of the collective self-defence ban.

Abe expertly changed the narrative surrounding the collective self-defence missions. To build institutional support for this narrative, he appointed key personnel within the bureaucracy, such as Yachi Shotaro as the National Security Advisor, Komatsu Ichiro as the Director of the Cabinet Legislation Bureau and Kanehara Nobukatsu as the Assistant Chief Cabinet Secretary in the Prime Minister's Office of Japan (Pugliese 2017: 159–61). In pursuing his reform agenda, Abe employed a less controversial strategy that focused on implementing the much-needed economic reforms to boost Japan's economy growth. This was well received by the Japanese public and was the determining factor in all Abe's election victories from 2012 onwards. Also, Abe received stronger support for his reform agenda from within his own party due to heightened nationalism among party members. This point was revealed in surveys of LDP candidates who were running for first past the post seats in the Lower House elections. While in 2009 only sixty-one out of 271 LDP candidates running had shared Abe's views on defence and constitutional reform, this number increased in the 2012 elections, when 189 out of 264 LDP candidates shared his views (Estéves-Abe 2014: 170). Though the Abe government started with the aim of revising Article 9, it subsequently settled for an interpretation of the Article to allow for the SDF to perform collective self-defence missions. This reinterpretation influenced the outcome of the US–Japan defence guidelines signed in April 2015 and the passage of the security bills in the National Diet in September 2015.

Owing to its controversial nature, the Abe government's reform agenda, including the lifting of the ban on collective self-defence missions, faced widespread opposition from inside and outside Japan. Though the opposition to Abe's reform agenda has been consistent since he became Prime Minister in 2006, its intensity increased when the security bills were introduced and debated in the National Diet in 2015. There were widespread demonstrations in Tokyo and elsewhere at levels never seen since the so-called Anpo riots of 1960 (student-led protests against the revision of the US–Japan Security Treaty), as these groups viewed the Abe government's pursuit of radical change as inimical to the Japanese Constitution.

The opposition political parties were concerned about the Abe government's push to legalise collective self-defence missions. The SDPJ was the boldest in its accusation, calling the security bill authorising collective self-defence missions for the SDF a 'war bill' that would revive Japanese militarism (Hughes 2017: 96–8). The DPJ saw the Abe government's decision to pursue reinterpretation rather than a revision as an illegitimate move (Hughes 2017: 97). The DPJ accused the Abe government of being too quick to pursue military initiatives and failing to consider limited measures, such as policing action, as alternative means to assist and protect US forces in an armed contingency. In the event of a crisis on the Korean Peninsula, the DPJ proposed that the SDF take seaborne policing action to defend US military vessels transporting Japanese nationals if they fell under attack (*Yomiuri Shimbun*, 11 July 2015). The opposition parties also highlighted the risks related to the SDF engaging in collective self-defence missions, even though the security policymaking elite had added conditions (discussed in greater detail below) to the final bill to limit the SDF's participation in collective self-defence missions. This was a problem for the opposition because it was left to the discretion of the government in power to determine what constitutes a 'threat to Japan's survival' (*Japan Times*, 30 March 2016). Accusing the Abe government of not being sincere in the risks and conditions related to the SDF's deployment on collective self-defence missions, Edano Yukio, leader of the Constitutional Democratic Party of Japan (CDPJ), accused the Abe government of taking a 'two-faced stance'; Tamaki Yuichiro, head of the opposition Kino no To (Hope), also described the Abe government as 'two-faced' (Aibara 2018).

A large majority of constitutional scholars opposed the Abe government too. One figure revealed that 99 per cent of constitutional scholars were opposed to the reinterpretation of Article 9 to allow for collective self-defence ('Hasebe Yasuo interview' 2015). Not only scholars, but also constitutional experts who were previously in the government were opposed to the proposed reinterpretation of Article 9. Before the Abe Cabinet's decision to reinterpret Article 9 to allow for collective self-defence in July 2014, a group that included former director-generals of the CLB (such as Sakata Masahiro and Omori Masasuke) was formed to challenge the final report of the Advisory Panel on Reconstruction of the Legal Basis for Security, released in May 2014, which had recommended the reinterpretation of Article 9 to allow for collective self-defence (*Asahi Shimbun*, 29 May 2014).[3]

The constitutional scholars and experts were not against collective self-defence but questioned the Abe government's decision to pursue reinterpretation instead of revision of Article 9. Sota Kimura, constitutional expert at Tokyo Metropolitan University, stated that: 'Use of military force when an armed attack on Japan has not been launched is by definition unconstitutional'; hence, the Japanese Constitution, as the interpretation stands, does not permit the use of military force in a collective self-defence operation (*Japan News*, 14 July 2015). For Hasabe Yasuo from Waseda University, allowing collective self-defence missions would go over the limit of minimum necessary use of force, as set by the Constitution. This applies even with the incorporation of the three conditions by the Abe government on when collective self-defence missions could be authorised. Even though Article 51 of the UN Charter allows for individual and collective self-defence, the Japanese Constitution has higher power of law compared to the UN Charter (Hasebe n.d.). For Hasebe, the only way to authorise collective self-defence is through revising the Constitution. Even though limited collective self-defence could be compatible with pacifism, Hasabe argued that it was necessary to conduct discussions and change the Constitution via a national referendum ('Hasebe Yasuo interview' 2015). Setsu Kobayashi, emeritus professor of constitutional law at Keio University, said: 'Article 9 of the constitution does not allow for the overseas deployment of the SDF. Having the SDF fly around the world to serve as an aide to the US military is unfathomable.' He added, 'The Prime Minister is taking away the Constitution that belongs to the public. I believe he is a thief' (*Asahi Shimbun*, 29 May 2014).

The general public was also largely against the Abe government's push to authorise collective self-defence missions. Most public opinion polls showed that more people were against the security bills than were in favour. In a survey conducted by *Asahi Shimbun* in 2013, 27 per cent were in favour of changing the reinterpretation of the Constitution to allow for the right to collective self-defence, while 59 per cent were against (*Asahi Shimbun*, 26 August 2013). In a poll conducted in June 2014 by *Asahi Shimbun*, when asked if in favour or opposed to the exercise of collective self-defence, the results were 28 per cent in favour and 56 per cent opposed (*Asahi Shimbun*, 23 June 2014). The opposition was visible even after the law took effect in March 2016. A *Kyodo News* poll showed that 49.9 per cent of the respondents said they 'do not value' the legislation, as opposed to 39 per cent who said they do (*Japan Times*, 30 March 2016). There were several reasons for this low support from the general public. One of the main reasons was that the government had failed to provide a clear explanation of the bills. According to Hosoya (2019: 39), the bills were written in a confusing manner that could only appeal to the experts on security. In a survey conducted by the conservative *Sankei Shimbun* and Fuji News Network, only 6.3 per cent said they understood the details of the collective self-defence bill, while 50 per cent said they understood it 'somehow' (*Sankei Shimbun*, 29 June 2015). In a poll conducted in June 2014 by *Asahi Shimbun*, when asked if the Abe administration had discussed the issue sufficiently, 8 per cent said yes and 76 per cent said no (*Asahi Shimbun*, 23 June 2014). Though aware of the importance of security, Japanese society was wary of expanding the role of the SDF overseas, especially to combat missions (Mori 2015). Finally, Japanese society was worried that the security bills challenged the pacifism and the Constitution of Japan (Hosoya 2019: 11–16). One of the most prominent civil society groups to oppose the Abe government's push to authorise collective self-defence missions was the student-led group known as Student Emergency Action for Liberal Democracy (SEALD). This group led regular demonstrations outside the National Diet, condemning the Abe government's top-down approach to changing the Japanese Constitution. With the aim of protecting the Constitution and pacifist security policy, this group demanded that the Abe government make decisions based on the Japanese Constitution (SEALD n.d.).

Externally, China and South Korea expressed reservations about Japan's intention to reinterpret the Constitution to allow collective self-defence missions for the SDF. When the Cabinet approved the reinterpretation of Article 9 to allow for collective self-defence, Xinhua, the official Chinese news agency, stated that 'Abe is manipulating a dangerous coup to overturn the country's postwar pacifism and democratic ideals, as he hones in on releasing the shackles of the nation's legally tethered military and war will from its war-renouncing Constitution' (Glosserman 2014). In a white paper published in 2015, China said: 'Japan is sparing no effort to dodge the postwar mechanism, overhauling its military and security policies. Such development has caused grave concerns among other countries in the [Asia-Pacific] region' (Igarashi 2015). South Korea stated that Japan's decision to allow for collective self-defence missions affecting security and national interests on the Korean Peninsula 'cannot be accepted unless we request it or agree to it' (Glosserman 2014).

Threat Construction

The lifting of the collective self-defence ban led the security policymaking elite to adopt a complex threat construction process. On the one hand, unlike in the previous case studies, the security policymaking elite was bold in calling out China's increased assertiveness in the maritime domain from the mid-2000s onwards, reflecting the internalisation of the China threat in Japan's security policy discourse. The first time China was explicitly cited in a defence document was in the 2004 NDPG published following the 2004 Chinese nuclear submarine incursion into Japanese waters (Przystup 2015: 14). As China was 'expanding its area of operation at sea', Japan had 'to remain attentive to its future actions' (MOD Japan 2004a: 2–3). Policymakers also started vocalising their concerns about China. In 2005, Aso Taro, Japan's Foreign Minister, said China was becoming a 'considerable threat' (Takahara 2005). A few months later, the DPJ leader Maehara Seiji described China's growing military might as 'a realistic concern' (Yoshida 2006b). The increased level of concern related to China's military activity led Japan and the US to commit to 'common strategic objectives', including the peaceful resolution of the Taiwan Strait issue, during a bilateral 2005 SCC meeting (Sasaki 2010: 576).

Japan's concerns over China became more explicit in the defence documents following the fishing trawler incident. This coincided with Japan's more hardline approach towards China due to the latter's growing assertiveness in the maritime domain and Japan's loss of its position as Asia's largest economy to China in 2010. When the Kan government released the 2010 NDPG a few months after the incident, Kitaoka Shin'ichi said the guidelines were 'primarily concerned about how to deal with China's rise' (Kitaoka 2014). Compared to the 2004 version, the reference made to China in the 2010 NDPG was stronger. It discussed China's increasing military budget, its modernising military force including power projection capabilities, widening naval activity in the surrounding waters, and insufficient transparency as matters of 'concern for the region and the international community' (MOD Japan 2010a: 4). In the 2011 Defense Ministry white paper, China's growing maritime activities were described as 'overbearing' (*Daily Yomiuri*, 3 August 2011), and it was noted that 'there is a concern over its future direction' (MOD Japan 2011: 72). There was also further discussion in the defence white paper of China's intensified maritime activities in the East China Sea and South China Sea. Here, these activities were described as a cause for concern 'in the region and within the international community' (MOD Japan 2011: 145–6). This continued in the 2012 defence white paper, when China's intensified maritime activities were described as a 'matter of concern' requiring 'prudent analysis' (MOD Japan 2012: 28). China also began to dominate Japan's security policy agenda more in Abe's second stint as Prime Minister than his first. The 2013 NSS published by the Abe government noted that Japan would respond 'calmly and resolutely to the rapid expansion and step-up of China's maritime and air activities' (T. B. 2013).

On the other hand, the Abe government was careful not to overstate the China threat. The threat construction process was divided into two phases. The threat from China, especially in the maritime domain, was central in the first phase of the threat construction process pursued by the security policymaking elite to lift the collective self-defence ban, first through the reinterpretation of Article 9 in July 2014, and then incorporating these missions into the bilateral defence guidelines signed in April 2015. While the 1978 guidelines had envisioned an invasion of Japan by the Soviet Union and the 1997 iteration envisioned contingencies on the Korean Peninsula, it was quite clear that the 2015 guidelines were targeted at China's assertive policies in the East China Sea and the South China Sea (Shiraishi 2015). Even though the defence of the Senkaku/Diaoyu Islands was a case for self/national defence, the security policymaking elite clearly linked the strengthening of the US–Japan alliance to the defence of the disputed islands. The lifting of the collective self-defence ban was perceived as a crucial means of achieving the goal of strengthening the bilateral security alliance with the US.

In fact, the push towards revising the bilateral defence guidelines came from Japan. Morimoto Satoshi was the first to propose revision of the defence guidelines when he served as defence minister in a DPJ government. However, there was no progress. Some reports claimed that the US was not keen on a revision. A senior MOD official stated, 'Some parts of the US have questioned the effectiveness and urgency of the re-revision' (*Shikoku News*, 3 January 2013). America's view was that there was still work to be done to achieve the outstanding goals of the 1997 defence guidelines. The 1997 version had too many 'opt-out clauses', and they were not binding (Finnegan 2009: 9; Przystup, personal communication, 16 June 2015; Schoff, personal communication, 20 May 2015). A Japanese official also stated that the US was hesitant because it did not want the guidelines to be agreed on and then subsequently watered down during the Diet deliberations (Matsumoto, personal communication, 15 June 2015). However, the push for revising the guidelines experienced a boost when Abe came back to power in 2012. He immediately instructed Defense Minister Onodera to push for the revision of the defence guidelines (Tamura 2016: 367–7), and both states agreed on the revision at the bilateral SCC meeting in October 2013.

The second phase of the threat narrative was directed at domestic society and centred on the debate in the National Diet on the proposed security bills. Here, the China threat was underplayed. Though regional threats such as China's maritime activities and the instability on the Korean Peninsula were mentioned, the threat narrative focused on global/international missions, including collective self-defence ones, that would require the SDF's involvement. This approach was intended to underplay the threatening environment around Japan and the possibility of the SDF becoming embroiled in a conflict alongside the US.

At the national level, various aspects of China's assertive behaviour in the maritime domain defined the threat narrative. One element that tied these aspects together was the concept of change. The first aspect was how China had changed, and how this affected Japan–China relations negatively. Before 2010, the assumption had been that Japan was willing to somewhat ignore the lack of transparency of China's military spending on the condition that it was becoming a responsible stakeholder in the international system (Hornung 2014: 104–5). However, this changed after the fishing trawler incident. The way China responded to the 2010 incident made Kitaoka conclude that Japan could 'hardly count on what China claims to be its peaceful rise' (Kitaoka 2010). A high-ranking policymaker, Takamizawa Nobushige, said that Japan had 'to look at the reality of China' (Takamizawa as cited in Hornung 2014: 105). Senior Vice Minister of Defense Watanabe Shu of the DPJ government said, 'the current enemy isn't Soviet or Russia; the enemy is China' (as cited in Hagström 2012: 290). Koji Kano, a senior defence ministry official, said that although Japan and China had faced many crises in the past, China's reactions to the 2010 and 2012 crises were 'different' and 'something has changed' (Kano, personal communication, 29 November 2012).

The change in China had severe consequences for Sino-Japanese relations. Mori Satoru said that the economic and security dimensions of Sino-Japanese relations, which had been kept separate in the past, became interconnected following the maritime incidents. This was shown by the widespread demonstrations in China following the two incidents (Mori, personal communication,

20 November 2012). The issue of sovereignty, which had been avoided in the past when discussing territorial disputes between Japan and China, made a return in defining Sino-Japanese relations following the 2010 and 2012 incidents (Kano, personal communication, 29 November 2012). The competitive nature of Japan–China relations, as described by a senior defence ministry official, became the 'new normal' in the bilateral relationship (Kimura, personal communication, 29 November 2012).

Still on the theme of change, China was described as more assertive. The 2013 NDPG, for the first time, described China's actions in the maritime domain as 'assertive' (Prime Minister of Japan and His Cabinet 2013b: 3). Other than the usual list of concerns (China's rising expenditures, military modernisation, China's unclear intentions and the lack of transparency of its military build-up), the 2013 NDPG raised new concerns related to China. It discussed China's strengthening of 'asymmetrical military capabilities to prevent military activity by other countries in the region by denying access and deployment of foreign militaries to its surrounding areas' (Prime Minister of Japan and His Cabinet 2013b: 3). The 2013 NDPG also, for the first time, made reference to the East China Sea and the South China Sea in discussing the 'expanding and intensifying [. . .] activities in the maritime and aerial domains in the region' (Prime Minister of Japan and His Cabinet 2013b: 3).

The threat narrative also focused on how China was changing the status quo in the maritime sphere. This was visible in its intention to widen its control of the maritime domain. Kitaoka Shin'ichi wrote in the *Daily Yomiuri*: 'In an attempt to change the status quo in its favor, Beijing has allowed Chinese fishing boats to converge on waters around the Senkakus' (Kitaoka 2010). The 2013 EASR (published by the MOD-funded National Institute of Defense Studies) stated that the repeated intrusions by China into Japanese territorial waters and airspace around the Senkaku Islands was intended to challenge Japan's administrative control over the disputed islands (*Daily Yomiuri*, 30 March 2013).

Not only was China attempting to change the status quo, it was achieving this goal through the use of force/coercion. In the MOD's annual white paper, the repeated intrusions by Chinese ships and aircrafts into Japanese territorial waters and airspace around the Senkaku/Diaoyu Islands were described as China's attempt 'to change the status quo by force based on its own assertion, which is incompatible with the existing order of international law' (MOD Japan 2013: 30). This was repeated in the NDPG 2013, which described China's actions in the maritime domain as 'attempts to change the status quo by coercion' (Prime Minister of Japan and His Cabinet 2013b: 3). Matsuda Yasuhiro, a leading expert on China, described the constant presence of Chinese coast guard ships in the contiguous zone supported by Chinese military ships as an indication of China challenging the status quo through coercion (Matsuda, personal communication, 5 December 2018). To show Chinese coercion, the Japanese government started disclosing information about China's military activities in the disputed East China Sea to highlight the challenges to Japan's national security occurring on a daily basis that required the government to respond and defend its national interests. The government readily shared the number of daily intrusions, the number of ships and the number of 'scrambles' by the Japanese air force required to address intrusions into Japanese airspace (see MOD Japan 2016).

China was also described as reckless, especially in terms of deliberately causing instability in the region. In response to China's directing fire-control radar at a Japanese destroyer, Japan's ambassador to the United Kingdom, Hayashi Keiichi, wrote in an op-ed that this action 'might be regarded as an act of war' in normal naval practice (Hayashi 2014). In characterising the Chinese use of force/coercion actions to change the status quo as dangerous, Abe said in an interview with the *Wall Street Journal* that 'There are concerns that China is attempting to change the status quo by force, rather than by rule of law. But if China opts to take that path, then it won't be able to emerge peacefully' (*Japan Times*, 27 October 2013). Ambassador Hayashi wrote that if China did not choose to seek dialogue and abide by the rule of law, it risked becoming the Voldemort of the region by 'letting loose the evil of an arms race and escalation of tensions' (Hayashi 2014).

The second threat element at the national level was related to the uncertainty resulting from China's assertive behaviour in the maritime domain, which, it was thought, could escalate into a contingency. The 2013 EASR stated that repeated Chinese intrusions into Japanese territorial waters and airspace around the Senkaku Islands could lead to an unexpected contingency (*Daily Yomiuri*, 30 March 2013). The 2013 defence white paper stated that some Chinese monitoring activities that intruded into Japan's territorial waters and airspace 'could cause a contingency situation, which are extremely regrettable' (MOD Japan 2013: 39). When China announced the ADIZ in November 2013, Kishida said, 'It was a one-sided action and cannot be allowed. It could well lead to an unforeseen situation' (*Straits Times*, 25 November 2013). In criticising the ADIZ, Japan's 2014 defence white paper described these measures as 'profoundly dangerous acts that unilaterally change the status quo in the East China Sea, escalating the situation, and that may cause unintended consequences' (*Japan News*, 6 August 2014). In defending the Abe government's push for the passage of security bills to authorise collective self-defence missions for the SDF despite widespread opposition, LDP Vice President Komura Masahiko said:

> As the security environment grows harsher, we need to keep up our diplomatic efforts and at the same time further our deterrent capabilities. A crisis could come at any time. We see it necessary to prepare as soon as we possibly can legislation to take preventive measures in anticipation of dire circumstances. (Matsushita 2015)

The third threat element was the vulnerability of Japan's national security to assertive Chinese maritime behaviour. When the 2013 NDPG was being prepared, the MOD secretly conducted assessments of the SDF's capability and equipment in the event of a contingency in the region. This capability was tested against several challenging scenarios for the region, including a Chinese invasion of the Senkaku/Diaoyu Islands. A senior ministry official said that the results on the readiness of the SDF, based on a computer analysis, were 'dismal' in the event the US did not come to Japan's aid (*Japan News*, 13 October 2013).

Japan's vulnerability was related to its inability to defend against 'gray zone' situations – defined as 'confrontations over territory, sovereignty, and economic interests that are not to escalate to wars' (MOD Japan 2010a: 3). As these situations had an unclear status in the 1997 bilateral defence guidelines, Japan was concerned that this left open the possibility of a forceful Chinese takeover of the Senkaku/Diaoyu Islands in such a way that an American military intervention could not be authorised. Hence, the gray zone situations, for the first time, were included in the 2013 NDPG. It underscored the alarming nature of gray zone situations, stating that 'gray-zone situations over territory, sovereignty and maritime economic interests tend to linger, raising concerns that they may develop into more serious situations' (Prime Minister of Japan and His Cabinet 2013b: 2). The 2013 NSS reiterated the increased importance of gray zone situations when it noted that '[t]here is a risk that these "gray-zone" situations could further develop into grave situations' (Prime Minister of Japan and His Cabinet 2013a: 11).

Another element related to Japan's vulnerability was how Chinese maritime behaviour was damaging to the US–Japan security alliance and the US-led order. China's assertive behaviour was viewed as testing the alliance in the context of the Senkaku/Diaoyu Islands disputes (Kimura, personal communication, 29 November 2012). A high-ranking Japanese official stated that China was one of the main challenges to the stability of the global commons, which is dependent on the power and influence of the US (Shimada, personal communication, 21 November 2012). This affected Japan's ability to rely on the US–Japan alliance, which remained critical in Japan's efforts to address China's assertive behaviour (Kurauchi, personal communication, 21 November 2012). The seriousness of this point was amplified by discussion on the perceived relative weakening of America's global power and influence, and how this directly affected Japan's national security. The 2013 NDPG said: 'The multi-polarization of the world continues as a result of shifts in the balance of power due to the further development of countries such as China and India and the relative change of influence of the United States' (Prime Minister of Japan and His Cabinet 2013b: 1). To safeguard Japan's national security in light of the rising assertiveness of China along with the changing influence of the US, the

Abe government was resolved to strengthening the deterrence of the US–Japan alliance, even if it meant taking bold and unpopular decisions such as the lifting of the collective self-defence ban. In an exchange with opposition leaders, Abe said that Japan 'needs to decide what needs to be decided' (*Japan Times*, 23 May 2015). In defending this commitment to deepening Japan's alliance with the US, Abe said: 'In several years, it may become impossible to protect the Senkaku Islands only with the Maritime Self-Defense Force. It will be too late when such a situation becomes a reality' (*Japan News*, 3 July 2014). At an Upper House Special Committee meeting, Abe underscored the urgency of the situation when he said: 'If we develop legislation after something happens, it's too late' (Kuromi and Okabe 2015).

Nearing the passage of the bills, Japan augmented the threat narrative by raising alarm around Chinese behaviour. The government's 2015 defence white paper was revised after its initial draft was rejected by the LDP's national defence panel in early July on the grounds that it was being 'too soft' on China (*Japan Times*, 27 July 2015). Hence, new issues surrounding China were raised in the final version of the white paper. One example was Japan's concerns towards China's construction of a new offshore platform near the median line between its shoreline and that of Japan in the East China Sea. The Japanese government released photos and a map showing China's construction of offshore platforms for gas field developments in the East China Sea. The Japanese government shared that these offshore facilities could be not only for China to steal deposits, but also for military purposes. A senior MOD official said: 'The offshore structures could become a foothold for developing militarized facilities' in the East China Sea (Kuromi and Takekoshi 2015). This conclusion was based on China's land reclamation and militarisation activities in the South China Sea (*Japan News*, 12 July 2015). At a Lower House special committee meeting on security legislation, Nakatani Gen, Japan's defence minister, said China 'could install a radar system on the platform, or use it as an operating base for helicopters or drones conducting air patrols' (*Japan News*, 12 July 2015). He added: 'If radar was installed on the platform, it would supplement the [ADIZ].' According to Nakatani, this 'would improve China's capacity for surveillance and warning, which could give them a better idea of the SDF's activities' – especially since China did not have the capability to cover the East China Sea from its mainland (*Japan News*, 12 July 2015).

These activities, along with China's maritime assertiveness in the East China Sea and the South China Sea, were included in the expanded 2015 defence white paper. The white paper stressed that the security situation surrounding Japan had become 'increasingly tough'. It said that China 'has been continuing activities seen as high-handed to alter the status quo by force and has attempted to materialize its unilateral claim without making compromise' (*Japan Times*, 27 July 2015). Regarding the East China Sea, the white paper explained that for the first time, territorial intrusions into Japanese waters surrounding the Senkaku/Diaoyu Islands by Chinese ships were becoming routine operations (*Japan News*, 22 July 2015). At a joint press conference after the summit with President Obama in April 2015, Abe singled out China when he said: 'I don't want to minimize, though, the fact that there are some real tensions that have arisen with China around its approach to maritime issues and its claims. That's the wrong way to go about it' (*Japan News*, 2 May 2015).

The international dimension was equally important for Japan's threat construction process. The first element was how the regional and international environment had become 'severe', either directly or indirectly due to China's attempts to change the status quo by coercion (Prime Minister of Japan and His Cabinet 2014b, 2015). The 2013 NDPG stated: 'As Japan has great concern about these Chinese activities, it will need to pay utmost attention to them, as these activities also raise concerns over regional and global security' (Prime Minister of Japan and His Cabinet 2013b: 4). In a press conference to announce the submission of the final report by the Advisory Panel in 2014, Prime Minister Abe discussed the severity of the regional environment caused by China's 'unilateral actions backed by coercion' in the maritime domain in the context of the South China Sea and East China Sea territorial disputes (Prime Minister of Japan and His Cabinet 2014a). The 2014 *Defense of Japan* (Japan's defence white paper) noted, 'Such trends in China have also caused security concerns for the Asia-Pacific region and the international community' (MOD Japan 2014: 143). The 2015 *Defense of Japan* warned of China's ambitions when it said 'China plans to further expand the sphere of its maritime activities, and further intensify its operations in waters surrounding Japan, including the East China Sea and the Pacific Ocean, as well as the South China Sea and the airspaces over these seas areas' (MOD Japan 2015b: 48).

The second element was how China's attempt to change the status quo using force was a risk to the 'global commons', in the sense of impeding 'free access to global commons, such as the sea, outer space, and cyberspace' (Prime Minister of Japan and His Cabinet 2013a: 8). According to Japan, this behaviour infringed international law. The 2013 NSS noted:

> While the seas are governed by international maritime law, in particular the United Nations Convention on the Law of the Sea (UNCLOS), there have been an increasing number of cases of unilateral actions in an attempt to change the status quo by coercion without paying respect to existing international law. (Prime Minister of Japan and His Cabinet 2013a: 8)

Japan used international platforms to underscore the importance of international law and illustrate China's repeated failure to conform to it. In a speech at the 13th Asian Security Summit, Prime Minister Abe said, 'To achieve this [peace and stability], all countries must observe international law.' Abe introduced three principles for rule of law at sea: (1) states shall make and clarify claims based on international law; (2) states shall not use force or coercion in trying to drive their claims; and (3) states shall seek to settle disputes by peaceful means (Abe 2014, parenthesis added). While praising the efforts of states that rely on peaceful methods that conform to international law to resolve maritime disputes (such as the Philippines' decision to resolve the dispute in the South China Sea through legal means), Abe challenged China without mentioning it. He said, 'Movement to consolidate changes to the status quo by aggregating one fait accompli after another can only be strongly condemned as something that contravenes the spirit of the three principles' (Abe 2014).

The Japanese security policymaking elite also stressed that China's intentions were dangerous to the international legal order. In the 2015 *Defense of Japan*, it noted:

> While advocating 'peaceful development', China, particularly over maritime issues where its interests conflict with others', based on its own assertions incompatible with the existing international legal order, continues to act in an assertive manner, including coercive attempts at changing the status quo, and is poised to fulfil its unilateral demands without compromise. China's actions include dangerous acts that may invite unintended consequences. (MOD Japan 2015b: 33)

The security policymaking elite utilised the fire-control radar locking incident as an illustration of China's dangerous actions that were outside international law. At a Lower House Budget Committee session, Onodera Itsunori, Japan's defence minister, shared that the ship's action should be considered a violation of the UN Charter because it was a preliminary step towards gunfire. He said, 'The incident could have developed into a dangerous situation such as an armed conflict [between the two countries]. China's actions should be regarded as a threat of force, banned under the UN Charter' (*Daily Yomiuri*, 8 February 2013, parenthesis from original).

The third element was to internationalise Japan's claims over the territorial disputes with China. This was no longer seen only as a bilateral matter, but an international one as well. Former Ambassador of Japan to the US Okawara Yoshio said that Japan should make the international community more aware of Japan's position in the Senkaku/Diaoyu territorial disputes – especially when a compromise with China was not conceivable (Okawara, personal communication, 2 October 2012).

To internationalise the East China Sea issue, the Abe government directly linked China's assertive behaviour and attempt to change the status quo in the

East China Sea to the South China Sea dispute. This was not only because of the importance of the South China Sea to Japan's interests (see Koga 2017), but also as a way to amplify China's assertive behaviour. In fact, according to a Japanese official, one could argue that the South China Sea was more important to Japan than the East China Sea in terms of economic growth (Matsumoto, personal communication, 15 June 2015). Hence, Japan was concerned about the blocking of the open and safe sealanes due to China's assertiveness in the South China Sea. Japan was also concerned about China's attempts to change the status quo in the South China Sea through its land reclamation of reefs and militarisation activities. The Japanese leadership was quick to alert Southeast Asian states of the possible implications of China's ADIZ. At the Japan–ASEAN Commemorative Summit to celebrate the 40th anniversary of Japan–ASEAN relations in Tokyo, Abe 'suggested his guests should consider China's establishment of the ADIZ in the East China Sea as a matter of concern for the entire region' (T. B. 2013).

The connection between the East China Sea and the South China Sea was important in raising the China threat among Japan's allies and partners. The way to deal with emergencies in the South China Sea was one of the topics discussed at the Obama–Abe summit that resulted in the signing of the bilateral guidelines in April 2015 (*Japan News*, 2 May 2015). Following talks at the Asia Security Summit in Singapore in 2015, the defence ministers of Japan, the US and Australia released a joint statement expressing 'serious concern' over China's ongoing land reclamation activities in the South China Sea. The statement by Defense Minister Nakatani Gen, US Defense Secretary Ashton Carter and Australian Defense Minister Kevin Andrews urged China to 'exercise self-restraint' regarding its unilateral action to conduct land reclamation and militarisation activities in the South China Sea. Defense Minister Nakatani said: 'If unlawfulness is left unchecked, it would ruin the [regional] order, resulting in the collapse of peace and security,' and continued: 'Regrettably, large-scale land reclamation and harbor and runway construction is continuing to rapidly advance at this very moment' (Okabe 2015).

Threat Deflation

Due to the controversial nature of the security bills to lift the collective self-defence ban, the Abe government adopted a strategy of threat deflation during the 220-hour debate in the National Diet. The Abe government underplayed China as a justification for Japan's adoption of collective self-defence missions and adopted a discourse that focused on less controversial scenarios that either involved accepted threat notions, such as North Korea, or those that would reinforce Japan's role as a responsible actor in the regional and international security environments through addressing global challenges.

Prime Minister Abe and the security policymaking elite raised several scenarios – or, more specifically, 'survival-threatening situations' – that justified the

SDF's deployment on collective self-defence missions. One such scenario was a ballistic missile attack on Japan. In defending Japan's need to engage in collective self-defence missions, Abe said, 'There is the clear danger of suffering irreversible and major damage through a first strike by a ballistic missile,' which could 'represent a survival-threatening situation' (Aibara 2018). Defense Minister Onodera said in the Diet in August 2017 that a ballistic missile attack by North Korea on Guam could be another scenario. This could weaken America's deterrence and military capabilities, which were important to defend Japan's national security. Abe and the security policymaking elite also mentioned a scenario in which US military personnel or ships deployed to protect Japan and its citizens were attacked near the Korean Peninsula, justifying assistance from the SDF. Another scenario Abe repeatedly raised was in the Middle East, especially in ensuring safe and open sealanes in the Strait of Hormuz. This was a vital transport route for petroleum, important to Japan's national security. In the event that mines were placed in the Strait, the security policymaking elite argued that the SDF would be justified in engaging in collective self-defence missions to ensure open and safe sealanes (Aibara 2018). Though other scenarios were persistently raised, Abe also made a reference to China during the Diet deliberations. He said, 'A country has been conducting reclamation activities in the South China Sea,' concerning situations that could significantly affect Japan. Abe continued, 'I'm going to refrain from going into specifics, but I will arrange for the use of the law if possible' (*Japan News*, 7 June 2015).

The Abe government also underplayed the frequency with which Japan would engage in collective self-defence missions. In a lecture in Naha in November 2015 (part of an LDP lecture series intended to win over public support to the controversial security bills), LDP's Vice President Komura likened Japan's deterrence power to a 'treasured sword' to be used only in cases of emergency. He said 'Japan has become able to exercise the right of collective self-defence in a limited manner, but I believe that decades and decades will pass without the right being exercised. I'm pretty sure about it' (*Japan Times*, 23 May 2015). At a press conference, Prime Minister Abe made it clear that the decision to allow for the military to engage in collective self-defence missions would only be implemented as a means of last resort. He said, 'even if Japan were hypothetically to take such action, it would be limited to when there is no other appropriate means available and it must be limited to the minimum extent necessary' (Prime Minister of Japan and His Cabinet 2014b). When the government defended a case in the Japanese high court against a lawsuit submitted by an active GSDF member who 'wanted to confirm there was no obligation to obey an order for defence deployment under a survival-threatening situation defined in the national security laws', the government responded to say that such a situation was 'an "abstract supposition" that could not be envisaged under current international circumstances' (Aibara 2018).

Prime Minister Abe regularly underplayed the potential risks and played up the benefits of the proposed security bills. In a one-on-one debate in the Lower House, Abe challenged the opposition parties who labelled the security bills as war legislation as 'irresponsible labeling' and 'totally misguided'. While Abe explained that the rules of the SDF's deployment were being changed so that they would be able to react more quickly to provide support to other forces, he also stated that SDF personnel would 'naturally choose to operate in areas where they would not face the risk of being involved in fighting as much as possible and where their safety is secured'. The change in the rules of the SDF's operation, he said, 'has nothing to do with risks' for the SDF members in such missions (*Japan Times*, 23 May 2015).

Prime Minister Abe also dismissed concerns related to Japan being drawn into military conflicts started by other countries, or being dragged into a war by the US if the SDF was authorised to engage in collective self-defence. He said, 'Japan would never be involved in combat activities against its will. It is impossible' (*Japan Times*, 23 May 2015). He gave an assurance when he said, 'Some people have vague concern that (Japan) will be dragged into a war the US engages in. I say to them clearly here that such a situation will never happen' (*Japan Times*, 15 May 2015). At the press conference announcing the Cabinet decision to reinterpret Article 9 on July 1, 2014, Abe said:

> There are no changes in today's Cabinet Decision from the basic way of thinking on the constitutional interpretation to date. Neither has the existing principle of not, as a general rule, permitting overseas deployment of the SDF changed in the slightest. It still remains the case that the SDF will never participate in such warfare as the Gulf War or the Iraq War in the past. (Prime Minister of Japan and His Cabinet 2014b)

Moreover, the Abe government underscored that collective self-defence was a 'right' for Japan rather than an obligation. Hence, Japan retains autonomy on when to engage in collective self-defence missions (The Advisory Panel on Reconstruction of the Legal Basis for Security 2008: 112). An indication that Japan will not go to war and is able to withstand American pressure was shown in Japan's resistance to participating in patrol activities in the South China Sea (Hosoya 2019: 43; Satake, personal communication, 4 December 2018; Toku-chi, personal communication, 4 December 2018).

Instead of Japan engaging in unwanted conflict, the Abe government argued that the lifting of the collective self-defence ban improved the government's ability to protect Japanese citizens and their livelihoods in the event of a crisis overseas that was not a direct attack on Japan (Prime Minister of Japan and His Cabinet 2014a, 2014b). At the Press Conference on 25 September 2015, Abe said:

> We will resolutely protect the lives and peaceful livelihoods of the Japanese people in any situation. To achieve this, it is vital that we strengthen the foundations of our national security while also striving harder than ever to push forward with peaceful diplomacy. (Prime Minister of Japan and His Cabinet 2015)

Abe and the security policymaking elite argued that the reinterpretation to allow for collective self-defence was a '"rationalization" of unified government stances within existing interpretations' (Hughes 2017: 95), and not a radical change in Japanese security policy (Green and Hornung 2014; Liff 2017; Oros 2014). The reinterpretation of Article 9 and the security bills added more political and legal constraints through 'closing the gap' to all the security policy changes that Japan had adopted since the onset of the post-Cold War period. The bills also addressed the inadequacies of the legal framework to support security policy expansion that could defend Japan's national security and play a responsible role in regional and international security affairs (Mori, personal communication, 6 December 2018; Prime Minister of Japan and His Cabinet 2014b). The Japanese government argued that the security legislation, including the authorisation of collective self-defence mission for the SDF, would strengthen deterrence of the US–Japan alliance and reduce the chances of any attack against Japan (Prime Minister of Japan and His Cabinet 2014a). At the press conference to announce the conclusion of the report by the Advisory Panel on 15 May 2014, Abe stressed the importance of the updated legal framework for Japan's security. He said:

> In fact, I perceive that precisely by having the ability to respond to every possible situation and developing legal system, which enables such responses, deterrence will be enhanced, and thus conflict will be prevented and Japan's embroilment in war will be eliminated. (Prime Minister of Japan and His Cabinet 2014a)

To add to the 'low risk' argument, Prime Minister Abe and the security policymaking elite stressed that Japan would not engage in collective self-defence unless the situation fulfilled three conditions set out in the legislation. These conditions were: the 'use of force to a minimum extent' when 'an armed attack against a foreign country that is in a close relationship with Japan occurs'; the attack 'threatens Japan's survival and poses a clear danger to fundamentally overturn the people's right to life, liberty and pursuit of happiness'; and 'when there is no other appropriate means available to repel the attack'. The Komeito, the LDP's ruling coalition member, played an important role as a check to the LDP's initial proposals and in influencing the outcome of the conditions that limited the SDF's engagement in collective self-defence missions. Abe referred to these conditions as 'strict brakes' to contain Japan from resorting to collective self-defence (*Japan Times*, 15 May 2015). He went on to say that 'generally Japan would not be permitted to enter the territory or territorial waters of other countries for the purpose of using force or engaging in combat missions' (*Japan Times*, 23 May 2015).

The conditions discussed above had a strong 'self-defence' focus (Liff 2017: 160–1).[4] When the Secretary-General of the Japan Innovation Party (JIP), Kakizawa Mito, proposed redefining self-defence to include not just individual but collective self-defence (*Yomiuri Shimbun*, 11 July 2015), he was strongly rebuked. At a national security special committee meeting at the National Diet's Lower House, Kakizawa argued that the development of military technology had blurred the lines between the right of individual self-defence and the right of collective self-defence (*Yomiuri Shimbun*, 11 July 2015). Since the SDF is permitted to use force only when there is a clear and imminent danger that an armed attack would be made on Japan, then it will also have the right to engage in collective self-defence missions if Japan adopts a widened conception of self-defence. This proposal was criticised by the MOFA and the LDP-Komeito ruling coalition. The Foreign Ministry bureau chief said at the committee meeting, 'Use of force cannot be justified under the right of individual self-defence unless an armed attack is made directly on Japan' (*Yomiuri Shimbun*, 11 July 2015). The ruling coalition said Japan would be criticised internationally if it made ambiguous the difference between the right of individual self-defence and the right of collective self-defence (*Yomiuri Shimbun*, 11 July 2015).

The SDF's involvement in the collective self-defence missions was also linked to Japan assuming a responsible role in global security affairs. Prime Minister Abe argued that the collective self-defence bills enabled the SDF to address every situation in a seamless manner to protect Japanese citizens. When the bills were passed, Abe said, 'The Cabinet today approved a package of security bills to ensure peace for Japan and the world.' Stressing the need for legislation to expand the scope of the SDF's overseas operations, he observed that 'We are in times in which no country can secure its safety alone,' amid an increasingly severe security environment (*Japan Times*, 30 March 2016). When the bills were enacted, Abe said that the implementation of the legislation was of 'historic importance that makes peace and security of our country even more secure' and 'upgrades our deterrence and enables the nation to proactively contribute more than ever to peace and stability of regional and international communities' (*Japan Times*, 30 March 2016).

Security Policy Development

The lifting of the collective self-defence ban has been a long-standing issue in Japan's domestic politics. However, the pressure to lift the ban significantly increased from the mid-2000s. Having successfully contributed to the OEF and OIF, there was a sense of anticipation within the Japanese government that the Bush administration would be expecting more from Japan during the second term of the Bush administration. A senior Foreign Ministry official said 'It's possible that the US will demand more of the [Japanese] government in [the Bush administration's] second term' (*Yomiuri Shimbun*, 5 November 2004, parentheses added). In fulfilling this demand, the Japanese government contemplated lifting the collective self-defence ban, along with other initiatives such as establishing a permanent law for the SDF's overseas dispatch (*Yomiuri Shimbun*, 5 November 2004). Though both states successfully updated the US–Japan alliance in the mid-2000s, there was no progress on the collective self-defence issue.

It was only when Abe Shinzo became Prime Minister in 2006 that collective self-defence became a legitimate strategy in Japan's official discourse. The Advisory Panel on Reconstruction of the Legal Basis for Security (also known as the Yanai commission), which was assembled by the Abe government, supported the lifting of the collective self-defence ban (The Advisory Panel on Reconstruction of the Legal Basis for Security 2008). This position was also supported by the less conservative DPJ government, as revealed in the DPJ's own private advisory panel's report to Prime Minister Kan in August 2010. Calling for Japan to change from a 'passive peace-loving nation' to a 'proactive peace-loving nation', the panel recommended constitutional reinterpretation to lift the collective self-defence ban (The Council on Security and Defense Capabilities in the New Era 2010). This shift in the position of the governments was critical in changing the discourse surrounding the controversial issue of collective self-defence. Nevertheless, lifting the ban on collective self-defence remained only a desired goal, even though Japan had arguably engaged in collective self-defence missions in the post-Cold War period without legal authorisation, such as in OEF.

According to a National Bureau of Asian Research report, this impasse contributed to the serious questioning of the utility of the alliance between the US and Japan. For the US, this utility was being challenged by a long-standing asymmetry in the alliance that referred to the unequal role of Japan compared to its alliance partner, as well as by the regular implementation of 'small adjustments'[5] to the alliance to address ongoing challenges (Finnegan 2009: 3). For Japan, it was unable to resolve the asymmetric nature of the alliance due to its entrenched social and legal constraints. However, Tokyo was more concerned about the continued utility of the alliance in addressing its security challenges – namely those related to China and North Korea. It was concerned about the sustainability of America's commitment to offer Japan a robust security guarantee, and the range of required capabilities for its national security. Even though the DPJ government was not fully responsible for the problems in the alliance, DPJ's tenure in government, according to Finnegan, brought about much-needed reflection by both states that led to the subsequent adjustments (Finnegan 2009: 5–6).

The questioning ended with Abe's return to power in 2012. He challenged the 'small adjustments' approach and pursued 'radical' policies to strengthen the alliance. In this context, collective self-defence missions, described as the 'Achilles' heel of any effort to increase US–Japan cooperation' in operational and strategic terms, were introduced in the alliance (Finnegan 2009: 13). The choice of the collective self-defence policy was important for Abe. This was not only a source of America's frustrations with Japan, but also matched Abe's long-term goal of revising the postwar regime and lifting the constraints on Japan's security policy. At a press conference on 1 July 2014, Prime Minister Abe mentioned that he had been questioned about Japan's seriousness in building a robust alliance with the US without the SDF having the ability to engage in collective self-defence missions. He said that a number of 'high-ranking US government officials' stated that while US forces would perform their duty to defend Japan, in line with Article 5 of the security treaty, Japan's inability to defend American vessels would affect US trust in the alliance (Prime Minister of Japan and His Cabinet 2014b).[6] Abe said, 'I was urged to seriously consider whether the US public would continue to trust Japan if a Self-Defense Forces' vessel did not take any action when a nearby US vessel that was protecting Japan came under attack' (*Japan News*, 3 July 2014). This message was repeated when Abe was defending the collective self-defence bill in the Diet. If Japan was authorised to defend US naval vessels that were attacked in a contingency near Japan even though Japan was not attacked, Abe stressed that 'the bond that binds the Japan–US alliance will be stronger' and that the alliance would provide a more effective deterrence for Japan's security (*Japan Times*, 23 May 2015).

China's assertive behaviour in the maritime domain manifested in the series of incidents that provided the Abe government with an opportunity or policy window to pursue this 'radical' policy (Finnegan 2009: 4; *Japan Times*, 27 October 2013; Matsuda, personal communication, 5 December 2018; Michishita, personal communication, 6 December 2018; Sahashi, personal communication, 5 December 2018; Satake, personal communication, 4 December 2018; Togo 2014). Using abandonment fears to justify the reinterpretation of Article 9, a member of the Prime Minister's advisory panel said: 'The United States does not want to fight for [Senkakus]. If Japan, when push comes to shove, does not prepare to work together with [Washington], then [Washington] will say goodbye to its participation in the defense of our islands' (*Asahi Shimbun* as cited in Liff 2017: 158, parenthesis added). A senior Defense Ministry official said, 'To avoid a clash with China, it is important to show that Japan and the United States are united' (Kuromi and Okabe 2015). In discussing the security bills in an interview with

Yomiuri Shimbun, Iokibe Makoto, the former president of the National Defense Academy, underscored that Japan should strengthen the Japan–US alliance and send a message to China that Japan and the US were inseparable. Iokibe said:

> Making it possible for Japan to exercise a limited right of collective self-defence is the very manifestation of the cooperative framework between Japan and the United States. If something happens to a US military vessel in this region, it is important that Japan defend the region together and not leave the Americans for dead. The second that Japan's Self-Defense Force turns a blind eye to such a situation, the Japan–US alliance would be over in the eyes of the American public. We should show that Japan is deeply connected with America. It protects the security of Japan and provides a potent means to force China to exercise self-restraint. (Fukumoto 2015)

In order to successfully implement a legal framework for the authorisation of collective self-defence missions for the SDF, the Abe government pursued internal and external (with the US) measures. Internally, Abe strengthened the supported structure around him – including by the formation of the National Security Secretariat led by a National Security Advisor, which coordinated security policy – and made strategic appointments of individuals sympathetic to adding collective self-defence to the SDF's mandate. Additionally, to bolster cooperation with the US, the Abe government speedily passed the national secrets law, which was meant to tighten control of state secrets to protect information and 'persuade the United States to share more sensitive military intelligence' (Fackler 2013). In April 2014, the Cabinet eased the principles and guidelines governing weapons exports and joint development of arms (except for exporting arms to countries involved in conflict or to those that violate UN resolutions). Abe reconvened the second government policy advisory panel on security issues in February 2013. It was again headed by Yanai Shunji and co-chaired by Kitaoka Shin'ichi. At the initial meeting that launched the panel, Abe said: 'I want to consider what Japan can do to make the US–Japan security alliance more effective' (Mie 2013). When the report was submitted two and half years later, it stated that the international environment around Japan had become more severe and Japan was unable to defend itself and address these threats alone. In this context, it was imperative that Japan widened its security role through not only individual self-defence, but also by lifting the ban on collective self-defence missions (Hughes 2017: 108, fn. 29).

Related to the lifting of the collective self-defence ban, the Abe government was also determined to revise the defence guidelines. Unlike the 1978 and 1997 versions, this time the push came from Japan (Harner 2013). Within two weeks of his return to office in December 2012, Abe pushed for a review of the country's defence guidelines, which had initially been agreed between Defense Minister Morimoto Satoshi and Defense Secretary Leon Panetta in August 2012 (*Daily Yomiuri*, 10 January 2013; de Koning and Lipscy 2013). The importance of this move was noted in the 2013 NDPG, which stated that 'Japan will revise the Guidelines for Japan–US Defense Cooperation' as one of the measures to strengthen the alliance (Prime Minister of Japan and His Cabinet 2013b: 9). The aim was to strengthen effective deterrence against a range of situations listed in the 2013 NDPG, especially those related to maritime security. The top two situations listed were 'ensuring security of the sea and airspace surrounding Japan' and 'response to an attack on remote islands'.[7]

The Japan–US SCC meeting in 2013 was held in Tokyo for the first time. Prime Minister Abe said: 'This is the first time a two-plus-two meeting was held in Japan with both the US secretary of state and defense secretary in attendance. It has historic significance' (Takahashi and Matsushita 2013). There was a sense of urgency surrounding this meeting due to 'a heightened sense of crisis shared by the two countries over China's looming presence' (Takahashi and Matsushita 2013). Foreign Minister Kishida Fumio said, 'China is challenging order in the region by use of force, along with significant expansion of military capabilities and activities' (Takahashi and Matsushita 2013). At this meeting Secretaries John Kerry and Chuck Hagel initially did not share Japan's serious concerns related to China's maritime assertiveness and 'avoided highlighting and endorsing Japan's position on the Senkaku/Diaoyu islands dispute' (Harner 2013). The US also did not want a direct reference on China in the joint statement issued. According to reports, this changed following Abe's push. It stated: 'Abe gave the ministers a strong direction to include the words "China" and "military expansion" and the United States agreed' (MOFA Japan 2013; Takahashi and Matsushita 2013).

The foreign and defence ministers of the US and Japan agreed to the revision of the Japan–US defence cooperation guidelines at this meeting. The American side agreed to this revision because of Japanese pressure and the uncertainty caused by China's increased activities in the maritime area (Przystup, personal communication, 16 June 2015). Expanding on the existing categories of circumstances when Japan and the US should respond in the defence guidelines (times of peace; an armed attack on Japan; and a contingency in areas surrounding Japan), the discussion focused on a 'seamless' or all-inclusive response covering every possible situation – including a situation on a remote island that cannot be easily identified as a contingency, referred to as a gray zone situation (Takahashi and Matsushita 2013). The negotiations on the defence guidelines were accelerated because both the US and Japan acknowledged the urgency of strengthening the defence of remote islands, including the Senkaku/Diaoyu Islands (Takahashi and Matsushita 2013). The SCC joint statement also outlined that Japan was considering lifting the collective self-defence ban to strengthen Japan's contribution to the US–Japan alliance (*Japan Times*, 7 October 2014). The lifting of the ban on collective self-defence became a source of trust between the US and Japan.

Using the Advisory Panel's findings as a basis, the Abe-led LDP subsequently conducted long discussions with its coalition partner, the Komeito, in May and June 2014 to attain its support (Hughes 2017: 109). Both reached an agreement on the principles and took the first step on 1 July 2014 to announce the Cabinet decision that reinterpreted Article 9 to allow for collective self-defence missions for the SDF. Abe invoked the importance of friendship based on trust between Japan and the US. This turned out to be the more important reason compared to the relevance of the collective self-defence bill to possible contingencies involving the Senkaku/Diaoyu Islands in the East China Sea, which could be dealt with by Japan through the exercise of its right to individual self-defence (*Japan Times*, 27 July 2015). When speaking about changing the constitutional interpretation, he said: 'If someone cannot help his or her friend, they are not friends' (*Japan News*, 3 July 2014).

Once the Japanese Cabinet approved the 'historic' reinterpretation of the Constitution to authorise collective self-defence missions, the next goal was for the LDP–Komeito coalition to formulate legislation authorising collective self-defence missions for the SDF to be deliberated at the Diet. However, it was important first that the historical Cabinet decision on July 2014 was incorporated within the Guidelines for US–Japan Defense Cooperation that were being negotiated. This was highlighted as a 'historic' step towards improving Japan's contribution to mutual defence commitments. When Defense Minister Onodera Itsunori met his US counterpart, Chuck Hagel, soon after the Cabinet decision, he said the Japanese government would proceed with the creation of laws based on the Cabinet's reinterpretation of Article 9. At a joint press conference after the meeting, Hagel said, 'When Japan's Diet passes the appropriate legislation, this bold, historic, landmark decision will enable Japan to significantly increase its contribution to regional and global security and expand its role on the world stage.' With the decision, Hagel added, 'We can raise our alliance to a new level, and we intend to do that' (Okabe 2014).

On 27 April 2015, President Obama and Prime Minister Abe signed the Guidelines for Japan–US Defense Cooperation. Rather than a revision or an update, the officials from both Washington and Tokyo referred to the revised defence guidelines as 'new'. This was because the document incorporated elements that signalled 'a new beginning' for US–Japan defence cooperation in light of the augmented threat from China in the maritime domain.

First, the 2015 guidelines stated that Japan and the US would cooperate in all situations, even when Japan was not attacked. Taking into account the 'complex' environment, it said, the two states 'will take measures to ensure Japan's peace and security in all phases, seamlessly, from peacetime to contingencies, including situations when an armed attack against Japan is not involved' (MOD Japan 2015a). Under the section entitled 'Actions in Response to an Armed Attack against a Country other than Japan' in the guidelines, it underscored the authorisation of the SDF's ability to use force to defend a country close to Japan, as it 'threatens Japan's survival and poses a clear danger to overturn fundamentally its people's right to life, liberty, and pursuit of happiness, to ensure Japan's survival, and to protect its people' – that is, collective self-defence (MOD Japan 2015a). To achieve this objective, the SDF was authorised to perform actions beyond conventional logistical support that included asset protection, search and rescue, maritime operations, operations to counter ballistic missile attacks, aerial refuelling and ammunition supply (*Japan News*, 7 June 2015; MOD Japan 2015a).

Second, compared to the 1997 version, the 2015 guidelines added more detailed points about peacetime cooperation between Japan and the US. It included sharing intelligence, surveillance and reconnaissance (ISR), asset protection and defence against ballistic missiles (*Japan News*, 15 April 2015). To coordinate such integrated operations, the 2015 guidelines introduced a permanent Alliance Coordination Mechanism that would provide a structure for officers from both Japan and the US to be stationed in each other's countries. This was intended to facilitate close cooperation not just during a contingency, but during peacetime as well (Shiraishi 2015).

Third, the guidelines removed any geographical boundary for Japan's defence cooperation with the US (Imai 2015). They stated: 'Japan and the United States will take a leading role in cooperation with partners to provide a foundation for peace, security, stability, and economic prosperity in the Asia-Pacific region and beyond' (MOD Japan 2015a). This was a clear evolution of the bilateral defence cooperation from the previous chapter, which explained how the scope of US–Japan defence cooperation expanded from a regional to a global focus. Fourth, not only in wider geographical terms, the guidelines expanded bilateral defence cooperation from the traditional areas into new areas deemed critical to the current strategic environment, such as cyber security and space, and in wider scenarios. Fifth, the new guidelines reinforced responses to gray zone incidents, which could raise tensions without having developed into armed conflict (*Japan News*, 15 April 2015). This was in special reference to the defence of remote Japanese islands such as the Senkaku/Diaoyu Islands (Shiraishi 2015). The addition of the defence of remote islands removed any ambiguity about a US engagement in the event of a contingency.

Following the signing of the revised guidelines, the LDP–Komeito ruling submitted a package of ten bills to the Diet on 24 May 2015 to gain a legal backing for the SDF's engagement in collective self-defence missions. The bills passed the Lower House, where the LDP–Komeito coalition held the majority, on 16 July 2015, although the opposition parties boycotted the vote. The ruling coalition then submitted the bills to the Upper House on 27 July 2015. With the support of three smaller parties – the Assembly to Energize Japan, the New Renaissance Party and the Party for Future Generations – LDP–Komeito managed to pass the bills through the committee stage on 17 September 2015 in the midst of an uproar involving the opposition parties and widespread demonstrations in Tokyo and elsewhere. The LDP–Komeito coalition passed the bills through the Upper House on 19 September 2015 that involved the opposition parties delaying the vote. The laws came into effect on 29 March 2016 (Hughes 2017: 94, fn. 2).

The bill that authorised the SDF to perform collective self-defence was known as the Law on Response to Contingencies. It allowed Japan to use force to assist other states, including the US, even when it was not attacked (MOFA Japan 2016). However, the law listed three conditions that had to be met before the SDF's deployment to such missions: (1) an armed attack occurs against a foreign country that is in a close relationship with Japan; (2) the attack threatens Japan's survival and poses a clear danger to fundamentally overturn people's right to life, liberty and pursuit of happiness; and (3) there is no other appropriate means available to repel the attack, ensure Japan's survival and protect its people.

To support Japan's participation in collective self-defence missions, two new situations were added to the legal framework that authorised the SDF's participation in collective self-defence missions.[8] First, the 'important-influence situation' replaced 'emergency in areas surrounding Japan', which removed geographical constraints on US–Japan defence constraints that aligned with the 2015 guidelines. This allowed the SDF to not only engage in contingencies in the 'areas surrounding Japan', such as the Korean Peninsula, but also in the Indian Ocean, the Strait of Hormuz or, even more controversially, the South China Sea. The rationale for this expansion was that contingencies beyond Japan's 'surrounding areas' could also affect Japan's national security (*Japan News*, 7 June 2015, 27 June 2015). The other situation added was the 'survival-threatening situation', which was defined as 'an armed attack . . . against a foreign country with which Japan has close relations, and Japan's survival is threatened with a clear danger that the people's right to life, liberty and the pursuit of happiness will be fundamentally undermined'. This meant Japan was authorised to participate in a contingency to assist the US and others even when Japan was not directly attacked, as long as the contingency was understood as damaging to Japan's national security (*Japan News*, 1 June 2015).

Along with the authorisation of collective self-defence missions, related laws were revised. The International Peace Support Law was passed, removing the need for Japan to enact separate laws for each SDF deployment to provide logistical and search and rescue support to multinational forces during UNPKOs. As part of the International Peace Cooperation Activities, additional roles were added for the SDF involved in UNPKOs. The tasks of protection of local populations and protection of individuals involved in the operation were added to a list that included the observation of cease-fire agreements, assistance in elections and assistance to people suffering due to conflict. Not only within the UN framework, the SDF was also authorised to be deployed to provide humanitarian assistance authorised by organisations other than the UN. Moreover, the ability of the SDF to use force was widened to conduct the missions effectively and protect the mission's mandate. The revised law also authorised the SDF to rescue Japanese and non-Japanese nationals caught up in emergency situations overseas with limited use of force. Finally, the ship inspection activities conducted by the SDF were expanded from limited situations 'in Japanese waters or on the surrounding high seas' to wider situations meant to achieve international peace and security purpose (*Japan Times*, 15 May 2015; MOFA Japan 2016). The net effect of all revisions brought about by the passage of the security bills was a stronger defence posture through strengthened deterrence offered by the US–Japan alliance, as well as an expanded security role for Japan in global security affairs.

NOTES

1. For information on the events discussed in this section, see Drifte (2013).
2. According to the JDA, Japan's sea-based Standard-3 interceptor missile could not shoot down missiles aimed at the US territory. This was because the missiles would be flying at a higher altitude compared to those targeted at Japan (Yoshida 2006a).
3. For the full report, see The Advisory Panel on Reconstruction of the Legal Basis for Security 2014.
4. Tetsuo Kotani has called the bills 'individual self-defence-plus' – underscoring the continued relevance of self-defence (Kotani, personal communication, 5 December 2018).
5. For the problem of the small adjustments to the alliance, see Finnegan (2009).
6. According to reports, Prime Minister Abe spoke with US National Security Adviser Susan Rice during President Obama's visit to Japan in April 2014. In his discussions with Rice, Abe mentioned the example of 'friends' and explained that Japan could not protect US vessels carrying civilians escaping some disaster under the current constitutional interpretation. In response, Rice said that such a relationship could not be called an alliance, and she called on Abe to review the constitutional interpretation to lift the ban on collective self-defence (*Japan News*, 3 July 2014).

7. These top two areas were followed by 'Response to ballistic missile attacks', 'Responses in outer space and cyberspace' and 'Responses to major disasters' (Prime Minister of Japan and His Cabinet 2013b: 14–15).

8. Traditionally, Japan's legal framework accepted the deployment of the SDF in two situations: (a) when Japan is attacked; and (b) when another country is perceived to be preparing an armed attack against Japan (known either as 'imminent armed attack situation' or 'anticipated armed attack situation) (*Japan News*, 1 June 2015).

7

SUMMARY, IMPLICATIONS AND US–CHINA COMPETITION

This book analysed the causes of change in Japanese post-Cold War security policy. This was interesting because it explained how change in Japanese security policy has occurred despite the existence of domestic (the entrenched social and legal constraints in domestic politics and society) and regional (suspicion from its neighbours of Japan's expanded security policy) constraints that have limited Japan's ability to pursue security policy like other states, especially in military terms. Nevertheless, Japan's post-Cold War security policy has evolved from its Cold War version. Instead of being driven mainly by economics features with limited involvement in political-strategic affairs, Japan's post-Cold War security policy has expanded with the widened use of the military in achieving its strategic objectives. The SDF's roles, missions and capabilities have expanded both outside and within the US–Japan alliance framework, even though the social and legal constraints continue to not only exist but also influence the national security debate and the security policymaking process.

Experts on Japanese security policy from the realism and social constructivism persuasions have used a range of international (international structure and international norms) and domestic (changes to the domestic political system, changes to the security identity, norms and risks) factors to explain this significant development in Japanese post-Cold War security policy. However, as argued here, these factors only created the context for change but failed to explain how the Japanese security policymaking elite negotiated the long-standing opposition to Japan's security policy expansion from selected political parties, selected

LDP members, civil society and NGO groups. To overcome this weakness, this research introduced external military crisis as the policy window that the security policymaking elite used to implement the initiatives that resulted in Japan's security policy expansion. The security policymaking elite shaped the threat narrative surrounding selected military crises, either through threat inflation or deflation, in order to circumvent domestic opposition from various segments of Japanese state and society wanting to defend Japan's peace-based security policy, as well as external opposition, especially from states that continue to harbour suspicion towards Japan's expanded security role due to the unresolved historical legacy. The military crises have been useful as they allowed the security policymaking elite to successfully expand the role of the SDF within Japanese security policy and gain legitimacy for a strengthened security policy.

To show the effects of external military crises, I focused on four key security policy initiatives of the post-Cold War period: the passage of the IPCL authorising the SDF to engage in international peacekeeping in 1992, the incorporation of a regional defence role into the SDF's mandate within the US–Japan alliance in 1997–9, the incorporation of global missions into the SDF's mandate within the US–Japan alliance in 2003–5 and the lifting of the collective self-defence ban for the SDF in 2014–15. For the implementation of international peacekeeping, the 1990–1 Persian Gulf Crisis was a critical impetus. The 1994 North Korean Nuclear Crisis, the 1996 Taiwan Strait Crisis and the 1999 Taepodong Crisis were critical in updating the US–Japan security alliance in the mid-1990s, which led to the incorporation of regional defence for the SDF within the alliance. The September 11th attacks and Japan's subsequent active participation in the US-led global war on terror (through the OEF and OIF campaigns) were critical in Japan's incorporation of global missions in the US–Japan alliance. The lifting of the collective self-defence ban in 2014–15 occurred in the context of China's maritime assertiveness in the East China Sea as manifested in the 2010 fishing trawler incident, the 2012 nationalisation of the Senkaku/Diaoyu Islands by Japan, Chinese maritime and military vessels frequent incursions into Japanese sea and air spaces, the fire-control radar locking incident and China's announcement of the ADIZ. This series of incidents collectively created an appropriate context for Abe and his government to achieve a milestone in Japan's security relations with the US, as well as strengthening deterrence against the threat posed by China's attempt to change the status quo through the use of force.

From the preceding analysis presented in the case study chapters, two points must be noted about understanding the effects of the six external military crises on change in Japanese post-Cold War security policy. First, it could be argued that the first five crises of the post-Cold War period (1991 Persian Gulf Crisis, 1994 North Korean Nuclear Crisis, 1996 Taiwan Strait Crisis, 1998 Taepodong Crisis and September 11th attacks) had the most significant influence in modifying Japanese post-Cold War security policy. These crises formed the foundation of the incremental Japanese security policy expansion in the post-Cold War period. A MOD official confirmed this point when he answered 'no' to the question of whether there were other critical military crises during the post-2001 period that were important in shaping Japanese security policy. He said that the earlier crises were more important as they shocked Japan and changed Japan's strategy fundamentally (Kano, personal communication, 29 November 2012). However, as the fourth case study chapter shows, the impact of external military crises did not stop in 2001. The post-2001 period saw a series of events surrounding China as being a critical impetus for change in Japanese security policy. Nevertheless, it is arguable that the utility of military crises as an impetus of change weakened over the course of the post-Cold War period. As Japan matures into an engaged and responsible security actor in regional and global affairs, the security policymaking elite relies less on external military crises to implement important security policy initiatives that challenge the peace-based security policy. Furthermore, the worsening of the regional and international security environment around Japan, and the weaker domestic opposition towards an expanded security policy, could make it less necessary for the security policymaking elite to rely on external military crises to pursue a strengthened security policy.

Second, the effects of the crises were uneven. One official from Japan's MOD said that the North Korean Nuclear Crisis and the Taiwan Strait Crisis were the most important crises for Japanese security policy in the post-Cold War period. The reason for this was that Japan was 'unaware of its strategic environment' and these crises made Japanese policymakers realise that the end of the Cold War would mean serious challenges ahead for the country (Kano, personal communication, 29 November 2012). This position was supported by another MOD official who argued that these crises set the stage for the crafting of a new role for the SDF, to defend the country from regional strategic challenges (Kimura, personal communication, 29 November 2012). Nishihara Masashira, a leading security policy expert, noted the importance of the Persian Gulf Crisis and the September 11th attacks on the US, which were probably the most important crises for Japanese post-Cold War security policy. These crises expanded Japan's security role at the global level (Nishihara, personal communication, 14 September 2012).

The analysis introduced an intervening mechanism, known as the threat construction process, which connected the external military crises and Japanese security policy expansion. An important point about the threat construction process, as revealed in the case study chapters, was that this process was not uniform for all crises and/or security policy initiatives. The threat construction process pursued by the security policymaking elite was either simple/direct or a complex process, depending on three conditions. The first condition was whether the threat posed by an external crisis was direct or indirect to Japan's national security. What this refers to is whether the security policymaking elite perceived the threat from the external crisis as a direct 'hit' on Japan's national security. A direct 'hit' perception would usually result in a simple/direct threat construction process and an indirect 'hit', in turn, in a complex process. The second condition was whether there was a consensus on the 'direct' nature of the threat posed by an external crisis on Japan's national security. This refers to a consensus held either by the international community or within Japanese society. However, the domestic consensus was more important than the international consensus for the security policymaking elite. This is because domestic constituents were the main audience for the security policymaking elite's threat construction process, along with being responsible for the legitimisation of the government's measures to expand Japan's security policy. A consensus at the domestic and/or international level(s) would lead to a simple/direct threat construction process and a lack of consensus would lead to a complex process. The final condition refers to the level of controversy related to either the crisis in which the SDF was considering participation, or the desired security policy initiative pursued by the security policymaking elite. For non-controversial missions and policy initiatives, the threat construction process is simple/direct, as opposed to the complex process for controversial missions and initiatives.

Based on the above-mentioned conditions, the 1994 North Korean Nuclear Crisis and the 1998 Taepodong Crisis had simple/direct threat construction processes. The threat from North Korea was perceived as direct and there was international (for the 1994 crisis only) and domestic consensus (for both crises) that North Korea was a serious threat to Japan's national security; hence, Japan had to implement measures to protect itself. An official from the MOD has said that when North Korea is involved, Japanese people become united in deterring the threat (Kurauchi, personal communication, 21 November 2012). For the 1991 Persian Gulf Crisis and 1996 Taiwan Strait Crisis, the threat construction process was complex. Both crises were not perceived as direct hits to Japan's national security. Even though there was an international consensus on the threat posed by Iraq's invasion of Kuwait, there was no domestic consensus in Japan about this threat, which prevented Japan from offering a 'human contribution' to the resolution of the crisis. There was no domestic consensus on the threatening nature of the Taiwan Strait Crisis on Japan's national security. Moreover, the security policy initiatives pursued by the policymaking elite related to these crises – international peacekeeping and incorporating regional defence for the SDF into the US–Japan alliance – were seen as controversial.

The September 11th attacks and China-related crises comprised both simple/direct and complex threat construction processes. To deploy the SDF to the OEF, the threat construction process was simple: the September 11th attacks were perceived as a direct hit on Japan, there was both international and domestic consensus on the level of threat posed by international terrorism, and the policy initiative in deploying the SDF to the Indian Ocean was not controversial. However, the deployment of the SDF to the OIF produced a complex threat construction process, as there was no international and domestic consensus on the threat posed by Iraq and the SDF's deployment to Iraq was perceived as controversial. In incorporating collective self-defence missions into the new guidelines signed in 2015, the security policymaking elite only required a simple threat construction process, as both the US and Japan perceived China's maritime assertiveness as a direct threat to Japan's national security and neither viewed the policy initiative as controversial. However, Abe and his government adopted a complex process when the security bills to authorise collective self-defence missions for the SDF were debated in the National Diet. At the National Diet, lifting the collective self-defence ban was clearly perceived as controversial and resulted in widespread opposition from both political parties and groups within Japanese society.

IMPLICATIONS FOR JAPANESE SECURITY POLICY PRACTICE

The argument of the book showed that an external impetus continues to be a critical explanation of change in Japanese post-Cold War security policy. To add to the range of external factors discussed in the extant literature, such as international and regional balance of power considerations, US pressure, and a range of crises such as natural disasters and economic crisis, this book adds external military crisis to the debate. To be sure, the argument does not discount the impact of domestic factors on influencing the outcome of Japan's security policy. In fact, Japan has displayed a greater sense of agency in the formation of its security objectives, interests and policy and has become less susceptible to pressure from external factors over the post-Cold War period. This occurred especially with the increasing dominance of the revisionist strand of normal nationalist politicians in the Japanese political systems and bureaucracy, along with the weakening of the political power of politicians who prefer a limited peace-based security policy. Moreover, the administrative and institutional reforms of the mid-1990s led to the centralisation of power over the security policymaking process within politicians (see Singh 2016). Despite this strengthened agency, the presence of social and legal constraints and society's weak support for Japan's security policy expansion continue to steer the security policymaking elite to rely on an external impetus, such as an external military crisis, to bring about security policy change.

Japan's security policy expansion has been evolutionary throughout the post-Cold War period. This was a product of the tensions that exist between the security policymaking elite's push for security policy expansion and the caution expressed by various domestic actors towards promoting an activist security policy on the grounds that Japan could be entrapped in military situations not directly related to its national security. However, it is important to note that this evolutionary approach has turned out to be positive for the security policymaking elite. The 'salami slicing' approach has led to some weakening of social and legal constraints and to a greater acceptance by Japanese society of an expanded role for the SDF both at home and abroad.

In response to a series of regional and global security challenges, the SDF has carved out a responsible role in terms of contributing to collective security efforts in new and diverse ways. The SDF's mandate has expanded to include activities such as minesweeping, humanitarian and disaster relief (HADR) activities, peacekeeping, anti-piracy patrols and ship inspections for anti-proliferation efforts. In fact, the SDF has gradually become bolder as it has participated in regional and international efforts that border on collective self-defence efforts (such as in the OEF mission and in the context of the BMD deployment) without a proper legal framework and even while the conflict was still underway (OIF). The SDF also strengthened its role within the US–Japan security alliance, especially in implementing measures to institutionalise collective responses to regional and international security challenges. The bilateral defence cooperation reveals a stronger convergence of strategic interests and strengthened interoperability between the militaries of the US and Japan. The lifting of the collective self-defence ban was an important milestone that further elevated the US–Japan security alliance. It added new situations in which the SDF could assist and even use force to protect the US military. These new roles and missions represent a clear break from Cold War practice and have become a permanent feature of the SDF's mandate and Japan's post-Cold War security policy.

Yet, it is important to note that the development in Japan's security policy in terms of security roles, scope and function in regional and global security affairs has occurred within limits. This is true for all the security policy initiatives discussed in the case study chapters. The reason for this is that the pacifist-based normative framework – which is made up of domestic social and legal constraints and supported by several opposition parties, civil society and NGO groups as well as a large segment of Japanese society – continues to influence security policy debates in the post-Cold War period. Even though the constraints have been renegotiated over the post-Cold War period (see Gustafsson et al. 2018), the security policymaking elite is still forced to address these constraints in formalising new security policies. The outcome is a negotiated policy that is attached with limits on the accepted roles for Japan's involvement in external security affairs. As long as Japan retains Article 9, which is the source of pacifism and limitations to security policy initiatives, it is arguable that it will never be able to exercise a 'normal' security policy like other states.

Hence, it is important to distance the security policy expansion from Japan's return to its militarist past of the 1930s. Such talk regularly appears when there is an announcement by any conservative Japanese government of a new security policy initiative that expands the SDF's role overseas. The more controversial the proposed security policy, the louder the allegations from opponents within and outside Japan that the conservative Japanese government is leading Japan to cause instability in the region, as it did in the past. Following the disastrous experience in World War Two, the US and Japanese postwar governments worked hard to institutionalise the idea of peace and pacifism into Japanese state and society. This approach was very successful, as it facilitated Japan's return to the international community; Japan achieved stunning economic growth and earned goodwill from the rest of the world. This collective idea of 'peace' remains strong within Japanese state and society in the post-Cold War period, even though Japan is facing an escalating intensity of strategic challenges around its neighbourhood. However, the means of achieving peace have changed. While the security policymaking elite relied on economic and soft power measures during the Cold War period, it added security measures to achieve and contribute to peace. The more Japan contributes to keeping the peace in the regional and global security environment, the less likely Japan will return to its militaristic past. Japan's integration into the regional and international security environment would be the best bulwark against the emergence of pre-war nationalistic values within Japan.

The US–Japan alliance remains a pillar of Japanese post-Cold War security policy. In explaining security policy expansion in the book, three out of the four case studies (regional defence, global defence and collective self-defence) were developments within the US–Japan alliance – underscoring the continued importance of the US in Japanese post-Cold War security policy. All post-Cold War Japanese governments, whether led by the LDP or the opposition parties, recognised the importance of the US being a guarantor for Japan's national security against conventional and nuclear threats. These governments have not only supported but strengthened the mutual agreement that ensures the US continues to provide for Japan's security in exchange for hosting American military bases (Tokuchi, personal communication, 14 September 2005; Yanai, personal communication, 24 May 2006). Despite the presence of numerous bilateral political, economic, security and social difficulties, the US–Japan security relationship was revised and reaffirmed in response to the demands of the new security challenges of the post-Cold War period. The significant change has come in Japan's roles, missions, capabilities and geographical scope within the Japan–US security relationship (A. Tanaka, personal communication, 6 September 2005). The changes to Japan's contribution to the alliance were crucial in addressing the asymmetry in the alliance between the American and Japanese militaries through building strategic and tactical cooperation in terms of tightened interoperability and strengthening deterrence effect against the rising uncertainty in Japan's neighbourhood, namely with reference to North Korea's and China's behaviour.

It is important to note here that support for the strengthening of the US–Japan alliance emerged internally due to the needs of Japan's national security and is not due to American pressure. The notion that Japan is 'free-riding' on the US or pursuing a buck-passing strategy in relation to the US security guarantee in the same way as in the Cold War period (see Lind 2004) is less applicable to Japan's role in the US–Japan alliance during the post-Cold War period. This is evident in the gradual expansion of Japan's security roles and contribution to the alliance through the security agreements signed by the two countries since 1996, as outlined in Chapters 4, 5 and 6. Hughes had warned that the strengthening of the US–Japan security relationship since the 2000s worsened the entrapment concerns for Japan, resulting in limited flexibility for Japan within the alliance – referred to as 'resentful realism' (Hughes 2016).[1] There is no doubt that the US–Japan security alliance remains a critical pillar of Japanese security policy as a source of protection of Japan's national security against regional and global challenges. However, Tokyo has always and will continue to exercise agency to ensure that Japan does not run out of options for its national security. Japan's diversification of security partners outside of the US–Japan alliance, including Australia, India and several other states and institutions, is an example of maintaining this flexibility (see Mukherjee 2018; Samuels and Wallace 2018; Satake and Hemmings 2018). A recent illustration of Japan's agency within the US–Japan alliance was Japan's refusal to engage in a US-led collective military effort in the Strait of Hormuz in 2019. Instead, Japan deployed a destroyer and surveillance aircraft to the international waters off Oman and Yemen for an 'investigation and research' mission.

JAPAN AND US–CHINA COMPETITION

The most important structural factor shaping contemporary regional and global strategic affairs, including Japanese security policy, is the intensifying US–China competition being played out in various areas such as technology, economics and strategy. This is an outcome of the changing structural balance of power due to the perceived waning of American power and leadership and China's strategic rise. Though the competition has existed from 2010, it peaked when the Trump administration took office in 2016. In fact, rather than just a Trump administration policy, the tough approach against China is now widely understood as having bipartisan support in American domestic politics (Zakaria 2020). If this rivalry is not managed well, a new Cold War will become inevitable. This evolving tense US–China relationship undoubtedly affects the security policies of all states, including Japan. The question is how Japan is responding to this evolving structural shift. This is important because of Japan's special position as the most important ally of the US in East Asia, and because it remains a close neighbour of China with deep economic interdependence. More importantly, for Japan, this competition raises questions about the sustainability of the US-led order in East Asia and the implications of East Asia being defined by a China-led order on Japan's national security.

In Japan, the Japanese government and academics are already thinking in binary terms – US-led order and Chinese-led order (Akita, personal communication, 16 January 2018; Michishita, personal communication, 16 January 2018).[2] Experts in Japan argue that China is dissatisfied with the current US-led order and is looking to rewrite the rules and norms of this order (Mori, personal communication, 18 January 2018; Yuzawa, personal communication, 17 January 2018). China has its own vision of regional order that is defined by a hierarchical system (similar to its internal order) and would like to replace the alliance network with a partnership system (Funabashi, personal communication, 18 January 2018; Mori, personal communication, 18 January 2018). Tokyo views these objectives as part of Beijing's long-term strategy to become one of the greatest powers in the world, as announced at the 19th Party Congress (*China Daily*, 4 November 2017). For experts in Japan, China has started creating a sphere of influence over Southeast Asia, and its actions have led many to conclude that China is changing the facts on the ground in the South China Sea. After Southeast Asia, it is believed that China will expand its influence over Northeast Asia (Funabashi, personal communication, 18 January 2018; Mori, personal communication, 18 January 2018). This expansion will be a gradual process, but the end goal is clear: that is, to form a regional tributary architecture based on the hierarchical system (Akita, personal communication, 16 January 2018).

However, experts in Japan note that China is aware that its preferred order will not be realised soon. China will therefore support the US-led liberal order for now, as it has and will continue to benefit from it (Funabashi, personal communication, 18 January 2018; Tokuchi, personal communication, 17 January 2018). In fact, China is showing a willingness to strengthen the existing order by addressing the extant weaknesses. Experts in Japan also note that Chinese initiatives do not have the capability to change the order, as it does not possess the power and influence of the US (Sahashi, personal communication, 16 January 2018; Tokuchi, personal communication, 17 January 2018).

At the same time, Tokyo is also worried about how the policies of the Trump administration are contributing to the weakening of the US-led order in East Asia. The Trump administration does not seem to have a coherent Asia strategy and this is forcing states to choose between the US and China (Sahashi, personal communication, 16 January 2018). Japanese policymakers are concerned about America's actions, which could suggest the weakening of its leadership role in East Asia and beyond. The withdrawal of the US from the Trans-Pacific Partnership (TPP) free trade agreement signed between twelve countries bordering the Pacific Ocean was a worrying development for Japan (Michishita, personal communication, 16 January 2018).[3] Also, Trump's 'America first' policy, which is an underlying driving principle in strengthening homeland defence and correcting unfair trade arrangements that America has with other states, is another point of concern for Japan (Mori, personal communication, 18 January 2018). Tokuchi, former Vice Minister for Defense (International Affairs), said in 2018 that although the US security system would remain robust, the Trump administration's policies weakened the soft power of the US. Trump's approach is arguably beneficial in the short run, but, Tokuchi added, it is not clear whether that will be the case in the long run (Tokuchi, personal communication, 17 January 2018).

In response to the US–China strategic rivalry, the present Abe government has adopted a flexible approach that allows Japan to be adaptive in achieving its national interests through the implementation of a range of internal and external policies.

Internally, the Abe government has taken bold steps in challenging the sacred restrictions that limited Japan to maintaining a minimum level of force necessary to protect itself against the 'severe' strategic environment it faces. To strengthen its military capability so that Japan is militarily prepared, the Abe government approved the conversion of its largest warship, the helicopter carrier JS *Izumo*, into an aircraft carrier that would have the capacity to carry F-35B fighter jets (Gady 2018). This not only strengthens Japan's ability against China's maritime assertiveness but also has the potential for the MSDF to project power beyond its territory. Abe has pushed to legitimise the status of the SDF in Japanese state and society as part of his drive to revise the postwar regime. Instead of revising Article 9, Abe resorted to adding a third paragraph into Article 9 that legitimises the existence of the SDF, while keeping the first two original paragraphs unchanged. Though the support for this change to Article 9 is mixed,[4] Abe is expected to continue his efforts to achieve this historical change in the remaining time of his term as prime minister.

Externally, Japan has pursued actions to reinforce its interests in the context of the US–China competition. There is a general consensus that Japan should work towards preserving the current liberal international order, along with the values and principles that sustain it (Akita, personal communication, 16 January 2018; Funabashi, personal communication, 18 January 2018; Michishita, personal communication, 16 January 2018; Mori, personal communication, 18 January 2018; Yuzawa, personal communication, 17 January 2018). Amid the uncertainty related to US leadership in East Asia, the Abe government is clear that Japan has to strengthen the US–Japan alliance through expanding its role within the alliance, and this would be a critical deterrent against regional challenges (Akita, personal communication, 16 January 2018; Michishita, personal communication, 16 January 2018; Tokuchi, personal communication, 17 January 2018). At the same time, Japan has had to step up as a leader in preserving the US-led order (Funabashi, personal communication, 18 January 2018). This was particularly visible in Japan's quick response towards the negative policies of the Trump administration regarding multilateralism and international trade agreements. When the Trump administration withdrew the US from the TPP, Abe-led Japan assumed leadership that was crucial in the eventual realisation of the TPP without the US (known as the Comprehensive and Progressive Agreement for the Trans-Pacific Partnership, or CPTPP). In fact, Japan has vigorously pushed forward the free trade agenda by signing the Japan–EU Economic Partnership Agreement (EPA) and has expressed strong support for the completion of the Regional Comprehensive Economic Partnership (RCEP).

Japan has also shown leadership in developing a new strategy or vision to formulate its security policy in response to stiffening US–China competition and China's strategic rise. This is known as the 'free and open Indo-Pacific' (FOIP) vision/concept. Though the details of FOIP are evolving, one could argue that this is Japan's first attempt to devise a grand strategy since the Yoshida Doctrine, which defined principles of Japan's postwar security policy that remained relevant until today.[5] Abe first introduced the Indo-Pacific vision/concept in 2007 during an address to the Indian Parliament entitled 'Confluence of the Two Seas'. He explained how the Indian and Pacific Oceans could be understood as one strategic space where there is strengthened connectivity between Asia and Africa (Abe 2007). Due to Abe's short stint as prime minister, this vision/concept failed to make an impact on Japanese security policy. However, Abe's return to power in 2012 saw not only a revival of this vision/concept, but its growing dominance of Japan's foreign and security policy discussions. It is arguable that FOIP has become one of the main defining features of Japanese security policy practice, along with the US–Japan alliance, in the contemporary period.

According to Japanese official documents, the main objective of FOIP is to promote Japan's proactive contribution to peace based on the principle of international cooperation. Three main areas are highlighted for Japan to achieve this objective. They are (a) the promotion and establishment of the rule of law, freedom of navigation and free trade; (b) the pursuit of economic prosperity through improved connectivity; and (c) a commitment to peace and stability through measures such as capacity building on maritime law enforcement and contributing to HADR operations, among several other means (MOFA Japan 2019).

However, it is important to underscore the strategic dimension of FOIP as well, especially in order to understand Japan's strategy towards addressing the challenges from the evolving US–China competition and China's strategic rise. The use of the Indo-Pacific allows Japan to achieve two major strategic objectives. The first, and probably the more important of the two, is to keep the US engaged in the region. The Trump administration's endorsement and incorporation of FOIP for America's security policy strategy was a landmark strategic development for Japan. Trump first announced America's support of the Indo-Pacific strategy and vision at the Asia-Pacific Economic Cooperation (APEC) Summit in Vietnam in November 2017 (White House 2017a). In December 2017, the US announced a National Security Strategy that formalised America's support and application of the FOIP to America's foreign policy (White House 2017b). This was followed by the renaming of the 'Pacific Command' as the 'Indo-Pacific Command', underscoring the importance of both allies and partners of the US in the Pacific and Indian Oceans in maintaining the stability of 'broader Asia' (*Straits Times*, 20 October 2018). FOIP has become a means for the US to remain engaged in the region and continue to provide for regional stability. It is also a centrepiece of the US–Japan alliance and a source of stronger bilateral security cooperation between both states to address the key challenges of the twenty-first century (US Embassy and Consulates in Japan 2020).

Second, the use of FOIP legitimates Tokyo's increasing reliance on other actors, namely Australia and India, to address Japan's concerns related to China's strategic rise and promote a collective effort to preserve the US-led order. The introduction of FOIP led to Japan's push for the revival of the Quadrilateral Security Dialogue (QSD), a collective made up of the US, Japan, India and Australia that was first initiated by Prime Minister Abe in 2007. This minilateral made up of four like-minded democracies (referred to as Asia's democratic security diamond) was understood by Abe as an important bulwark to guard the maritime commons of the Indian and Pacific Oceans against China's strategic rise and serve as a conduit to boost America's strategic presence in the region (Abe 2012).

Though Abe and his government have boldly expressed their concerns about China and taken the range of internal and external measures discussed above, Japan under Prime Minister Abe (and this will also be true for the post-Abe governments) is still cognisant of the importance of cultivating a stable bilateral relationship with its neighbour (Smith 2020). This is unlike the Trump administration's policy, which views its bilateral relationship through a zero-sum lens (White House 2017b). The quick deterioration of Sino-Japanese relations during the 2010–13 period was arrested in 2014 when the two leaders met for a landmark meeting in Beijing. Japan and China agreed to a non-binding four-point consensus on relations including practical measures to mitigate tensions at sea. One of these measures was starting bilateral negotiations on formulating a crisis management mechanism that included a hotline between the two states. In November 2017, Abe met Xi on the sidelines of the APEC summit and both leaders agreed to make a 'fresh start' to the bilateral relationship (*Japan Times*, 6 December 2017). It was in this context that Japan and China agreed to officially implement a maritime and aerial communication mechanism (officially launched in 2018) that would avert unintended clashes in and above the East China Sea through diplomatic means. The Abe government also reversed its opposition to engage in China-led initiatives such as the Asian Infrastructure and Investment Bank and the Belt and Road Initiative. Tokyo argued that it was only through participation in these initiatives that it would be able to push reforms from within, ensure quality and transparency in the processes and gain access to capital for infrastructure building to allow Japanese businesses to take advantage of the opportunities (Mori, personal communication, 18 January 2018). The momentum of strengthening Sino-Japanese relations has continued even at the height of US–China tensions. Abe and Xi met in Beijing in December 2019, and Xi was scheduled to make his first state visit to Japan in 2020.

As we move into the 2020s and Japan enters the new imperial era named *Reiwa* (following the accession of Crown Prince Naruhito to the Emperor throne on 1 May 2019), Japan's strategic environment is expected to become even more challenging as a result of growing US–China competition and the escalating seriousness of China's strategic rise to Japanese national security. Though strengthening strategic cooperation with both the US and China will continue to be an important part of Japan's strategy, Japan will also boost bilateral and multilateral cooperation with partners outside of the US–Japan alliance – a strategy known as 'diversified dual hedge' – to deal with the two structural challenges (Wallace 2013). Although this process of diversifying strategic partners started under the DPJ government, it picked up speed under the Abe government, especially in response to intensifying US–China tensions. Two key strategic partners and stakeholders of regional stability for Japan have been Australia and India. With both of these nations Japan has signed joint security declarations and even action plans to advance security cooperation through a range of measures, such as regular ministerial meetings including the 'Two-plus-Two Meeting', the exchange of personnel from the militaries and other security-related agencies, and joint exercises. This diversification strategy revealed the adaptable nature of Japan's security policy practice – an inherent feature of Japan's foreign and security policy since its response to the Sinocentric Order (see Pyle 2007). Despite a range of domestic challenges such as an ageing population, a shrinking population and fiscal deficits, it is arguable that Japan has successfully adapted to the evolving regional and international security environment defined by ongoing US–China competition and China's strategic rise. This strategy allows Japan to gain strategic autonomy in light of worsening US–China competition without raising any opposition from the US or suspicion from China, and yet emerge as a reliable and credible strategic actor.

NOTES

1. For abandonment/entrapment concerns of Japan in relation to the US–Japan alliance, see Izumikawa (2010).
2. The discussion on Japan's view of the impact of the US–China competition on the East Asian order is adapted from Singh et al. (2019: 29–31).

3. The TPP was signed in February 2016 between the US, Japan, Malaysia, Vietnam, Singapore, Brunei, Australia, New Zealand, Canada, Mexico, Chile and Peru.
4. Media polls show that a majority of voters believe that the SDF's existence is constitutional. In a 2017 Kyodo News poll, 56 per cent of respondents supported the legitimate status of the SDF in Article 9. However, when asked whether they supported revising the constitution under the Abe government, the voters were split – 44.5 per cent in support and 43.4 per cent against (*Japan Times*, 21 May 2017).
5. The Yoshida Doctrine, named after Prime Minister Yoshida Shigeru, is defined by the following three features: the concentration of national energies on economic development; the maintenance of a limited defence capability; and reliance on the US for Japan's national security (see Pyle 1987). Due to space constraints, the characterisation of FOIP as a grand strategy will be elaborated in more detail in future research.

BIBLIOGRAPHY

Abe, S. (2006), *Utsukushii kuni e* [*Toward a Beautiful Country*], Tokyo: Bungei Shunju.

Abe, S. (2007), 'Confluence of the two seas', *Ministry of Foreign Affairs of Japan*, 22 August, <https://www.mofa.go.jp/region/asia-paci/pmv0708/speech-2.html> (last accessed 13 December 2019).

Abe, S. (2012), 'Asia's democratic security diamond', *Project Syndicate*, 31 December, <https://www.project-syndicate.org/onpoint/a-strategic-alliance-for-japan-and-india-by-shinzo-abe> (last accessed 27 January 2020).

Abe, S. (2013), 'Japan is back', *Ministry of Foreign Affairs of Japan*, 22 February, <http://www.mofa.go.jp/announce/pm/abe/us_20130222en.html> (last accessed 24 November 2019).

Abe, S. (2014), 'The 13th IISS Asian Security Summit – The Shangri-La Dialogue keynote address', *Ministry of Foreign Affairs of Japan*, 30 May, <https://www.mofa.go.jp/fp/nsp/page4e_000086.html> (last accessed 30 November 2019).

Agamben, G. [2003] (2005), *State of Exception*, trans. K. Attell, Chicago: The University of Chicago Press.

Aibara, R. (2018), 'Abe government called two-faced over threats to Japan's survival', *Asahi Shimbun*, 26 February, Factiva database (last accessed 12 December 2019).

Akaha, T. (1998), 'Beyond self-defense: Japan's elusive security role under the new guidelines for US–Japan defense cooperation', *The Pacific Review*, 11:4, 461–83.

Aoki, N. (1999), 'Diet panel approves Japan–US defense bills', *Kyodo News*, 26 April.

Armacost, M. H. (1996), *Friends or Rivals? The Insider's Account of US–Japan Relations*, New York: Columbia University Press.

Armacost, M. H. and K. B. Pyle (2001), 'Japan and engagement of China: challenges for US policy coordination', *NBR Analysis*, 12:5, 5–62.

Armitage, R. L. and J. S. Nye (2012), 'The US–Japan alliance: anchoring stability in Asia', *A Report of the CSIS Japan Chair*, August, <https://csis-prod

.s3.amazonaws.com/s3fs-public/legacy_files/files/publication/120810_
Armitage_USJapanAlliance_Web.pdf> (last accessed 12 December 2019).

Asahi Shinbun (2006), 'Japan's new blue water navy: a four-year Indian Ocean mission recasts the constitution and the US–Japan alliance', *Japan Focus*, 4:1, trans E. Osaki and M. Penn, <https://apjjf.org/-The-Asahi-Shimbun-Culture-Research-Center-/1812/article.html> (last accessed 12 December 2019).

Austin, G. and S. Harris (2001), *Japan and Greater China: Political Economy and Military Power in the Asian Century*, Honolulu: University of Hawaii Press.

Baerwald, H. H. (1977), 'The Diet and foreign policy', in R. A. Scalapino (ed.), *The Foreign Policy of Modern Japan*, Berkeley: University of California Press, 37–54.

Bennett, A., J. Lepgold and D. Unger (1994), 'Burden-sharing in the Persian Gulf war', *International Organization*, 48:1, 39–75.

Berger, T. U. (1996), 'Norms, identity, and national security in Germany and Japan', in P. J. Katzenstein (ed.), *The Culture of National Security: Norms and Identity in World Politics*, New York: Columbia University Press, 317–56.

Berger, T. U. (1998), *Cultures of Antimilitarism: National Security in Germany and Japan*, Baltimore: Johns Hopkins University Press.

'Beyond Abenomics: Japan's grand strategy' (2013), *Strategic Comments*, 19:4, v–vi.

Blaker, M. (1993), 'Evaluating Japan's diplomatic performance', in G. L. Curtis (ed.), *Japan's Foreign Policy after the Cold War: Coping with Change*, Armonk, NY: M. E. Sharpe, 1–42.

Blustein, P. (1991), 'In Japan, the politics of hesitation', *Washington Post*, 17 February, C2.

Boin, A. (2004), 'Lessons from crisis research', *International Studies Review*, 6:1, 165–74.

Boyd, J. P. and R. J. Samuels (2005), 'Nine lives?: The politics of constitutional reform in Japan', *Policy Studies*, 19, Washington, DC: East–West Center.

Brecher, M. (1977), 'Toward a theory of international crisis behavior: a preliminary report', *International Studies Quarterly*, 21:1, 39–74.

Brecher, M. and F. P. Harvey (1998), 'Conflict, crisis and war: cumulation, criticism, rejoinder', in F. P. Harvey and B. D. Mor (eds), *Conflict in World Politics: Advances in the Study of Crisis, War and Peace*, New York: St Martin's Press, 3–29.

Brecher, M. and J. Wilkenfeld (2000), *A Study of Crisis*, Ann Arbor: University of Michigan Press.

Brown, E. (1991), 'Contending paradigms of Japan's international role: elite views of the Persian Gulf crisis', *Journal Of Northeast Asian Studies*, 10:1, 3–18.

Bukh, A. (2015), 'Shimane Prefecture, Tokyo and the territorial dispute over Dokdo/Takeshima: regional and national identities in Japan', *The Pacific Review*, 28:1, 47–70.

Burton, J. (1994), 'South Korea steps up state of readiness', *Financial Times*, 7 June, 4.

Burton, J. and G. Graham (1994), 'S Korean forces go on alert as N-plant row with North grows', *Financial Times*, 23 March, 24.

Cabinet Office, Secretariat of the International Peace Cooperation Headquarters (n.d. (a)), 'International peace cooperation assignments', <http://www.pko.go.jp/pko_e/operations/pko.html> (last accessed 7 December 2019).

Cabinet Office, Secretariat of the International Peace Cooperation Headquarters (n.d. (b)), 'International humanitarian relief operations', <http://www.pko.go.jp/pko_e/operations/human.html> (last accessed 7 December 2019).

Calder, K. E. (1988a), *Crisis and Compensation: Public Policy and Political Stability in Japan, 1949–1986*, Princeton: Princeton University Press.

Calder, K. E. (1988b), 'Japanese foreign economic policy formation: explaining the reactive state', *World Politics*, 40:4, 517–41.

Calder, K. E. (1991), 'Japan in 1990: limits to change', *Asian Survey*, 31:1, 21–35.

Calder, K. E. (1992), 'Japan in 1991: uncertain quest for a global role', *Asian Survey*, 32:1, 32–41.

Calder, K. E. (2009), *Pacific Alliance: Reviving US–Japan Relations*, New Haven: Yale University Press.

Calder, K. E. and M. Ye (2010), *The Making of Northeast Asia*, Stanford: Stanford University Press.

Campbell, D. (1998), *Writing Security: United States Foreign Policy and the Politics of Identity*, Minneapolis: University of Minnesota Press.

Campbell, J. C. (1989), 'Democracy and bureaucracy in Japan', in T. Ishida and E. S. Krauss (eds), *Democracy in Japan*, Pittsburgh: University of Pittsburgh Press, 113–37.

Capoccia, G. and R. D. Kelemen (2007), 'The study of critical junctures: theory, narrative, and counterfactuals in historical institutionalism', *World Politics*, 59: 3, 341–69.

Castellano, M. (1999), 'China and Taiwan overshadows ASEAN Regional Forum meeting', *JEI Report*, 9, 30 July, <http://www.jei.org/Archive/JEIR99/9929w3.html> (last accessed 30 May 1999).

Catalinac, A. (2016), *Electoral Reform and National Security in Japan: From Pork to Foreign Policy*, Cambridge: Cambridge University Press.

Center for Nonproliferation Studies (n.d.), 'Overview of North Korea's ballistic missile program', *Monterey Institute of International Studies*, <http://cns.miis.edu/research/korea/overview.htm> (last accessed 6 August 2006).

Checkel, J. T. (2005), 'International institutions and socialization in Europe: introduction and framework', *International Organization*, 59:4, 801–26.

Choe, S. H. (1998), 'N. Korea missile capability condemned', *Associated Press*, 5 September, <http://www.nautilus.org/archives/napsnet/dr/9809/SEP04.html> (last accessed 25 May 2005).

Collier, D. (2011), 'Understanding process tracing', *PS: Political Science and Politics*, 44:4, 823–30.

Cronin, P. M., P. S. Giarra and M. J. Green (1999), 'The alliance implications of theater missile defense', in M. J. Green and P. M. Cronin (eds), *The US–Japan Alliance: Past, Present, and Future*, New York: Council on Foreign Relations Press, 170–88.

Cronin, R. P. (1994), 'North Korea's nuclear weapons program: US policy options', *Congressional Research Service Report*, 1 June, <http://www.fas.org/spp/starwars/crs/94-470f.htm#constraints> (last accessed 17 June 2006).

Dayton, B. W. (ed.) (2004), 'Managing crises in the twenty-first century', *International Studies Review*, 6:1, 165–94.

de Koning, P. and P. Y. Lipscy (2013), 'The land of the sinking sun', *Foreign Policy*, 30 July, <https://foreignpolicy.com/2013/07/30/the-land-of-the-sinking-sun> (last accessed 12 December 2019).

Deming, R. (2004), 'Japan's constitution and defense policy: entering a new era?', *Strategic Forum*, 213, Washington, DC: Institute for National Strategic Studies, National Defense University.

DiFilippo, A. (2002), *The Challenges of the US–Japan Military Arrangement: Competing Security Transitions in a Changing International Environment*, Armonk, NY: M. E. Sharpe.

Dobson, H. (2003), *Japan and United Nations Peacekeeping: New Pressures, New Responses*, London: RoutledgeCurzon.

Dowty, A. (1984), *Middle East Crisis: US Decision-Making in 1958, 1970, and 1973*, Berkeley: University of California Press.

Drifte, R. (1996), *Japan's Foreign Policy in the 1990s: From Economic Superpower to What Power?*, Basingstoke: Macmillan Press.

Drifte, R. (2013), 'The Senkaku/Diaoyu Islands territorial dispute between Japan and China: between the materialization of the "China threat" and Japan "reversing the outcome of World War II"?', *UNISCI Discussion Papers*, 32.

Edelman, M. (1988), *Constructing the Political Spectacle*, Chicago: The University of Chicago Press.

Emerson, T. and H. Takayama (1998), 'Pyongyang's test paces the rogue missile powers', *Newsweek*, 14 September, 44.

Estéves-Abe, M. (2014), 'Feeling triumphalist in Tokyo', *Foreign Affairs*, 93:3, 165–71.

Fackler, M. (2013), 'Secrecy bill could distance Japan from its postwar pacifism', *New York Times*, 28 November, <https://www.nytimes.com/2013/11/29/world/asia/secrecy-bill-could-distance-japan-from-its-postwar-pacifism.html> (last accessed 12 December 2019).

Federation of American Scientists (n.d.), 'Response of the Defence Agency to the missile launch by North Korea', <http://www.fas.org/nuke/guide/dprk/td-1-japan99.htm> (last accessed 24 May 2005).

Finnegan, M. (2009), 'Managing unmet expectations in the US–Japan alliance', *NBR Special Report*, 17, <https://www.nbr.org/publication/managing-unmet-expectations-in-the-u-s-japan-alliance> (last accessed 17 December 2019).

Fujishige, A. (2016), 'New Japan Self-Defense Force missions under the "proactive contribution to peace" policy: significance of the 2015 legislation for peace and security', *Center for Strategic and International Studies*, 21 July, <https://www.csis.org/analysis/new-japan-self-defense-force-missions-under-%E2%80%9Cproactive-contribution-peace%E2%80%9D-policy> (last accessed 7 December 2019).

Fukumoto, T. (2015), 'Right of collective self-defense protects Japan', *The Japan News*, 6 August, 5.

Fukui, H. (1977), 'Policy-making in the Japanese foreign ministry', in R. A. Scalapino (ed.), *The Foreign Policy of Modern Japan*, Berkeley: University of California Press, 3–35.

Fukui, Y. and S. Miwa (2015), 'Japan to reinforce SDF anti-piracy base in Djibouti for broader Middle East responses', *Asahi Shimbun*, 19 January, <http://ajw.asahi.com/article/behind_news/politics/AJ201501190036> (last accessed 20 January 2015).

Fukushima, A. (1999), *Japanese Foreign Policy: The Emerging Logic of Multilateralism*, Basingstoke: Macmillan Press.

Funabashi, Y. (1991), 'Japan and the new world order', *Foreign Affairs*, 70:5, 58–74.

Funabashi, Y. (1999), *Alliance Adrift*, New York: Council on Foreign Relations Press.

Gady, F. S. (2018), 'Japan to convert *Izumo*-class into F-35-carrying aircraft carrier', *The Diplomat*, 12 December, <https://thediplomat.com/2018/12/japan-to-convert-izumo-class-into-f-35-carrying-aircraft-carrier> (last accessed 23 December 2019).

George, A. (1993), 'Japan's participation in UN peacekeeping operations: radical departure or predictable response?', *Asian Survey*, 33:6, 560–75.

George, A. L. and A. Bennett (2005), *Case Studies and Theory Development in the Social Sciences*, Cambridge, MA: MIT Press.

Gilson, J. (2007), 'Building peace or following the leader? Japan's peace consolidation diplomacy', *Pacific Affairs*, 80:1, 27–47.

Glosserman, B. (2014), 'Japan and collective self-defense: less than meets the eye', *PacNet*, 49, 2 July.

Gordon, M. R. (1994), 'US is bolstering forces in Korea', *New York Times*, 27 March, 9.

Gourevitch, P. (1986), *Politics in Hard Times: Comparative Responses to International Economic Crises*, London: Cornell University Press.

Green, M. J. (1998), 'State of the field report: research on Japanese security policy', *AccessAsia Review*, 2:1.

Green, M. J. (2000), 'The forgotten player', *National Interest*, 60, 42–9.

Green, M. J. (2001), *Japan's Reluctant Realism: Foreign Policy Challenges in an Era of Uncertain Power*, New York: Palgrave.

Green, M. J. and J. Hornung (2014), 'Ten myths about Japan's collective self-defense change', *The Diplomat*, 10 July, <https://thediplomat.com/2014/07/ten-myths-about-japans-collective-self-defense-change> (last accessed 12 December 2014).

Green, M. J. and B. L. Self (1996), 'Japan's changing China policy: from commercial liberalism to reluctant realism', *Survival*, 38:2, 35–58.

Greenhouse, S. (1994), 'South Korean cautious on sanctions', *New York Times*, 12 February, 3.

Grimes, W. W. (2003), 'Institutionalized inertia: Japanese foreign policy in the post-cold war', in G. J. Ikenberry and M. Mastanduno (eds), *International Relations Theory and the Asia-Pacific*, New York: Columbia University Press, 353–85.

Grønning, B. E. M. (2014), 'Japan's shifting military priorities: counterbalancing China's rise', *Asian Security*, 10:1, 1–21.

Gustafsson, K., L. Hagström and U. Hanssen (2018), 'Japan's pacifism is dead', *Survival*, 60:6, 137–58.

Gustavsson, J. (1999), 'How should we study foreign policy change?', *Cooperation and Conflict*, 34:1, 73–95.

Haferkamp, H. and N. J. Smelser (1992), 'Introduction', in H. Haferkamp and N. J. Smelser (eds), *Social Change and Modernity*, Berkeley: University of California Press, 1–33.

Hagström, L. (2012), '"Power shift" in East Asia? A critical reappraisal of narratives on the Diaoyu/Senkaku Islands incident in 2010', *The Chinese Journal of International Politics*, 5:3, 267–97.

Hagström, L. and K. Gustafsson (2015), 'Japan and identity change: why it matters in International Relations', *The Pacific Review*, 28:1, 1–22.

Hagström, L. and U. Hanssen (2015), 'The North Korean abduction issue: emotions, securitisation and the reconstruction of Japanese identity from "aggressor" to "victim" and from "pacifist" to "normal"', *The Pacific Review*, 28:1, 71–93.

Harner, S. (2013), 'Abe boldly placing Japan on a path to foreign and defense policy independence', *Forbes*, 24 October, <https://www.forbes.com/sites/stephenharner/2013/10/24/abe-boldly-placing-japan-on-a-path-to-foreign-and-defense-policy-independence> (last accessed 12 December 2019).

Hart, P. (1993), 'Symbols, rituals and power: the lost dimensions of crisis management', *Journal of Contingencies and Crisis Management*, 1:1, 36–50.

Hasebe, Y. (n.d.), 'Can the nation's survival be entrusted to this administration? The right of collective self-defense – problems with changing constitutional interpretation', *Waseda Online*, <http://www.yomiuri.co.jp/adv/wol/dy/opinion/gover-eco_140707.html> (last accessed 12 December 2019).

'Hasebe Yasuo interview with the Kochi Shimbun' (2015), *I-CONnect*, 30 June, <http://www.iconnectblog.com/2015/06/hasebe-yasuo-interview-with-the-kochi-shimbun> (last accessed 12 December 2019).

Hay, C. (1996), 'Narrating crisis: the discursive construction of the "winter of discontent"', *Sociology*, 30:2, 253–77.

Hayashi, K. (2014), 'China risks becoming Asia's Voldemort', *Telegraph*, 5 January, <https://www.telegraph.co.uk/news/worldnews/asia/japan/10552351/China-risks-becoming-Asias-Voldemort.html> (last accessed 12 December 2019).

Heinrich, W. L., A. Shibata and Y. Soeya (1999), *United Nations Peace-Keeping Operations: A Guide to Japanese Politics*, Tokyo: United Nations University Press.

Hellman, D. C. (1977), 'Japanese security and postwar Japanese foreign policy', in R. A. Scalapino (ed.), *The Foreign Policy of Modern Japan*, Berkeley: University of California Press, 321–40.

Hermann, C. F. (1969), 'International crisis as a situational variable', in J. N. Rosenau (ed.), *International Politics and Foreign Policy: A Reader in Research and Theory*, New York: Free Press, 409–21.

Hermann, C. F. (1990), 'Changing course: when governments choose to redirect foreign policy', *International Studies Quarterly*, 34:1, 3–21.

Hickey, D. V. V. (2000), *The Armies of East Asia: China, Taiwan, Japan and the Koreas*, Boulder, CO: Lynne Rienner.

Hisada, K. (1999), 'Missile crisis moves stepped up', *Asahi Shimbun*, 14 August.

Hoge, J. F., Jr and G. Rose (2001), 'Introduction', in J. F. Hoge, Jr and G. Rose (eds), *How Did This Happen? Terrorism and the New War*, New York: PublicAffairs, ix–xiv.

Hook, G. D. (1996), *Militarization and Demilitarization in Contemporary Japan*, London: Routledge.

Hornung, J. W. (2014), 'Japan's growing hard hedge against China', *Asian Security*, 10:2, 97–122.

Hosoya, Y. (2014), 'Bringing "internationalism" back', *Nippon.com*, 23 June, <https://www.nippon.com/en/currents/d00122/bringing-international-ism-back.html> (last accessed 12 December 2019).

Hosoya, Y. [2016] (2019), *Security Politics in Japan: Legislation for a New Security Environment*, trans. T. Cannon, Tokyo: Japan Publishing Industry Foundation for Culture.

Hughes, C. W. (1996), 'The North Korean nuclear crisis and Japanese security', *Survival*, 38:2, 79–103.

Hughes, C. W. (1999), *Japan's Economic Power and Security: Japan and North Korea*, London: Routledge.

Hughes, C. W. (2002), 'Sino-Japanese relations and ballistic missile defence (BMD)', in M. Söderberg (ed.), *Chinese–Japanese Relations in the Twenty-First Century: Complementarity and Conflict*, London: Routledge, 69–87.

Hughes, C. W. (2004), *Japan's Re-emergence as a 'Normal' Military Power*, Oxford: Oxford University Press.

Hughes, C. W. (2007), 'Not quite the "Great Britain of the Far East": Japan's security, the US–Japan alliance and the "war on terror" in East Asia', *Cambridge Review of International Affairs* 20:2, 325–38.

Hughes, C. W. (2009), *Japan's Remilitarisation*, Oxford: Routledge.

Hughes, C. W. (2016), 'Japan's "resentful realism" and balancing China's rise', *The Chinese Journal of International Politics*, 9:2, 109–50.

Hughes, C. W. (2017), 'Japan's strategic trajectory and collective self-defense: essential continuity or radical shift?', *The Journal of Japanese Studies*, 43:1, 93–126.

Hughes, C. W. and A. Fukushima (2003), 'US–Japan security relations – toward bilateralism plus?', in E. S. Krauss and T. J. Pempel (eds), *Beyond Bilateralism: US–Japan Relations in the New Asia-Pacific*, Stanford: Stanford University Press, 55–86.

Hughes, C. W. and E. S. Krauss (2007), 'Japan's new security agenda', *Survival*, 49:2, 157–76.

ICB Project (n.d.), 'International crisis behavior', <http://sites.duke.edu/icb-data> (last accessed 30 November 2019).

Igarashi, A. (2015), 'China slams US surveillance in S. China Sea; white paper hints Beijing alarmed by Abe's security policies', *Japan News*, 27 May, 1.

Imai, T. (2015), 'Global expectations', *Japan News*, 29 April, 2.

Ina, H. (1994), 'Korean issue played a part in SDP walkout', *Nikkei Weekly*, 2 May, 2.

Inoguchi, T. (1993), *Japan's Foreign Policy in an Era of Global Change*, London: Pinter.

Inoguchi, T. (1998), 'Japan's United Nations peacekeeping and other operations', in E. R. Beauchamp (ed.), *Japan's Role in International Politics since World War II*, New York: Garland Publishing, 85–103.

Inose, H. (1996), 'China missiles wake-up call to Japan? Regional friction eases security-issue taboo', *Nikkei Weekly*, 18 March, 1.

Isaka, S. (1993), 'Tokyo remains hesitant over sanctions against North Korea: diplomatic efforts urged as alternative', *Nikkei Weekly*, 8 November, 4.

Isaka, S. (1994), 'Japan courts China as key to N. Korea impasse', *Nikkei Weekly*, 6 June, 1.

Ishihara, N. (1995), *Kantei 2668 nichi: seisakukettei no butaiura* [2668 Days in the Prime Minister's Residence: Backstage of Decision-making], Tokyo: NHK Shuppan.

Ishizuka, K. (2004), 'Japan and UN peace operations', *Japanese Journal of Political Science*, 5:1, 137–57.

Izumikawa, Y. (2010), 'Explaining Japanese antimilitarism: normative and realist constraints on Japan's security policy', *International Security*, 35:2, 123–60.

James, P. (2004), 'Systemism, social mechanisms, and scientific progress: a case study of the International Crisis Behavior Project', *Philosophy of Social Sciences*, 34:3, 352–70.

Japan Defense Agency [JDA] (1996), *Defense of Japan*, Tokyo: Japan Times.

JDA (1997), *Defense of Japan*, Tokyo: Japan Times.

JDA (1998), *Defense of Japan*, Tokyo: Japan Times.

JDA (1999), *Defense of Japan*, Tokyo: Japan Times.

JDA (2000), *Defense of Japan*, Tokyo: Japan Times.

JDA (2001), *Defense of Japan*, Tokyo: Japan Times.

JDA (2002), *Defense of Japan*, Tokyo: Japan Times.

JDA (2003), *Defense of Japan*, Tokyo: Japan Times.

Jimbo, T. (1991), 'Japanese cabinet approves despatch of minesweepers to Gulf', *Associated Press*, 24 April, LexisNexis Academic database (last accessed 3 April 2006).

Kamiya, M. (2001), 'Japanese reactions to the missile proliferation in Northeast Asia', paper presented at the CSBM and North Pacific Working Groups Joint Meeting, Council for Security Cooperation in the Asia-Pacific (CSCAP), Paris, 28–9 June.

Katahara, E. (2001), 'Japan: from containment to normalization', in M. Alagappa (ed.), *Coercion and Governance: The Declining Political Role of the Military in Asia*, Stanford: Stanford University Press, 69–91.

Kato, H. and S. Naka (1994), 'Tough choices for Hata over Korean issue', *Nikkei Weekly*, 23 May, 4.

Katzenstein, P. J. (1996), *Cultural Norms and National Security: Police and Military in Postwar Japan*, Ithaca, NY: Cornell University Press.

Kaufmann, C. (2004), 'Threat inflation and the failure of the marketplace of ideas: the selling of the Iraq war', *International Security*, 29:1, 5–48.

Kawaguchi, Y. (2003), 'A foreign policy to consolidate peace', *Japan Echo*, 30:2, 24–9.

Keeler, J. T. S. (1993), 'Opening the window for reform: mandates, crises, and extraordinary policy-making', *Comparative Political Studies*, 25:4, 433–86.

Keohane, R. O. (1984), *After Hegemony: Cooperation and Discord in the World Political Economy*, Princeton: Princeton University Press.

Kihl, Y. W. (1997), 'Confrontation or compromise? Lessons from the 1994 crisis', in Y. W. Kihl and P. Hayes (eds), *Peace and Security in Northeast Asia: The Nuclear Issue and the Korean Peninsula*, Armonk, NY: M. E. Sharpe, 181–204.

Kitaoka, S. (2010), 'Establish quiet, firm defense policy', *Daily Yomiuri*, 4 October, 15.

Kitaoka, S. (2014), 'The turnabout of Japan's security policy: toward "proactive pacifism"', *Nippon.com*, 2 April, <https://www.nippon.com/en/currents/d00108/the-turnabout-of-japan%E2%80%99s-security-policy-toward-proactive-pacifism.html> (last accessed 12 December 2019).

Koga, K. (2017), 'Japan's strategic interests in the South China Sea: beyond the horizon?', *The Pacific Review*, 72:1, 16–30.

Kohno, M. (2007), 'The domestic foundations of Japan's international contribution', in T. U. Berger, M. M. Mochizuki and J. Tsuchiyama (eds), *Japan in International Politics: The Foreign Policies of an Adaptive State*, Boulder, CO: Lynne Rienner, 23–46.

Kosaka, M. (1991), 'The Iraqi challenge to the world order', *Japan Echo*, 18:1, 6–13.

Krasner, S. D. (1984), 'Approaches to the state: alternative conceptions and historical dynamics', *Comparative Politics*, 16:2, 223–46.

Krauss, E. S. and B. Nyblade (2005), '"Presidentialization" in Japan? The prime minister, media and elections in Japan', *British Journal of Political Science*, 35:2, 357–68.

Krauss, E. S. and R. J. Pekkanen (2011), *The Rise and Fall of Japan's LDP: Political Party Organizations as Historical Institutions*, Ithaca, NY: Cornell University Press.

Kurashina, Y. (2005), 'Peacekeeping participation and identity changes in the Japan Self-Defense Forces: military service as "dirty work"', PhD thesis, University of Maryland.

Kuromi, S. (2015), 'Japan must face risks for its future security', *Japan News*, 13 September, 5.

Kuromi, S. and Y. Okabe (2015), 'Japan's security policy enters new stage', *Japan News*, 20 September, 1.

Kuromi, S. and M. Takekoshi (2015), 'China sets sights on East China Sea; fears grow Beijing could monitor all of ADIZ', *Japan News*, 24 July, 2.

Kwan, W. K. (1997), 'China's military giving Japan the jitters', *Straits Times*, 16 July, 18.

Layne, C. (1993), 'The unipolar illusion: why new great powers will rise', *International Security*, 17:4, 5–51.

Lebow, R. N. (1981), *Between Peace and War: The Nature of International Crisis*, Baltimore: Johns Hopkins University Press.

Lee, B. (1999), *The Security Implications of the New Taiwan*, Oxford: Oxford University Press.

Lee, Y. W. (2012), 'Synthesis and reformulation of foreign policy change: Japan and East Asian financial regionalism', *Review of International Studies*, 38:4, 785–807.

Leheny, D. (2006), *Think Global, Fear Local: Sex, Violence, and Anxiety in Contemporary Japan*, London: Cornell University Press.

Leitenberg, M. (1996), 'The participation of Japanese military forces in United Nations peacekeeping operations', *Asian Perspective*, 20:1, 5–50.

Liff, A. P. (2017), 'Policy by other means: collective self-defense and the politics of Japan's postwar constitutional reinterpretations', *Asia Policy*, 24, 139–72.

Lim, R. (2003), *The Geopolitics of East Asia*, London: RoutledgeCurzon.

Lind, J. M. (2004), 'Pacifism or passing the buck? Testing theories of Japanese security policy', *International Security*, 29:1, 92–121.

Mahoney, J. (2010), 'After KKV: the new methodology of qualitative research', *World Politics*, 62:1, 120–47.

Manning, R. A. (2002), 'United States–North Korean relations: from welfare to workfare?', in S. S. Kim and T. H. Lee (eds), *North Korea and Northeast Asia*, Lanham, MD: Rowman and Littlefield Publishers, 61–88.

Maoz, Z. (1990), *National Choices and International Processes*, Cambridge: Cambridge University Press.

Maslow, S., R. Mason and P. O'Shea (eds) (2015), *Risk State: Japan's Foreign Policy in an Age of Uncertainty*, Farnham: Ashgate.

Mason, R. (2014), *Japan's Relations with North Korea and the Recalibration of Risk*, London: Routledge.

Matsushita, M. (2015), 'Komura: security bills to deter "real threat"', *Japan News*, 12 September, 5.

Mazarr, M. J. (1995), 'Going just a little nuclear: nonproliferation lessons from North Korea', *International Security*, 20:2, 92–122.

Mazarr, M. J., D. M. Snider and J. A. Blackwell, Jr (1993), *Desert Storm: The Gulf War and What We Learned*, Boulder, CO: Westview Press.

Midford, P. (2000), 'Japan's leadership role in East Asian security multilateralism: the Nakayama proposal and the logic of reassurance', *The Pacific Review*, 13:3, 367–97.

Midford, P. (2002), 'The logic of reassurance and Japan's grand strategy', *Security Studies*, 11:3, 1–43.

Mie, A. (2013), 'Article 9 panel revived in collective defense bid', *Japan Times*, 8 February, <https://www.japantimes.co.jp/news/2013/02/08/national/politics-diplomacy/abe-revives-article-9-panel-for-collective-defense-rethink> (last accessed 12 December 2019).

Mie, A. (2016), 'Security laws usher in new era for pacifist Japan', *Japan Times*, 29 March, <https://www.japantimes.co.jp/news/2016/03/29/national/politics-diplomacy/japans-contentious-new-security-laws-take-effect-paving-way-collective-self-defense> (last accessed 7 December 2019).

Ministry of Defense of Japan [MOD Japan] (2004a), *National Defense Program Guidelines, FY 2005–*, 10 December, <https://www.mod.go.jp/e/d_act/d_policy/pdf/national_guidelines.pdf> (last accessed 12 December 2019).

MOD Japan (2004b), *Mid-Term Defense Program (FY 2005–2009)*, <http://www.mod.go.jp/e/d_act/d_policy/pdf/mid-term_defense_program.pdf> (last accessed 12 September 2011).

MOD Japan (2010a), *National Defense Program Guidelines for FY 2011 and Beyond*, 17 December, <https://www.mod.go.jp/e/d_act/d_policy/pdf/guidelinesFY2011.pdf> (last accessed 12 December 2019).

MOD Japan (2010b), *Defense of Japan 2010*, Tokyo: Ministry of Defense, Japan.

MOD Japan (2011), *Defense of Japan 2011*, Tokyo: Ministry of Defense, Japan.

MOD Japan (2012), *Defense of Japan 2012*, Tokyo: Ministry of Defense, Japan.

MOD Japan (2013), *Defense of Japan 2013*, Tokyo: Ministry of Defense, Japan.

MOD Japan (2014), *Defense of Japan 2014*, Tokyo: Ministry of Defense, Japan.

MOD Japan (2015a), 'The guidelines for Japan–US defense cooperation', 27 April, <http://www.mod.go.jp/e/d_act/anpo/shishin_20150427e.html> (last accessed 23 November 2019).

MOD Japan (2015b), *Defense of Japan 2015*, Tokyo: Ministry of Defense, Japan.

MOD Japan (2016), 'Handout on missions and operations of the SDF' (unpublished).

Ministry of Foreign Affairs of Japan [MOFA] (1991), 'Japan and ASEAN: seeking a mature partnership for the new age', policy speech by Prime Minister Kaifu Toshiaki, Singapore, 3 May, <http://www.mofa.go.jp/policy/other/bluebook/1991/1991-appendix-2.htm> (last accessed 9 April 2006).

MOFA Japan (1992), *Diplomatic Bluebook 1992*, Tokyo: Ministry of Foreign Affairs, Japan.

MOFA Japan (1993), *Diplomatic Bluebook 1993*, Tokyo: Ministry of Foreign Affairs, Japan.

MOFA Japan (1995a), 'Participation by Japan in United Nations peace-keeping operations', <http://www.mofa.go.jp/policy/economy/apec/1995/issue/info9.html> (last accessed 14 February 2005).

MOFA Japan (1995b), 'National defense program outline in and after FY1996', <http://www.mofa.go.jp/region/n-america/us/q&a/ref/6a.html> (last accessed 5 June 2006).

MOFA Japan (1996a), 'Japan–US joint declaration on security: alliance for the 21st century', 17 April, <http://www.mofa.go.jp/region/n-america/us/security/security.html> (last accessed 9 June 2014).

MOFA Japan (1996b), 'Japan's participation on UN peace-keeping operations and international humanitarian relief operations – "paths to peace"', December, <http://www.mofa.go.jp/policy/un/pko/pamph96/index.html> (last accessed 20 February 2005).

MOFA Japan (1996c), 'Press conference by the press secretary', 12 March, <http://www.mofa.go.jp/announce/press/1996/3/312.html#2> (last accessed 17 May 2005).

MOFA Japan (1996d), 'Press conference by the press secretary', 30 January, <http://www.mofa.go.jp/announce/press/1996/1/130.html#6> (last accessed 17 May 2005).

MOFA Japan (1996e), 'Press conference by the press secretary', 8 March, <http://www.mofa.go.jp/announce/press/1996/3/308.html#1> (last accessed 17 May 2005).

MOFA Japan (1997), 'The guidelines for Japan–US defense cooperation', 23 September, <http://www.mofa.go.jp/region/n-america/us/security/guideline2.html> (last accessed 26 July 2006).

MOFA Japan (1998), 'Toward achieving peace, development, and United Nations reform', statement by H. E. Mr Keizo Obuchi, Prime Minister of Japan, at the 53rd session of the General Assembly of the United Nations, 21 September, <http://www.mofa.go.jp/announce/announce/1998/9/921.html> (last accessed 21 March 2005).

MOFA Japan (1999a), 'Press conference by the press secretary', 26 March, <http://www.mofa.go.jp/announce/press/1999/3/326.html#4> (last accessed 21 March 2005).

MOFA Japan (1999b), 'Press conference by the press secretary', 9 April, <http://www.mofa.go.jp/announce/press/1999/4/409.html#3> (last accessed 21 March 2005).

MOFA Japan (1999c), 'Foreign policy speech by Minister for Foreign Affairs Masahiko Komura to the 145th session of the Diet', 19 January, <http://www.mofa.go.jp/announce/announce/1999/1/119-3.html> (last accessed 21 March 2005).

MOFA Japan (1999d), 'Press conference by the press secretary', 29 January, <http://www.mofa.go.jp/announce/press/1999/1/129.html#7> (last accessed 21 March 2005).

MOFA Japan (2001a), 'Japan's measures in response to the simultaneous terrorist attacks in the United States', statement by the prime minister, 19 September, <https://japan.kantei.go.jp/koizumispeech/2001/0919terosoti_e.html> (last accessed 12 December 2019).

MOFA Japan (2001b), 'Remarks by Prime Minister Koizumi Junichiro at the ceremony for all victims of terrorist attacks in US', 23 September, <http://www.mofa.go.jp/region/n-america/us/terro0109/010923_e.html> (last accessed 28 March 2005).

MOFA Japan (2001c), 'Campaign against terrorism: Japan's measures', <http://www.mofa.go.jp/region/n-america/us/terro0109/policy/index.html> (last accessed 10 October 2001).

MOFA Japan (2001d), 'Basic plan regarding response measures based on the anti-terrorism special measures law', 16 November, <http://www.mofa.go.jp/region/n-america/us/terro0109/policy/plan.html> (last accessed 13 October 2004).

MOFA Japan (2001e), 'Policy speech by Prime Minister Koizumi Junichiro to the 153rd session of the Diet', 27 September, <http://www.mofa.go.jp/announce/pm/koizumi/state0927.html> (last accessed 28 March 2005).

MOFA Japan (2002a), 'Press conference', 17 December, <http://www.mofa.go.jp/announce/press/2002/12/1217.html#8> (last accessed 29 March 2005).

MOFA Japan (2002b), 'Campaign against terrorism – Japan's measures', February, <http://www.mofa.go.jp/region/n-america/us/terro0109/policy/campaign.html> (last accessed 18 July 2006).

MOFA Japan (2002c), 'Policy speech by Minister for Foreign Affairs Yoriko Kawaguchi to the 154th session of the Diet', 4 February, <http://www.mofa.go.jp/announce/fm/kawaguchi/speech0204.html> (last accessed 28 March 2005).

MOFA Japan (2002d), 'Japan–US alliance in the 21st century: three challenges', speech by Prime Minister Koizumi Junichiro, Council on Foreign Relations, New York City, 10 September, <http://www.mofa.go.jp/region/n-america/us/alliance.html> (last accessed 28 March 2005).

MOFA Japan (2002e), *Diplomatic Bluebook 2002*, Tokyo: Ministry of Foreign Affairs, Japan, <http://www.mofa.go.jp/policy/other/bluebook/2002/chap1-b.pdf> (last accessed 12 December 2019).

MOFA Japan (2003a), 'The outline of measures based on the action guidelines', 20 March, <http://www.mofa.go.jp/region/middle_e/iraq/issue2003/measure.html> (last accessed 18 July 2003).

MOFA Japan (2003b), *Diplomatic Bluebook 2003*, Tokyo: Ministry of Foreign Affairs, Japan, <http://www.mofa.go.jp/policy/other/bluebook/2003/chap1.pdf> (last accessed 12 December 2019).

MOFA Japan (2003c), 'The global challenge of international terrorism', speech by Mr Toshimitsu Motegi, Senior Vice Minister for Foreign Affairs, Japan at the Munich Conference on Security Policy, 8 February, <http://www.mofa.go.jp/policy/terrorism/speech0302.html> (last accessed 29 March 2005).

MOFA Japan (2003d), 'Prime Minister Junichiro Koizumi's interview on the issue of Iraq', 18 March, <http://www.mofa.go.jp/region/middle_e/iraq/pm_int0303.html> (last accessed 28 March 2005).

MOFA Japan (2003e), 'Press conference by Prime Minister Junichiro Koizumi', 20 March, <http://www.mofa.go.jp/region/middle_e/iraq/issue2003/pmpress0320.html> (last accessed 28 March 2005).

MOFA Japan (2003f), 'Statement by Prime Minister Junichiro Koizumi', 9 December, <http://www.mofa.go.jp/region/middle_e/iraq/issue2003/pmstate0320.html> (last accessed 28 March 2005).

MOFA Japan (2003g), 'Press conference by Prime Minister Junichiro Koizumi', 9 December, <http://www.mofa.go.jp/region/middle_e/iraq/issue2003/pmpress0312.html> (last accessed 28 March 2005).

MOFA Japan (2004a), *Diplomatic Bluebook 2004*, Tokyo: Ministry of Foreign Affairs, Japan, <http://www.mofa.go.jp/policy/other/bluebook/2004/chap1.pdf> (last accessed 12 December 2019).

MOFA Japan (2004b), 'Policy speech by Minister for Foreign Affairs Yoriko Kawaguchi to the 159th session of the Diet', 19 January, <http://www.mofa.go.jp/announce/fm/kawaguchi/speech040119.html> (last accessed 28 March 2005).

MOFA Japan (2004c), 'Press conference', 27 February, <http://www.mofa.go.jp/announce/press/2004/2/0227.html#1> (last accessed 25 August 2011).

MOFA Japan (2005), 'US–Japan alliance: transformation and realignment for the future', 29 October, <http://www.mofa.go.jp/region/n-america/us/security/scc/doc0510.html> (last accessed 12 September 2011).

MOFA Japan (2007), 'Alliance transformation: advancing United States–Japan security and defense cooperation', 1 May, <https://www.mofa

.go.jp/region/n-america/us/security/scc/joint0705.html> (last accessed 11 December 2019).

MOFA Japan (2010), 'Joint statement of the US–Japan security consultative committee', 28 May, <http://www.mofa.go.jp/region/n-america/us/security/scc/joint1005.html> (last accessed 3 December 2011).

MOFA Japan (2011), 'Toward a deeper and broader US–Japan alliance: building on 50 years of partnership', 21 June <http://www.mofa.go.jp/region/n-america/us/security/pdfs/joint1106_01.pdf> (last accessed 29 December 2011).

MOFA Japan (2013), 'Toward a more robust alliance and greater shared responsibilities', 3 October, <https://www.mofa.go.jp/files/000016028.pdf> (last accessed 12 December 2019).

MOFA Japan (2016), *Japan's Legislation for Peace and Security: Seamless Responses for Peace and Security of Japan and the International Community*, March, <https://www.mofa.go.jp/files/000143304.pdf> (last accessed 12 December 2019).

MOFA Japan (2019), *Free and Open Indo-Pacific*, 21 November, <https://www.mofa.go.jp/files/000430632.pdf> (last accessed 19 December 2019).

MOFA Japan (n.d.), *Japan Disaster Relief Teams Deployed from 1987 to Apr. 2019*, <https://www.mofa.go.jp/files/000207528.pdf> (last accessed 7 December 2019).

Mizuno, M. (1993), 'Hosokawa cautious on N. Korean sanctions', *Daily Yomiuri*, 8 November, 1.

Mochizuki, M. M. (1983/4), 'Japan's search for strategy', *International Security*, 8:3, 152–79.

Mochizuki, M. M. (1997), 'A new bargain for a stronger alliance', in M. M. Mochizuki (ed.), *Toward a True Alliance: Restructuring US–Japan Security Relations*, Washington, DC: Brookings Institution Press, 5–40.

Mori, S. (2015), 'The new security legislation and Japanese public reaction', *The Tokyo Foundation for Policy Research,* 2 December, <https://www.tkfd.or.jp/en/research/detail.php?id=542> (last accessed 12 December 2019).

Morimoto, S. (1997), 'A tighter Japan–US alliance based on greater trust', in M. M. Mochizuki (ed.), *Toward a True Alliance: Restructuring US–Japan Security Relations*, Washington, DC: Brookings Institution Press, 137–48.

Morimoto, S. (1999), 'Confronting the North Korean threat', *Japan Echo*, 26:1, 25–9.

Moto, S. (1991), 'Japan's choice in the Gulf: participation or isolation', *Japan Echo*, 18:1, 14–19.

Mukherjee, R. (2018), 'Japan strategic outreach to India and the prospects of a Japan–India alliance', *International Affairs*, 94:4, 835–59.

Mulgan, A. G. (2004), 'Beyond self-defence? Evaluating Japan's regional security role under the new defence cooperation guidelines', in E. Krauss and B. Nyblade (eds), *Japan and North America: The Postwar, Vol. 2*, London: RoutledgeCurzon, 152–86.

Murata, K. (2000), 'Do the new guidelines make the Japan–US alliance more effective?', in M. Nishihara (ed.), *The Japan–US Alliance: New Challenges for the 21st Century*, Tokyo: Japan Center for International Exchange, 19–38.

Nabeshima, K. (2007), 'Unshackling Japan's defense', *Japan Times*, 22 January, <http://www.japantimes.co.jp/text/eo20070122kn.html> (last accessed 21 March 2012).

Nakai, Y. (1999), 'Turbulence threatens', *The World Today*, 55:11, 16–19.

Nakai, Y. (2000), 'Policy coordination on Taiwan', in M. Nishihara (ed.), *The Japan–US Alliance: New Challenges for the 21st Century*, Tokyo: Japan Center for International Exchange, 71–102.

Nakamoto, M. (1994), 'Korean worries mount in Japan', *Financial Times*, 8 April, 4.

National Institute for Defense Studies (2005), *East Asian Strategic Review 2005*, Tokyo: Japan Times.

Niksch, L. A. and R. G. Sutter (1991), 'Japan's response to the Persian Gulf crisis: implications for US–Japan relations', *Congressional Research Service*, 23 May, <http://www.fas.org/man/crs/91-5-23.htm> (last accessed 28 April 2005).

Nishihara, M. (2000), 'The Japan–US alliance: defense cooperation and beyond', in M. Nishihara (ed.), *The Japan–US Alliance: New Challenges for the 21st Century*, Tokyo: Japan Center for International Exchange, 9–18.

Nishimura, M. (1992), 'Peace-keeping operations: setting the record straight', *Japan Echo*, 19:3, 50–6.

Oberdorfer, D. (1999), *The Two Koreas: A Contemporary History*, Reading, MA: Addison-Wesley.

Ogawa, S. (2009), 'Japan, US out of step on DPRK; ties a cornerstone of East Asian security, but cracks seen emerging', *Daily Yomiuri*, 8 May, 4.

Okabe, Y. (2014), 'Guidelines to cite collective self-defense', *Japan News*, 13 July, 1.

Okabe, Y. (2015), 'Japan, US, Australia air concern over South China Sea; China urged to exercise self-restraint on reclamation', *Japan News*, 1 June, 1.

Okazaki, H. and S. Sato (1991), 'Redefining the role of Japanese military power', *Japan Echo*, 18:1, 20–5.

Ollapally, D. and M. Mochizuki (2011), 'Identity and Asian powers: what does it mean for International Relations of Asia and beyond?', *International Studies*, 48:3/4, 197–9.

Oros, A. L. (2008), *Normalizing Japan: Politics, Identity and the Evolution of Security Practice*, Stanford: Stanford University Press.

Oros, A. L. (2014), 'Japan's Cabinet seeks changes to its peace constitution – issues new "interpretation" of Article Nine', *Asia Pacific Bulletin*, 1 July, <https://www.eastwestcenter.org/sites/default/files/private/apb270_0.pdf> (last accessed 12 December 2019).

Oros, A. L. (2017), *Japan's Security Renaissance: New Policies and Politics for the Twenty-First Century*, New York: Columbia University Press.

Owada, H. (1995), 'A Japanese perspective on peacekeeping', in D. Warner (ed.), *New Dimensions of Peacekeeping*, Dordrecht: M. Nijhoff Publishers, 103–16.

Ozawa, I. (1994), *Blueprint for a New Japan: The Rethinking of a Nation*, Tokyo: Kodansha International.

Page, B. I. and R. Y. Shapiro (1992), *The Rational Public: Fifty Years of Trends in Americans' Policy Preferences*, Chicago: The University of Chicago Press.

Pan, L. (2005), *The United Nations in Japan's Foreign and Security Policy-making, 1945–1992: National Security, Party Politics, and International Status*, Cambridge, MA: Harvard University Asia Center.

Park, S. H. (1994), 'North Korea and the challenge to the US–South Korean alliance', *Survival*, 36:2, 78–91.

Parker, R. W. (1977), 'An examination of basic and applied international crisis research', *International Studies Quarterly*, 21:1, 225–46.

Patalano, A. (2014), 'Seapower and Sino-Japanese relations in the East China Sea', *Asian Affairs*, 45:1, 34–54.

Pekkanen, R. and E. S. Krauss (2005), 'Japan's "coalition of the willing" on security policies', *Orbis*, 49:3, 429–44.

Pempel, T. J. (2005), 'Introduction: emerging webs of regional connectedness', in T. J. Pempel (ed.), *Remapping East Asia: The Construction of a Region*, Ithaca, NY: Cornell University Press, 1–28.

Priest, D. (1998), 'N. Korea may have launched satellite', *Washington Post*, 5 September, A21.

Prime Minister of Japan and His Cabinet (1946), 'The Constitution of Japan', 3 November, <https://japan.kantei.go.jp/constitution_and_government_of_japan/constitution_e.html> (last accessed 4 December 2019).

Prime Minister of Japan and His Cabinet (2013a), *National Security Strategy*, 17 December, <http://japan.kantei.go.jp/96_abe/documents/2013/__icsFiles/afieldfile/2013/12/17/NSS.pdf> (last accessed 23 November 2019).

Prime Minister of Japan and His Cabinet (2013b), *National Defense Program Guidelines for FY2014 and Beyond*, 17 December, <http://japan.kantei.go.jp/96_abe/documents/2013/__icsFiles/afieldfile/2013/12/17/NDPG%28Summary%29.pdf> (last accessed 24 November 2019).

Prime Minister of Japan and His Cabinet (2014a), 'Press conference by Prime Minister Abe', 15 May, <https://japan.kantei.go.jp/96_abe/statement/201405/0515kaiken.html> (last accessed 12 December 2019).

Prime Minister of Japan and His Cabinet (2014b), 'Press conference by Prime Minister Abe', 1 July, <https://japan.kantei.go.jp/96_abe/statement/201407/0701kaiken.html> (last accessed 12 December 2019).

Prime Minister of Japan and His Cabinet (2015), 'Press conference by Prime Minister Shinzo Abe', 25 September, <https://japan.kantei.go.jp/97_abe/statement/201509/1213465_9928.html> (last accessed 12 December 2019).

Przystup, J. J. (2015), 'The US–Japan alliance: review of the guidelines for defense cooperation', *Strategic Perspectives*, 18, Washington, DC: Institute for National Strategic Studies, National Defense University.

Pugliese, G. (2017), 'Kantei diplomacy? Japan's hybrid leadership in foreign and security policy', *The Pacific Review*, 30:2, 152–68.

Purrington, C. and A. K. (1991), 'Tokyo's policy responses during the Gulf crisis', *Asian Survey*, 31:4, 307–23.

Pyle, K. B. (1987), 'In pursuit of a grand design: Nakasone betwixt the past and the future', *The Journal of Japanese Studies*, 13:2, 243–70.

Pyle, K. B. (1992), *The Japanese Question: Power and Purpose in a New Era*, Washington, DC: AEI Press.

Pyle, K. B. (2007), *Japan Rising: The Resurgence of Japanese Power and Purpose*, New York: PublicAffairs.

Radlin, C. A. (1994), 'Neighbours of North Korea appear to move toward action', *Boston Globe*, 5 June, 12.

Reid, T. R. (1991), 'New frustration; Tokyo says its Gulf role was misunderstood', *Washington Post*, 17 March, A21.

Richardson, B. (2004), 'Japan's Iraq deployment gets little airtime at home', *Christian Science Monitor*, 20 January, <https://www.csmonitor.com/2004/0120/p08s01-woap.html> (last accessed 12 December 2019).

Rix, A. (1988), 'Bureaucracy and political change in Japan', in J. A. A. Stockwin, A. Rix, A. George, J. Horne, D. Ito and M. Collick, *Dynamic and Immobilist Politics in Japan*, Basingstoke: Macmillan Press, 54–76.

Rose, C. (2000), 'Japanese role in PKO and humanitarian assistance', in T. Inoguchi and P. Jain (eds), *Japanese Foreign Policy Today: A Reader*, New York: Palgrave, 122–35.

Rose, G. (1998), 'Neoclassical realism and theories of foreign policy', *World Politics*, 51:1, 144–72.

Saltzman, I. Z. (2015), 'Growing pains: neoclassical realism and Japan's security policy emancipation', *Contemporary Security Policy*, 36:3, 498–527.

Samuels, R. J. (2007), *Securing Japan: Tokyo's Grand Strategy and the Future of East Asia*, Ithaca, NY: Cornell University Press.

Samuels, R. J. (2013), *3.11: Disaster and Change in Japan*, Ithaca, NY: Cornell University Press.

Samuels, R. J. and C. Wallace (2018), 'Introduction: Japan's pivot in Asia', *International Affairs*, 94:4, 703–10.

Sanger, D. E. (1994a), 'Japan split over role in a North Korea showdown', *New York Times*, 24 April, 3.

Sanger, D. E. (1994b), 'Tokyo raids to halt aid for North Korea on missiles', *New York Times*, 15 January, 5.

Sanger, D. E. (1994c), 'Tokyo reluctant to levy sanctions on North Koreans', *New York Times*, 9 June, 1.

Sanger, D. E. (1998), 'US to send North Korea food despite missile launching', *New York Times*, 10 September, <https://www.nytimes.com/1998/09/10/world/us-to-send-north-korea-food-despite-missile-launching.html> (last accessed 13 December 2019).

Sasaki, T. (2010), 'China eyes the Japanese military: China's threat perception of Japan since the 1980s', *The China Quarterly*, 203, 560–80.

Satake, T. and J. Hemmings (2018), 'Japan–Australia security cooperation in the bilateral and multilateral contexts', *International Affairs*, 94:4, 815–34.

Scobell, A. (2003), *China's Use of Military Force: Beyond the Great Wall and the Long March*, Cambridge: Cambridge University Press.

SEALDs (n.d.), 'Students Emergency Action for Liberal Democracys', <http://sealdseng.mystrikingly.com> (last accessed 12 December 2019).

Shinoda, T. (2002), 'Japan's response to terrorism and the implications for the Taiwan Strait issue', *Japan–Taiwan Research Forum*, 22 January, <http://taiwansecurity.org/TS/2002/JTRF-Shinoda-0102.htm> (last accessed 27 June 2005).

Shinoda, T. (2003), 'Koizumi's top-down leadership in the anti-terrorism legislation: the impact of political institutional changes', *The SAIS Review of International Affairs*, 23:1, 19–34.

Shinoda, T. (2004), 'Ozawa Ichiro as an actor in foreign policy-making', *Japan Forum*, 16:1, 37–61.

Shinoda, T. (2007), *Koizumi Diplomacy: Japan's Kantei Approach to Foreign and Defense Affairs*, Seattle: University of Washington Press.

Shiraishi, Y. (2015), 'Japan, US plan defense, eyeing China; guidelines cover remote island defense, maritime cooperation', *Japan News*, 29 April, 2.

Singh, B. (2010), 'Peacekeeping in Japanese security policy: international–domestic contexts interaction', *European Journal of International Relations*, 17:3, 429–51.

Singh, B. (2013), *Japan's Security Identity: From a Peace State to an International State*, New York: Routledge.

Singh, B. (2016), 'Japan embraces internationalism: explaining Japanese security policy expansion through an identity-regime approach', *Japanese Journal of Political Science*, 17:4, 589–613.

Singh, B., S. Teo, S. Ho and H. Tsjeng (2019), 'Contending visions of East Asian regional order: insights from the United States, China, Japan, and Indonesia', *Asian Affairs: An American Review*, 46:1, 19–41.

Smith, S. A. (2015), *Intimate Rivals: Japanese Domestic Politics and a Rising China*, New York: Columbia University Press.

Smith, S. A. (2020), 'Japan's interests in an era of US–China strategic competition', in A. J. Tellis, A. Szalwinski and M. Wills (eds), *Strategic Asia 2020: US–China Competition for Global Influence*, Seattle: The National Bureau of Asian Research, 44–72.

Snyder, G. H. and P. Diesing (1977), *Conflict Among Nations: Bargaining, Decision Making, and System Structure in International Crises*, Princeton: Princeton University Press.

Soeya, Y. (1998a), 'Japan: normative constraints versus structural imperatives', in M. Alagappa (ed.), *Asian Security Practice: Material and Ideational Influences*, Stanford: Stanford University Press, 198–233.

Soeya, Y. (1998b), 'Japan's dual identity and the US–Japan alliance', Asia/Pacific Research Center, Stanford University.

Soifer, H. D. (2012), 'The causal logic of critical junctures', *Comparative Political Studies*, 45:12, 1572–97.

Special Study Group on Japan's Role in the International Community, LDP (1992), 'Kokusai shakai ni okeru nihon no yakuwari' [Japan's role in the international community], *Japan Echo*, 19:2, 49–58.

Stanwood, F., P. Allen and L. Peacock (1991), *The Gulf War: A Day-by-Day Chronicle*, London: BCA.

Stokes, B. and J. J. Shinn (1998), *The Tests of War and the Strains of Peace: The US–Japan Security Relationship*, New York: Council on Foreign Relations Press.

Stone, D. A. (1989), 'Causal stories and the formation of policy agendas', *Political Science Quarterly*, 104:2, 281–300.

Subotić, J. (2015), 'Narrative, ontological security, and foreign policy change', *Foreign Policy Analysis*, 12:4, 610–27.

Swaine, M. (2013), 'US security policy towards China and the role of Japan', in A. Hashimoto, M. Mochizuki and K. Takara (eds), *The Okinawa Question: Futenma, the US–Japan Alliance and Regional Security*, Washington, DC: Elliott School of International Affairs, 65–78.

Takahara, K. (2005), 'China posing a threat: Aso', *Japan Times*, 23 December, <https://www.japantimes.co.jp/news/2005/12/23/national/china-posing-a-threat-aso> (last accessed 12 December 2019).

Takahara, K. (2015), 'Japan needs to seek out regional allies, view US as "second resort", says head of think tank', *Japan Times*, 9 December <https://www.japantimes.co.jp/news/2015/12/09/national/japan-needs-seek-regional-allies-view-u-s-second-resort-says-head-think-tank> (last accessed 23 November 2019).

Takahashi, J. (2002), 'Iraq issue casts shadow on post-9/11 solidarity', *Japan Times*, 4 September, <https://www.japantimes.co.jp/news/2002/09/04/national/iraq-issue-casts-shadow-on-post-911-solidarity> (last accessed 13 December 2019).

Takahashi, K. and M. Matsushita (2013), [No title], *Japan News*, 5 October, 1.

Takeda, Y. (1998), 'Japan's role in the Cambodian peace process: diplomacy, manpower and finance', *Asian Survey*, 38:6, 553–68.

Takeuchi, H. (2014), 'Sino-Japanese relations: power, interdependence, and domestic politics', *International Relations of the Asia-Pacific*, 14:1, 7–32.

Tamamoto, M. (2004), 'A nationalist's lament: the slippery slope of Koizumi's foreign policy', in *The People vs. Koizumi? Japan–US Relations and Japan's Struggle for National Identity*, Asia Program Special Report, 119, 10–15.

Tamura, S. (2016), *Nihon no bouei seisaku*, dai 2 han [*The Defense Policy of Japan*, 2nd edn], Tokyo: Naigai Syuppan.

Tanaka, A. (1999), 'A worrisome neighbor', *Japan Echo*, 26:1, <http://www.japanecho.com/sum/1999/260108.html> (last accessed 13 August 2006).

Tanter, R. (1978), 'International crisis behavior: an appraisal of the literature', *The Jerusalem Journal of International Relations*, 3:2/3, 340–74.

T. B. (2013), 'Japan and national security: island defence', *The Economist*, 16 December, <https://www.economist.com/banyan/2013/12/16/island-defence> (last accessed 12 December 2019).

The Advisory Panel on Reconstruction of the Legal Basis for Security (2008), *Report of the Advisory Panel on Reconstruction of the Legal Basis for Security*, 24 June, <https://www.kantei.go.jp/jp/singi/anzenhosyou/report.pdf> (last accessed 12 December 2019).

The Advisory Panel on Reconstruction of the Legal Basis for Security (2014), *Report of the Advisory Panel on Reconstruction of the Legal Basis for Security*, 15 May, <https://www.kantei.go.jp/jp/singi/anzenhosyou2/dai7/houkoku_en.pdf> (last accessed 30 June 2020).

The Council on Security and Defense Capabilities in the New Era (2010), *Japan's Visions for Future Security and Defense Capabilities in the New Era: Toward a Peace-Creating Nation*, August, <https://www.kantei.go.jp/jp/singi/shin-ampobouei2010/houkokusyo_e.pdf> (last accessed 12 December 2019).

Togo, K. (2010), 'The assertive conservative right in Japan: their formation and perspective', *The SAIS Review of International Affairs*, 30:1, 77–89.

Togo, K. (2014), 'Revision of Article 9 and its implications', *PacNet*, 70, 2 September, <https://www.pacforum.org/analysis/pacnet-70-revision-article-9-and-its-implications> (last accessed 12 December 2019).

Ueki, Y. (1993), 'Japan's UN diplomacy: sources of passivism and activism', in G. L. Curtis (ed.), *Japan's Foreign Policy after the Cold War: Coping with Change*, Armonk, NY: M. E. Sharpe, 347–70.

Unger, D. (1997), 'Japan and the Gulf war: making the world safe for Japan–US relations', in A. Bennett, J. Lepgold and D. Unger (eds), *Friends in Need: Burden Sharing in the Gulf War*, Basingstoke: Macmillan Press, 137–58.

USG Department of Defense (1995), *United States Security Strategy for the East Asia-Pacific Region*, Washington, DC: Department of Defense, Office of International Security Affairs.

USG Department of State (1991), 'The Gulf war: impact on Japan and US–Japan relations', cable by Ambassador Michael Armacost, 14 March, <http://www.gwu.edu/~nsarchiv/NSAEBB/NSAEBB175/japan2-13.pdf> (last accessed 18 April 2006).

US Embassy and Consulates in Japan (2020), 'Joint statement on 60th anniversary of the signing of the US–Japan Treaty of Mutual Cooperation and Security', January, <https://jp.usembassy.gov/joint-statement-60th-anniversary-us-japan> (last accessed 28 January 2020).

Ushiba, A. (1992), 'The minesweeping mission: a job well done', *Japan Echo*, 14:1, 43–50.

Walby, S. (2015), *Crisis*, Cambridge: Polity Press.

Wallace, C. J. (2013), 'Japan's strategic pivot south: diversifying the dual hedge', *International Relations of the Asia-Pacific*, 13:3, 479–517.

Walt, S. M. (1987), *The Origins of Alliances*, Ithaca, NY: Cornell University Press.

Waltz, K. N. (1979), *Theory of International Politics*, Reading, MA: Addison-Wesley.

Waltz, K. N. (1993), 'The emerging structure of international politics', *International Security*, 18:2, 44–79.

Waltz, K. N. (2000), 'Structural realism after the Cold War', *International Security*, 25:1, 5–41.

Weisman, S. R. (1991), 'Japan counts the costs of Gulf action – or inaction', *New York Times*, 27 January, 2.

Weldes, J. (1996), 'Constructing national interests', *European Journal of International Relations*, 2:3, 275–318.

Weldes, J. (1999), *Constructing National Interests: The United States and the Cuban Missile Crisis*, Minneapolis: University of Minnesota Press.

Weldes, J., M. Laffey, H. Gusterson and R. Duvall (eds) (1999), *Cultures of Insecurity: States, Communities, and the Production of Danger*, Minneapolis: University of Minnesota Press.

Wendt, A. (1992), 'Anarchy is what states make of it: the social construction of power politics', *International Organization*, 46:2, 391–425.

Wendt, A. (1999), *Social Theory of International Politics*, Cambridge: Cambridge University Press.

White House (2017a), 'Remarks by President Trump at APEC CEO Summit', 10 November, <https://www.whitehouse.gov/briefings-statements/remarks-president-trump-apec-ceo-summit-da-nang-vietnam> (last accessed 13 December 2019).

White House (2017b), *National Security Strategy of the United States of America*, December, <https://www.whitehouse.gov/wp-content/uploads/2017/12/NSS-Final-12-18-2017-0905.pdf> (last accessed 13 December 2019).

WuDunn, S. (1998), 'North Korea fires missile over Japanese territory', *New York Times*, 1 September, A6.

Yamaguchi, J. (1992), 'The Gulf war and the transformation of Japanese constitutional politics', *The Journal of Japanese Studies*, 18:1, 155–72.

Yamamoto, Y. (1999), 'Defence white paper focuses on threat from North Korea', *Nikkei Weekly*, 2 August, 4.

Yoshida, R. (1994), 'Debate on SDF rescue missions heats up', *Japan Times*, 20 May.

Yoshida, R. (2006a), 'National security debate mushrooming since October 9', *Japan Times*, 25 November, <http://www.japantimes.co.jp/text/nn20061125a2.html> (last accessed 22 March 2012).

Yoshida, R. (2006b), 'DPJ positions to change with new guard', *Japan Times*, 1 April, Factiva database (last accessed 12 December 2019).

Yoshida, R. (2007), 'Collective defense: what it means for Japan', *Japan Times*, 19 May, Nexis Uni database (last accessed 12 December 2019).

Zakaria, F. (2020), 'The new China scare: why America shouldn't panic about its latest challenger', *Foreign Affairs*, 99:1, <https://www.foreignaffairs.com/articles/china/2019-12-06/new-china-scare> (last accessed 22 February 2020).

Zaller, J. R. (1992), *The Nature and Origins of Mass Opinion*, Cambridge: Cambridge University Press.

NEWSPAPERS

Agence France-Presse
Asahi Shimbun
Associated Press
Boston Globe
China Daily
Christian Science Monitor
Daily Yomiuri
Financial Times

Japan Economic Journal
Japan News
Japan Times
Jiji Press Ticker Service
Korea Times
Kyodo News
Mainichi Daily News
New York Times
Newsweek
Nihon Keizai Shimbun
Nikkei Top Articles
Nikkei Weekly
Reuters
Sankei Shimbun
Shikoku News
St Louis Post
Straits Times
Telegraph
USIA Transcript
Washington Post
Yomiuri Shimbun

INTERVIEWEE LIST

Akita, Hiroyuki, personal communication, 16 January 2018, Tokyo
Akutsu, Hiroyasu, personal communication, 14 November 2012, Tokyo
Asari, Hideki, personal communication, 25 September 2012, Tokyo
Auslin, Michael, personal communication, 5 May 2015, Washington, DC
Bono, Naruhiro, personal communication, 26 August 2005, Tokyo
Bush, Richard, personal communication, 30 April 2015, Washington, DC
Funabashi, Yoichi, personal communication, 24 September 2012 and 18 January 2018, Tokyo
Izawa, Osamu, personal communication, 19 September 2012, Tokyo
Kano, Koji, personal communication, 29 November 2012, Tokyo
Kimura, Ayako, personal communication, 29 November 2012, Tokyo
Kojima, Tomoyuki, personal communication, 14 September 2005, Tokyo
Kokubun, Ryosei, personal communication, 30 October 2012, Kanagawa
Kotani, Tetsuo, personal communication, 5 December 2018, Tokyo
Kurauchi, Koji, personal communication, 21 November 2012, Tokyo
Matsuda, Yasuhiro, personal communication, 5 December 2018, Tokyo
Matsumoto, Kyosuke, personal communication, 15 June 2015, Washington, DC
Michishita, Narushige, personal communication, 21 September 2015, 16 January 2018 and 6 December 2018, Tokyo

Mizumoto, Yoshihiko, personal communication, 26 August 2005, Tokyo

Mori, Satoru, personal communication, 20 November 2012, Tokyo, 18 January 2018 and 6 December 2018, Tokyo

Nishihara, Masashi, personal communication, 14 September 2012, Tokyo

Okawara, Yoshio, personal communication, 2 October 2012, Tokyo

Przystup, James, personal communication, 16 June 2015, Washington, DC

Sahashi, Ryo, personal communication, 16 January 2018 and 5 December 2018, Tokyo

Samuels, Richard J., personal communication, 16 September 2005, Tokyo

Satake, Tomohiko, personal communication, 17 January 2018 and 4 December 2018, Tokyo

Schoff, Jim, personal communication, 20 May 2015, Washington DC

Serizawa, Kiyoshi, personal communication, 29 November 2012, Tokyo

Shimada, Kazuhisa, personal communication, 21 November 2012, Tokyo

Smith, Sheila A., personal communication, 13 May 2015, Washington, DC

Soeya, Yoshihide, personal communication, 22 September 2005, Tokyo

Sutter, Robert, personal communication, 16 April 2015, Washington, DC

Szechenyi, Nicholas, personal communication, 18 June 2015, Washington, DC

Takahashi, Sugio, personal communication, 2 October 2012, Tokyo

Takamizawa, Nobushige, personal communication, 28 September 2012, Tokyo

Tanaka, Akihiko, personal communication, 6 September 2005, Tokyo

Tanaka, Hitoshi, personal communication, 8 September 2012, Tokyo

Tatsumi, Yuki, personal communication, 27 April 2015, Washington, DC

Tokuchi, Hideshi, personal communication, 14 September 2005, 17 January 2018 and 4 December 2018, Tokyo

Yanai, Shunji, personal communication, 24 May 2006, Tokyo

Yuzawa, Takeshi, personal communication, 17 January 2018, Tokyo

INDEX

EU representative:
Easy Access System Europe
Mustamäe tee 50, 10621 Tallinn, Estonia
Gpsr.requests@easproject.com

www.ingramcontent.com/pod-product-compliance
Lightning Source LLC
Chambersburg PA
CBHW070845300326
41935CB00039B/1448